COPYRIGHT NOTICE

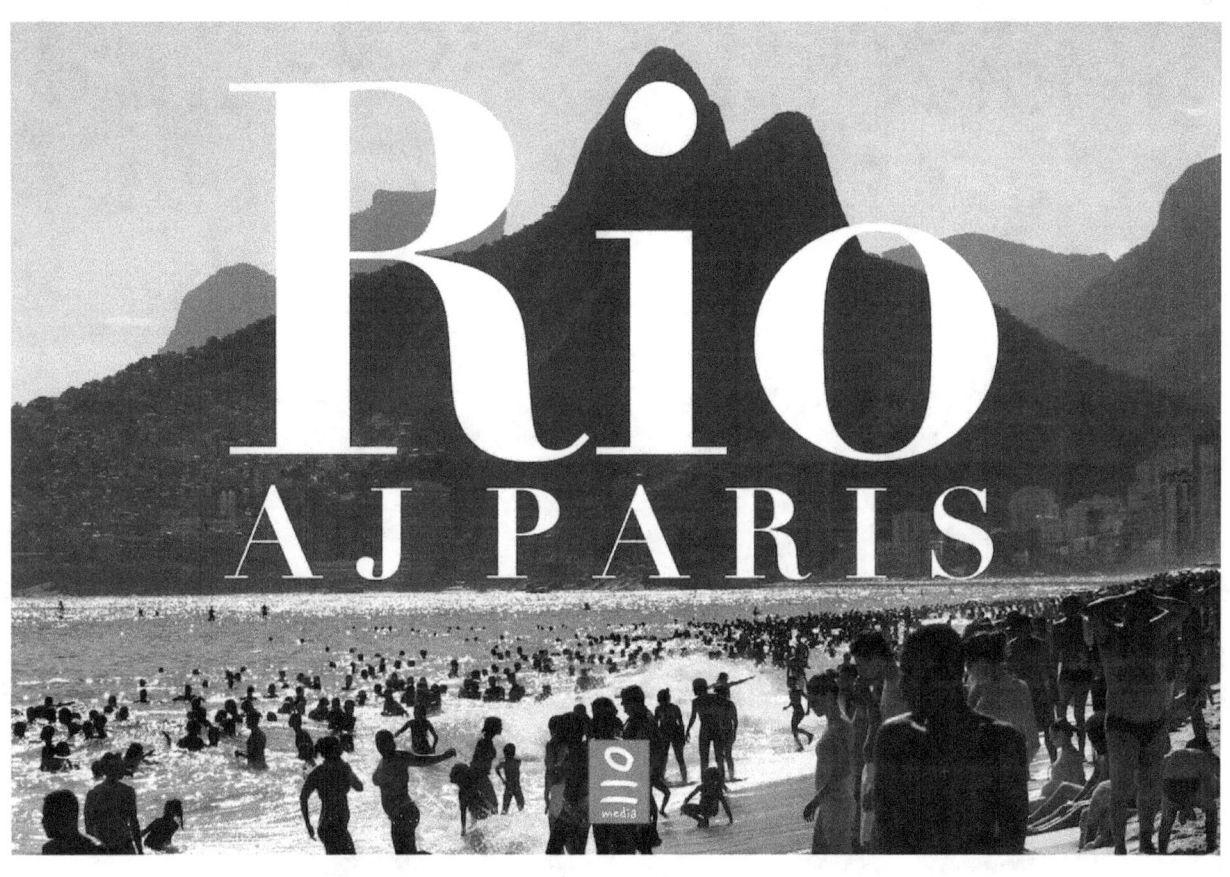

This Book Is

I love Rio de Janeiro.

I call it simply "Rio."

I have dreamed of this city ever since I was a child when I saw many things related to it. When I had the chance to visit later as a young man I realized it was much more than I had ever imagined. It was beyond my expectations. It was beyond the photos. It was beyond the dreams.

Rio is a beautiful city. No, really, it is. It is a visually beautiful city that celebrates all that I love about the planet: beautiful waters, long and beautiful beaches; beautiful mountains, which seem to be adorned all over the city; and beautiful people, colorful and diverse.

This book, therefore, is about my love for Rio.

I love to travel, take photos, and write.

As such this is a photo book with some writings rather than a book of writings with some photos. There are over 100 photos in the book. They occupy full pages. Yet, you will find a little bit of information about *my* Rio. That means I share information about the land, the people, the culture *my* way.

I ask you not to expect a guidebook, although there is a lot of information that you could use to enjoy a trip. You might find information to help you when to visit, what to expect, and where to go. However, it is not given to you that way. I'm just living my life and sharing what I love.

That is all.

So, then what is the book about?

The book is about the men of Rio, their land, their culture, and their people as I experience them. The men in this book are really diverse. There are different ethnicities. There are different ages. There are different sexualities. There are different economical groups. What they have in common is their relationship to the city, from being born in the city to being a tourist.

One day I will have a book about the women of Rio, too, because that is also a different experience for me. A city, in my opinion, is not about what is for everyone but what is experienced with different groups.

I hope you enjoy it.

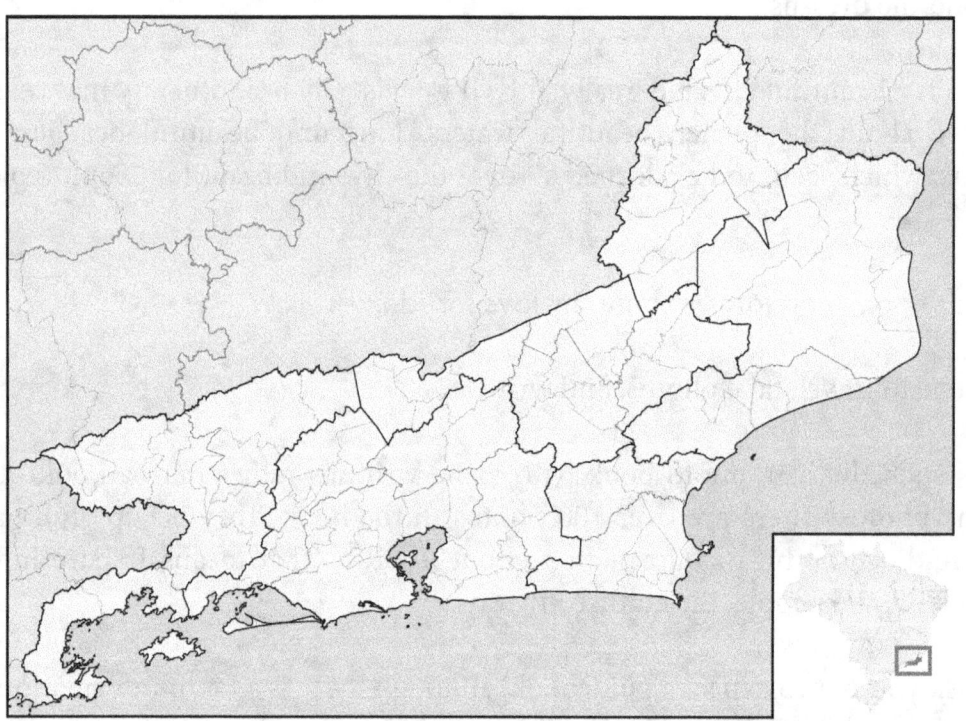

A Map of Rio de Janeiro

Quick History of Rio

On January 1, 1502 the Portuguese landed on Guanabara Bay. This led to the city being called "River of January" (Rio de Janeiro) because of the formation of the bay out of the river and their erroneous thinking that the bay was a river.

Since that time other Europeans tried to get a hold of this area, including the French who had an intense war with the Portuguese for two years.

The European interest in the area stemmed from its sugarcane resources, as well as the gold and other minerals later discovered.

Because of this fact, and the fact that it was practically better to ship things out of it than Salvador, which was the capital of that time, Rio de Janeiro became the capital of the Portuguese Americas in the mid 1700s.

In the early 1800s the city was so important to the Portuguese Empire that the Royal family, as well as their court, moved to the city as they escaped from Napoleon. When the country changed hands from Portuguese kings to Brazilian kings, Rio remained the capital just as it did after the country moved from monarch to republic.

Rio played an important part in the Atlantic Slave Trade.

Brazil was the largest importer of African slaves, importing nearly 5 million Africans. This led to the fact that today Brazil is home to the largest community of people of African descent in the world not counting Nigeria. Before Africans were imported, and during, the Portuguese also enslaved local natives.

In the 20th Century, Rio became an important cultural city.

Ipanema

In the **Tupí** language, which belonged to a group of people who are believed to be the original inhabitants of the area and whose language has since gone extinct, "Ipanema" means "stinky lake."

I assure you, nothing stinks in Ipanema these days. It's probably the most stylish *bairro* or neighborhood of the city, and it's simply too expensive to be stinking.

The first time I went to Brazil I wanted to stay in Ipanema. I was chasing that "Girl from Ipanema" song experience. I wanted to be as fabulous as her. I thought someone would notice me if I stayed there, and perhaps even ended up having a song written in my honor.

None of that happened.

Oh, well. At least I got you some photos.

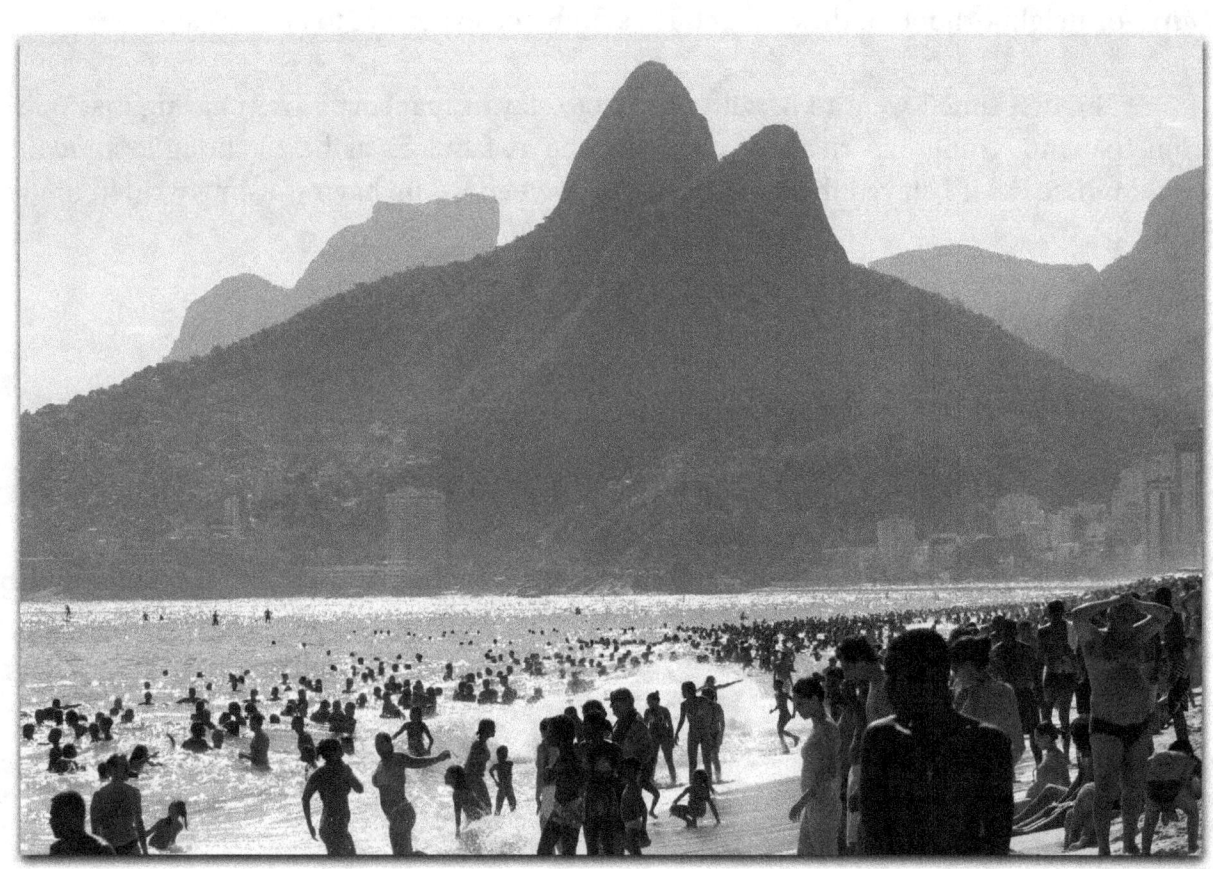

João checking out a bikini-clad Brazilian beauty in the water.

Ipanema Beach

Ipanema is full of interesting people.

They may not all be able to afford living in those expensive apartments, and they may not all be able to eat in those exquisite restaurants, but these people make the beach colorful, exciting, and simply beautiful.

"I live in Cantagalo," said the young man, smiling, "It takes me maybe ten or fifteen minutes to come down to the beach," he began to laugh, adding, "I don't pay the high rent of this neighborhood, though. I love the women here, they are so open and they love their bodies. I would never go anywhere else."

That was João.

"It is John," he explained his name, "Like,

He lives in a **favela**, a shantytown, just above Ipanema. There's an elevator that whisks you up to the hill in no time. In fact, you might arrive home in Cantagalo faster than the cool tourists from Copacabana. João pays less than $200 a month for rent, which is something he would have paid at a cheap night's hotel in Ipanema.

Brazil is a country full of many inequalities. Yet, at the beach everyone seems to find his or her place. Parents are giving their kids much needed experiences at a diverse society. Young people are eyeing each other like young people do. Entrepreneurs of all kinds are giving their luck a good go. In a country full of noise you might even spot that young mind seeking solitude with the waves, far from the noisy shores.

Bem vindo a Ipanema!

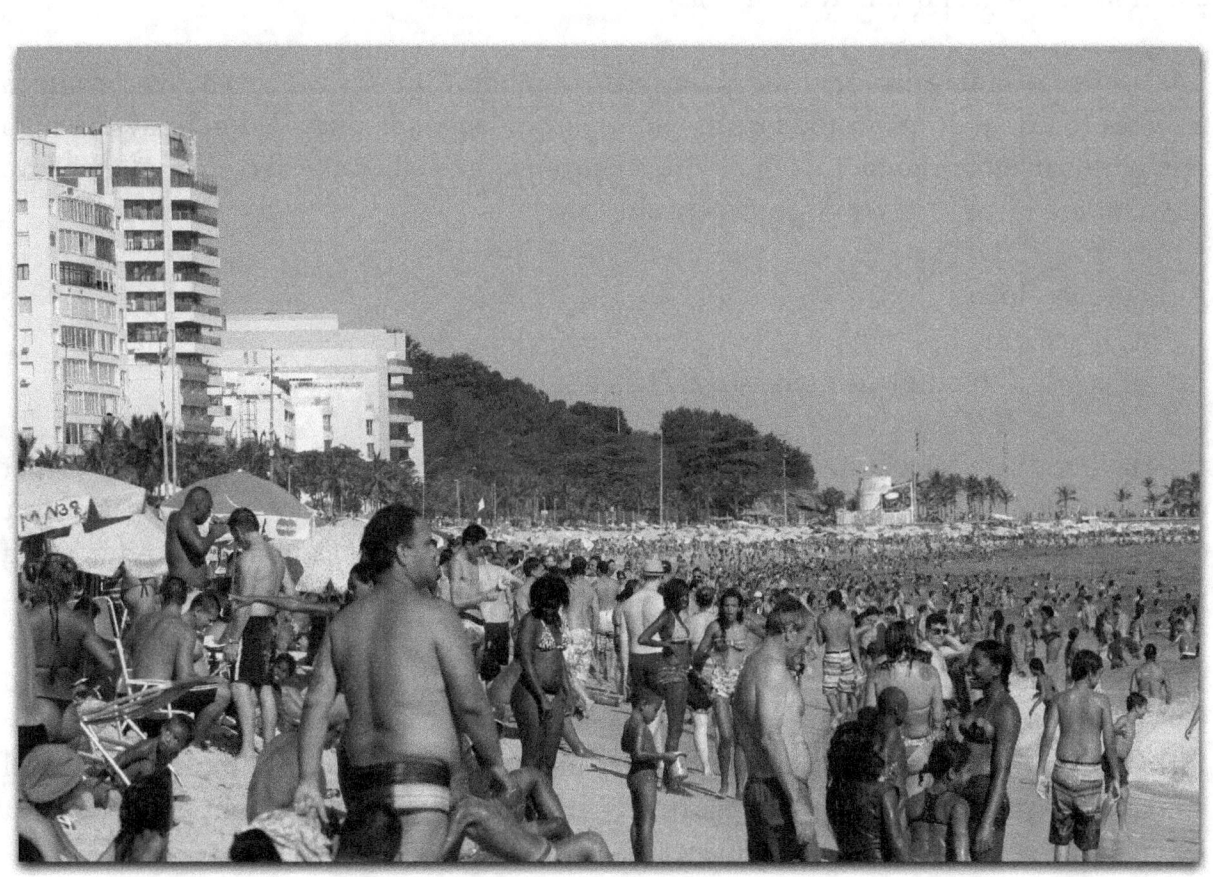

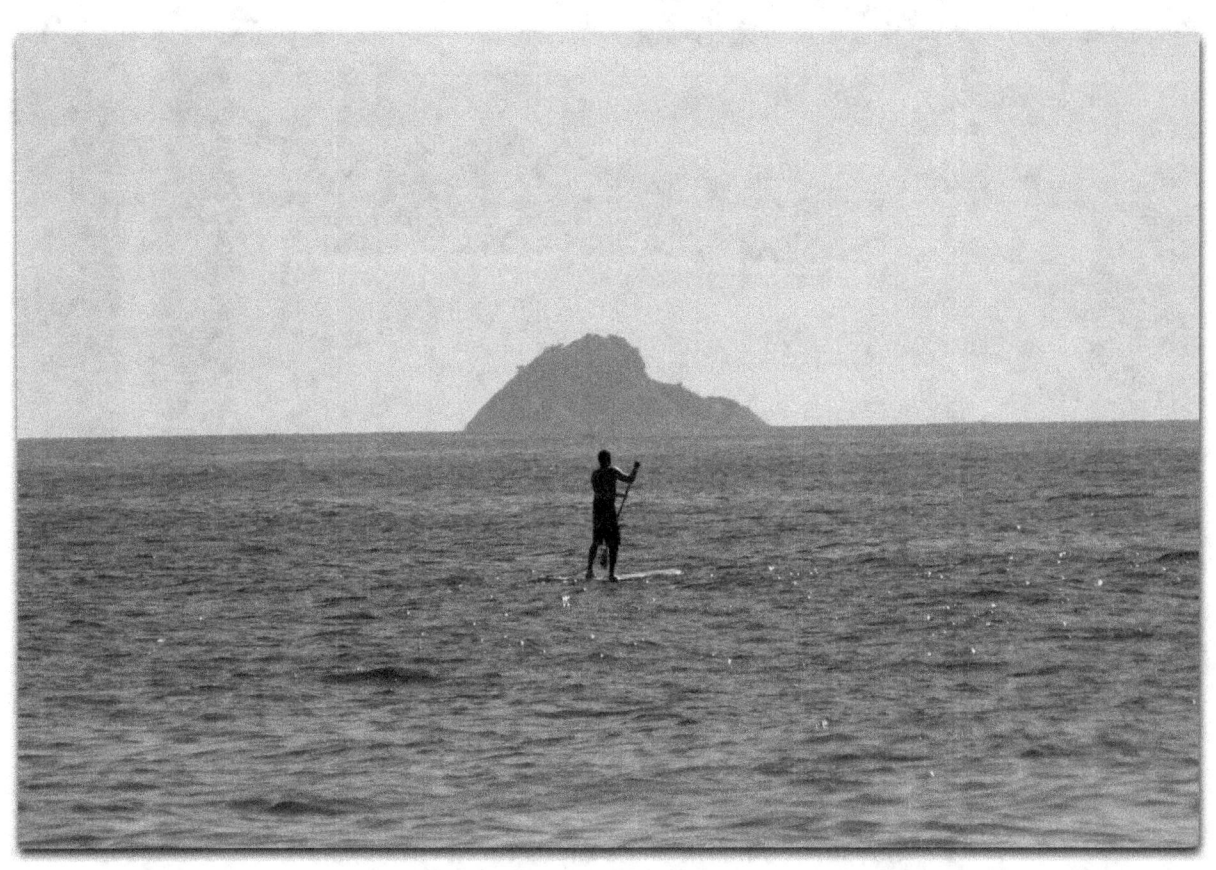

Fabio paddle boarding half way to Cagarras Islands.

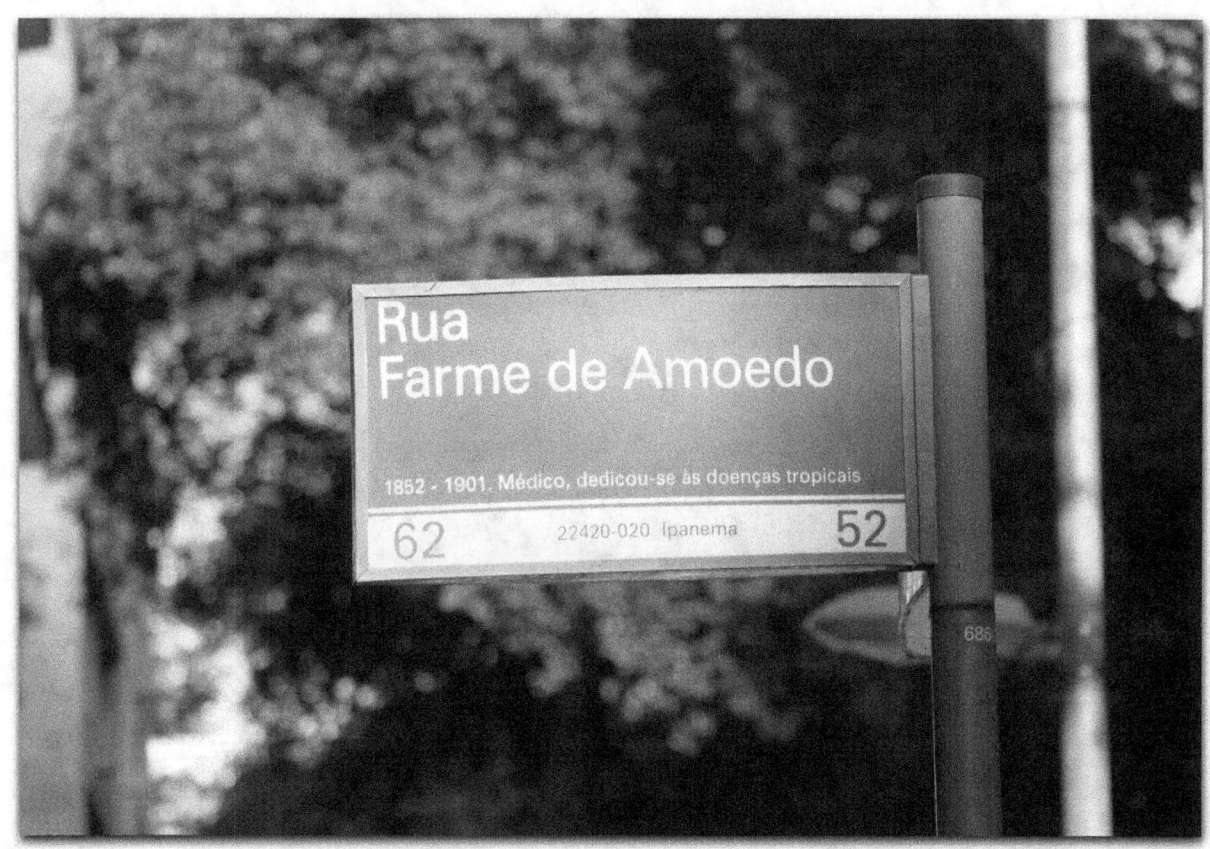

The Gayborhood: This is the gay street in Ipanema, from
Vieira Souto to Alberto de Campos.

Gays at the Beach

There are many spots for gays in Rio, but there is no place like the area near the street Rua Farme de Amoedo. According to the travel website **GayCities**, the "gays are concentrated around Farme de Amoedo, also called Farme Gay, where the muscle men and pretty boys flock."

In 2012 the New York-based popular paper **The Village Voice** reported how Rio was chosen as the best gay beach city in the world. After the beach in the early evening many gay guys walk over to the LGBT friendly establishments on and around Rua Farme de Amoedo such as Bofetada Bar, A Casa da Lua, and Gringo Café.

"It's my favorite street in the world," a young tourist from Dubai named Mohamed told me at Bofetada Bar, as he watched young guys walk on the street, "I love being here, the atmosphere is completely open and relaxed and accepting," he added, smiling, "I would say there isn't a better place to be."

During the weekend, especially on Saturday night, there are literally thousands and thousands of people on these streets. They will stay there until it's time to go to the popular nightclubs like The Week in the Saúde neighborhood.

Watch this video made by the **Rio de Janeiro Tourism Office** for LGBT visitors: https://youtu.be/uV_y3v6SJRg

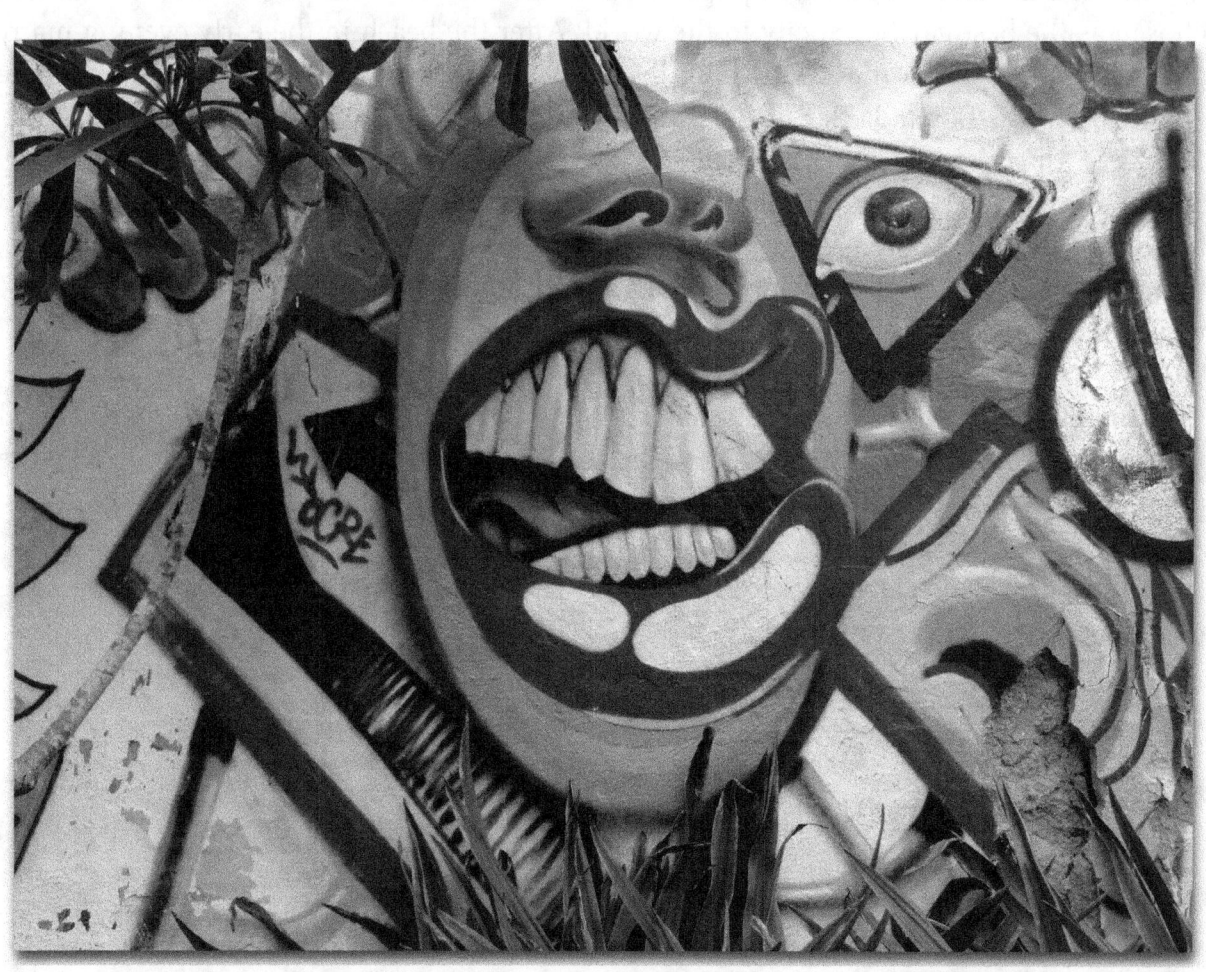

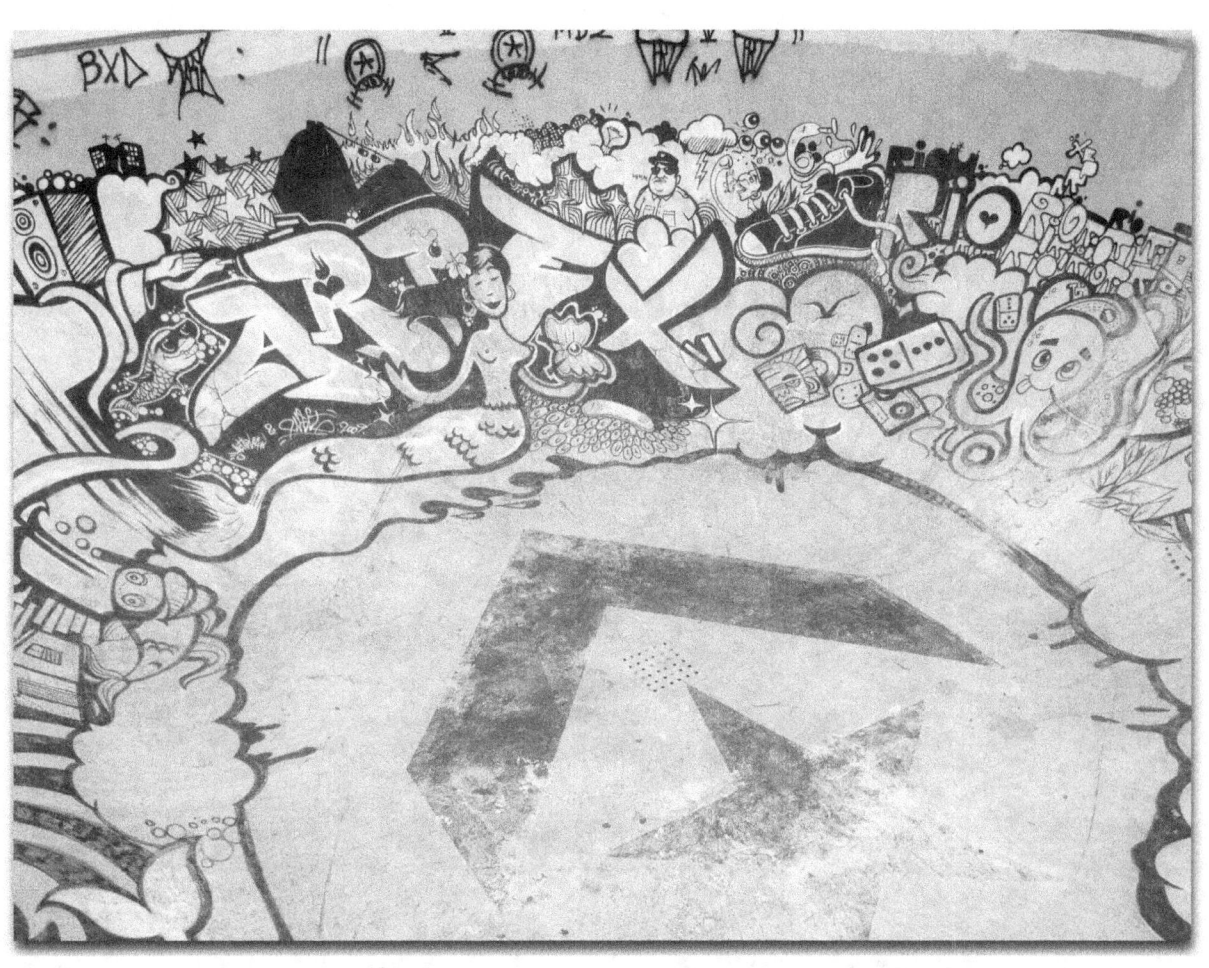

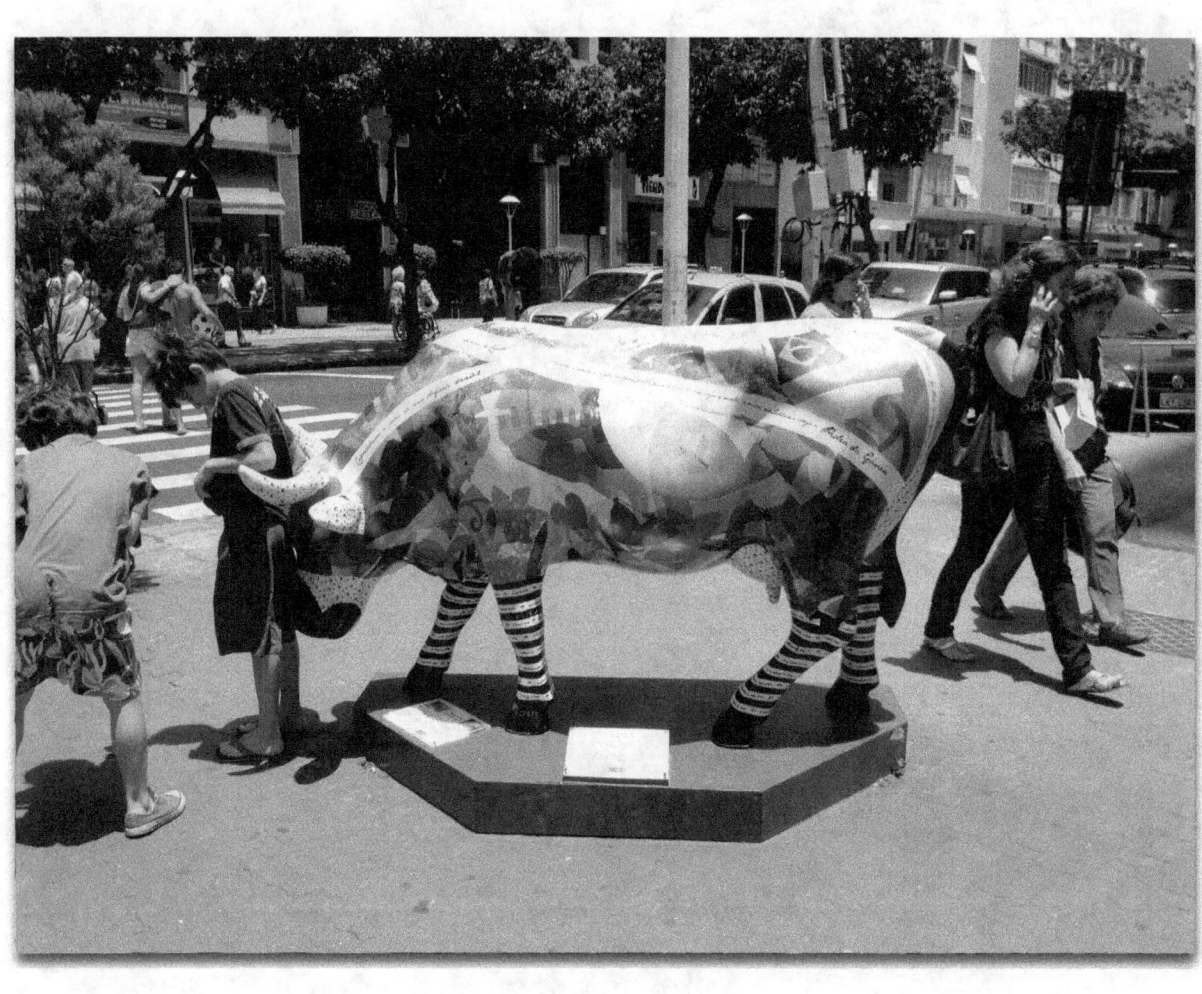

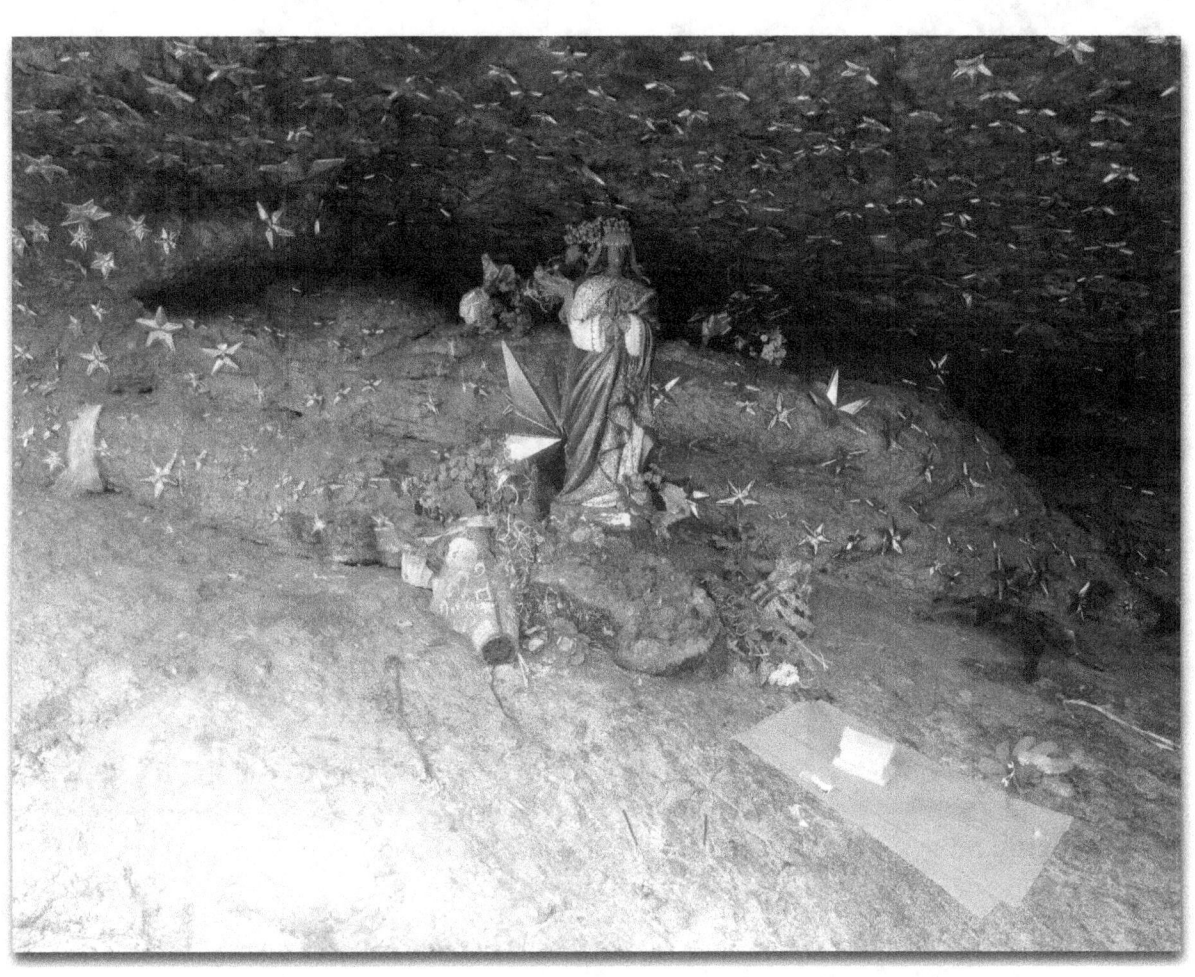

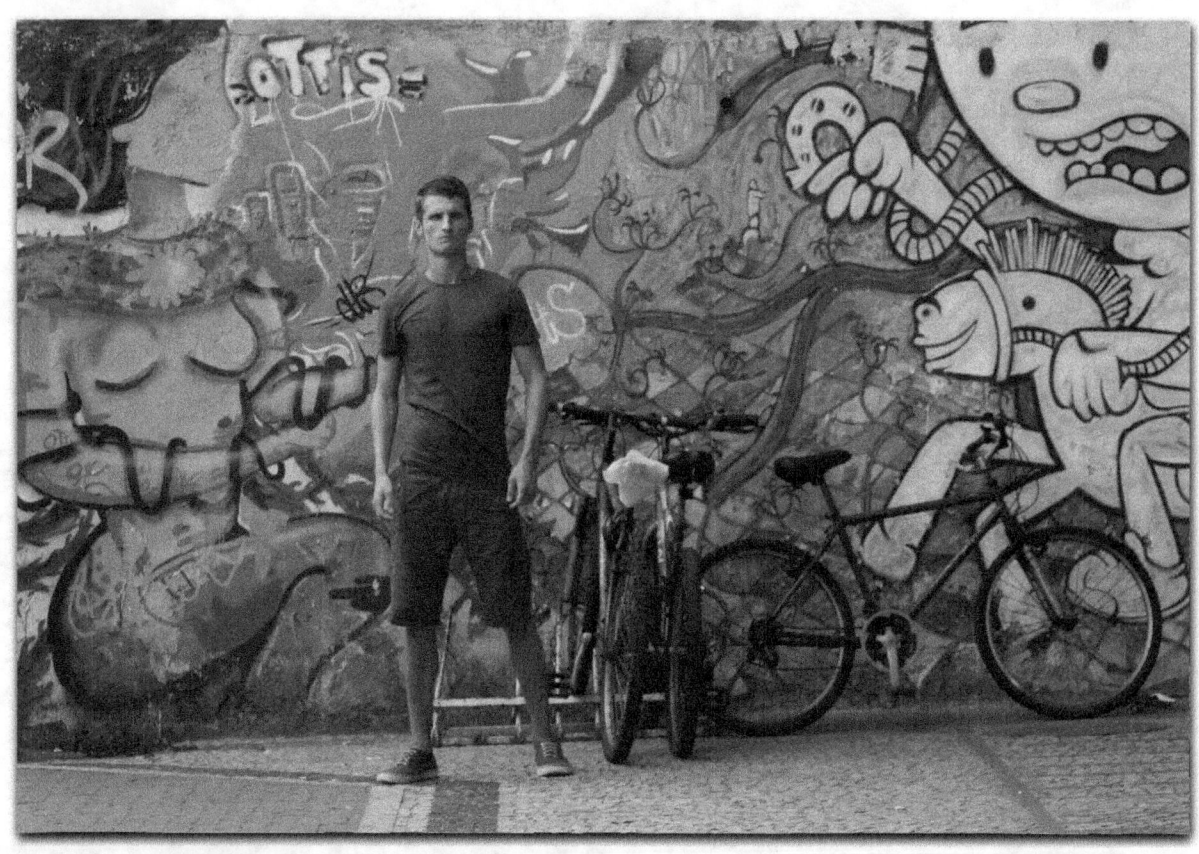

Artful Streets: like many parts of Rio this neighborhood has a lot of street art.

Street Art

In 2009 the city of Rio passed a law that made it legal for street artists to have fun, provided that the owners of such spaces agree to it.

"As progressive of a policy as this may sound," wrote Michelle Young for the **Huffington Post**, "the legislation is actually a reflection of the evolving landscape in Brazilian street art, an emerging and divergent movement in the global street art landscape."

Street art is a major artistic part of the Brazilian culture, and even foreign countries are now inviting Brazilian street artists to come and make their own cities colorful.

"I like the street art in Ipanema, particularly," Luciano, a young man who lives in the northern part of the city and whom I photographed, told me, "I think it's beautiful how they make the area more interesting."

Street art in Brazil is about many different things. Paulo Ito's 2014 image of a young boy crying at the table, holding a knife and fork firmly against the table while a soccer ball sits on the plate –– that image went globally viral.

Ito posted the mural on the door of a school just a month before the World Cup.

It has been shared millions of times on across social media, was featured on many international media outlets, and has taken on the ultimate response to something the rest of the world looked at positively.

Watch this **BBC** coverage of Paulo Ito's image: https://youtu.be/Qmw3cRYx0Lw

In other words art is alive in Rio!

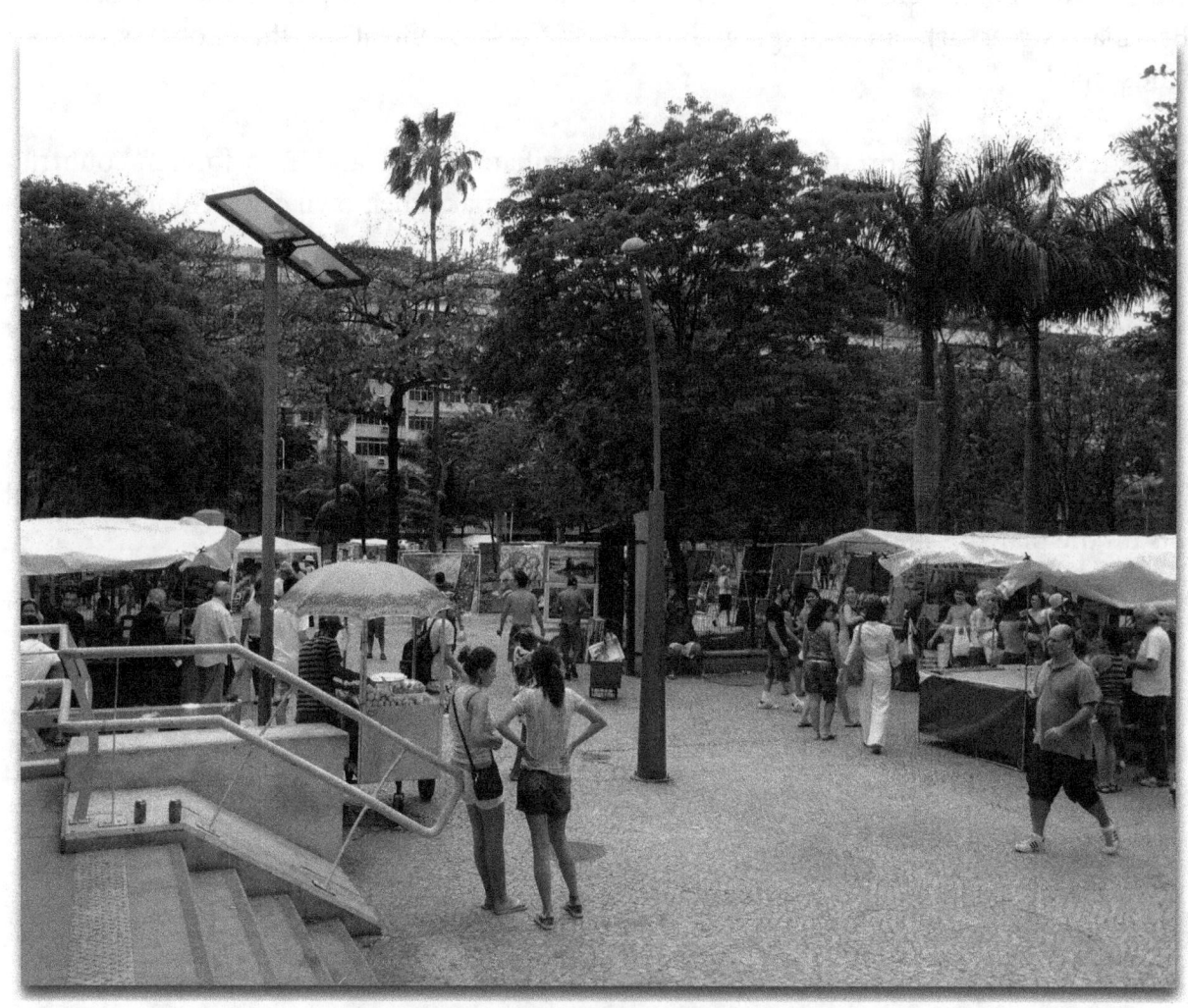

Street Market: **Feira Hippe** or Hippie Market.

Street Market

The **Hippie Market**, known locally as the *Feira Hippe de Ipanema*, is on Sundays and is generally open from 9am to 5pm, although you might find some people up to two hours before and after.

Located on Praça General Osório, which is just two blocks away from the beach on the main Ipanema drag and right on the metro station of the same name, this is a must see for anyone visiting Rio.

Founded in 1968, this quirky flea market has been operating continuously ever since without any problems.

The exhibitors are licensed through the city's Department of Finance, Fair Sector or *Secretaria Municipal de Fazenda, setor Feirarte*. You will find art, souvenirs, clothes, and there are a few stalls to try out unique foods such as acarajé or açaí.

To get a glimpse, watch this 2010 video by **GeoBeats** on YouTube: https://youtu.be/J6VbF2gBhGU

Happy shopping!

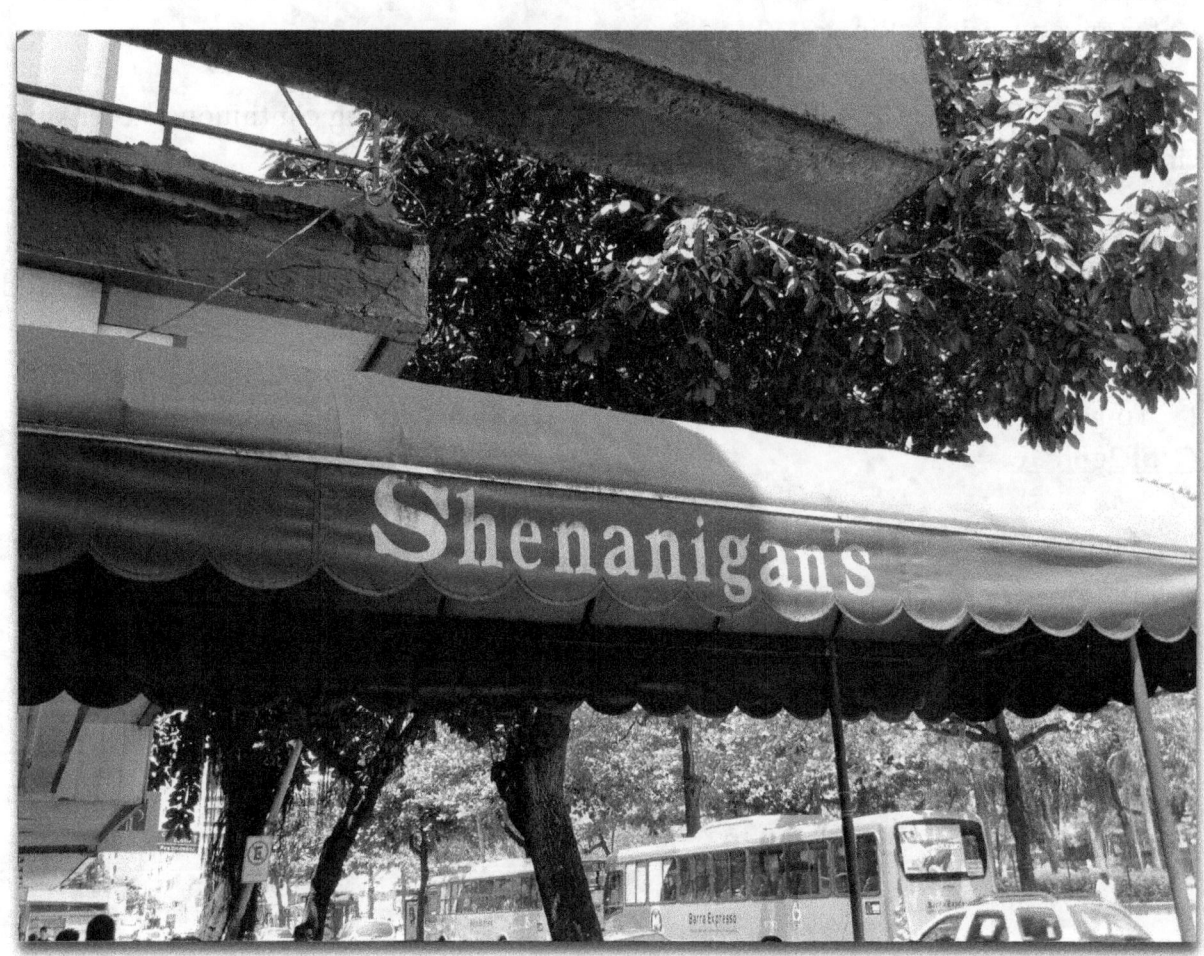

Irish pub.

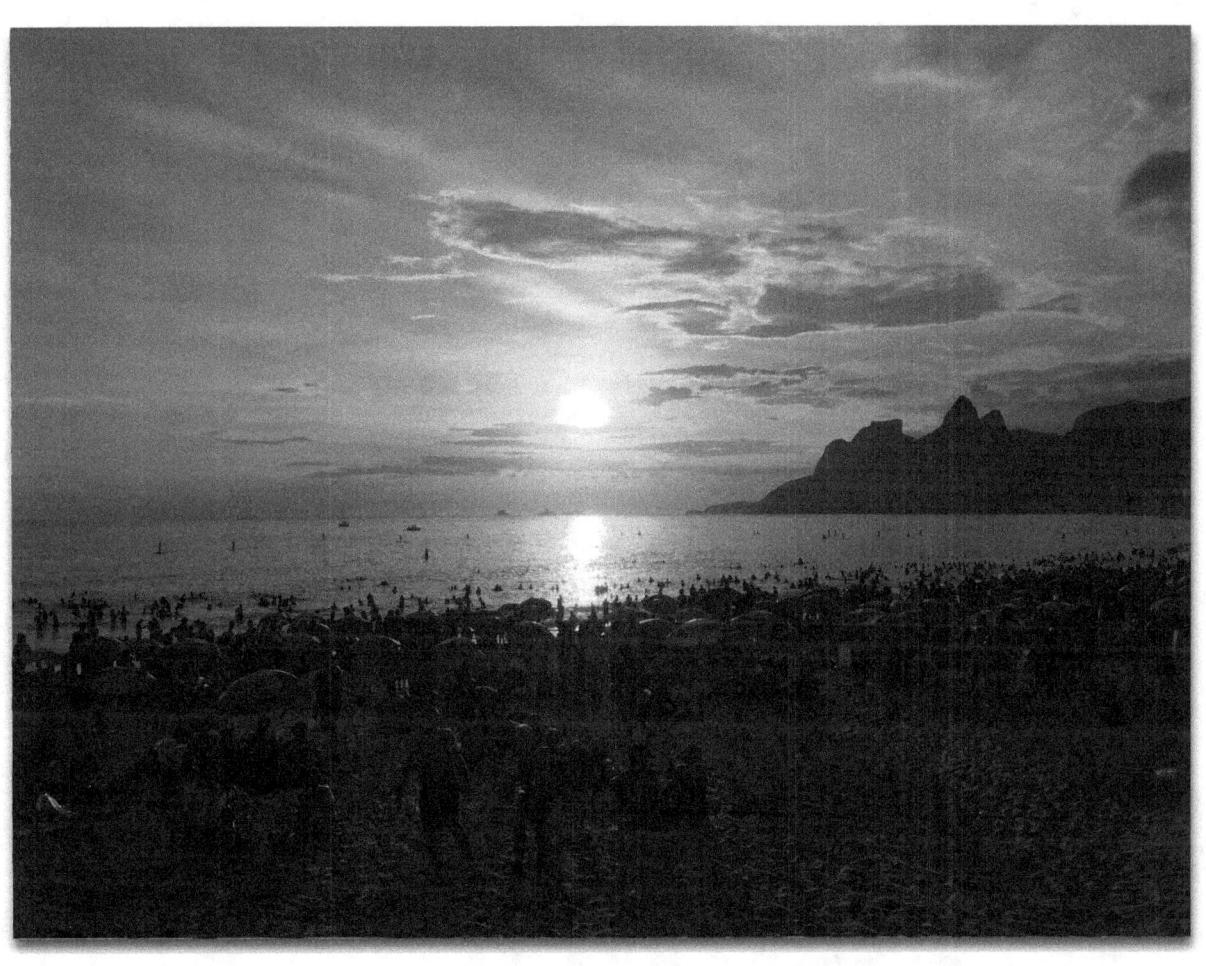

Copacabana

Before it was renamed in the 18th Century after a newly built chapel that held a replica of the Virgen de Copacabana, who by the way happens to be the patron saint of Bolivia, Copacabana was known as *Sacopenapā* or the Way of the Socós Bird in the local Tupi language.

The chapel was on the southern end of the district on land that now belongs to the Fort Copacabana, which was built in 1908 by the army to protect that part of the city.

These days, of course, no one thinks of birds or saints when they think about Copacabana. Instead, its 4-kilometer or 2 ½-mile beach life is what comes to mind.

Two things, I would say, characterize Copacabana: beach and luxury life.

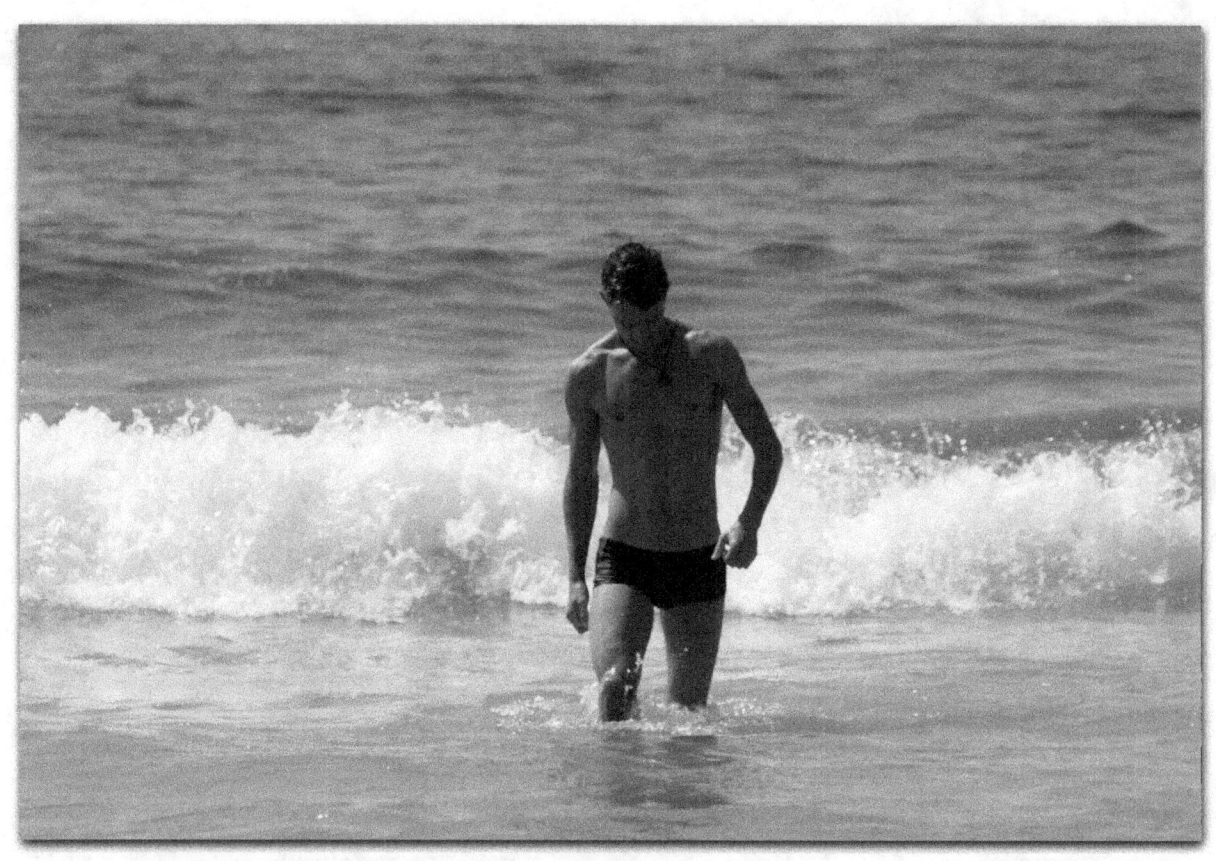

Copacabana Beach: Lucio rising out of the most famous beach in the world.

Copacabana Beach

Copacabana Beach is not just a place to go and sun tan; it is a big part of life for many locals. The people of this city love this beach so much they have nicknamed it **Princesinha do Mar** or Princess of the Sea.

Although the majority of the people at the beach are off of the water, doing things like playing sports or just having conversations, a large number of people are in the water in any given time of the daylight hours.

Generally, the warm weather of Rio makes it easy to swim any time of the year. Yet, these waters are cool enough that sharks don't like to swim. As such, far less shark attacks happen in Rio area than would in places like Recife.

To give you an example, the last fatal shark attack in Copacabana happened in 1947!

You may find many young men playing football or soccer at the beach, but don't think water sports are absent from this dynamic beach. There are several competitions taking place throughout the year like **Travessia dos Fortes** (Crossing of the Forts), which sees many people swim between the two forts, and the **Rei e Rainha do Mar** (King and Queen of the Sea), which is a national competition of swimmers.

The beach is also a place to go and meet, have a cool drink, and to be part of the distinct fun energy of this neighborhood. There are many kiosks on the mosaic-covered promenade of Avenida Atlântica. There are also tons of street artists, painting the sand, or selling their hand-made products like crafts or jewelry.

Finally, important beach parties like **New Year's Eve** celebration make the beach of this neighborhood a must even after the sun goes down.

In other words, Copacabana Beach is a place for many occasions.

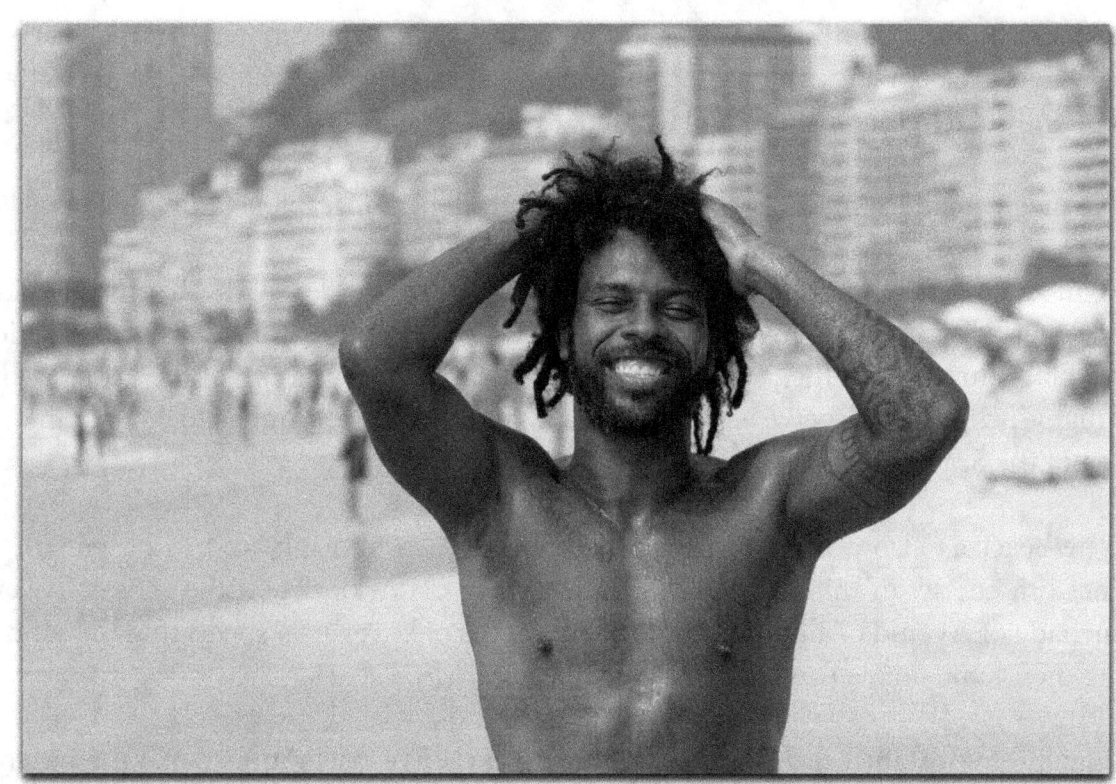

Italo out of the warm water.

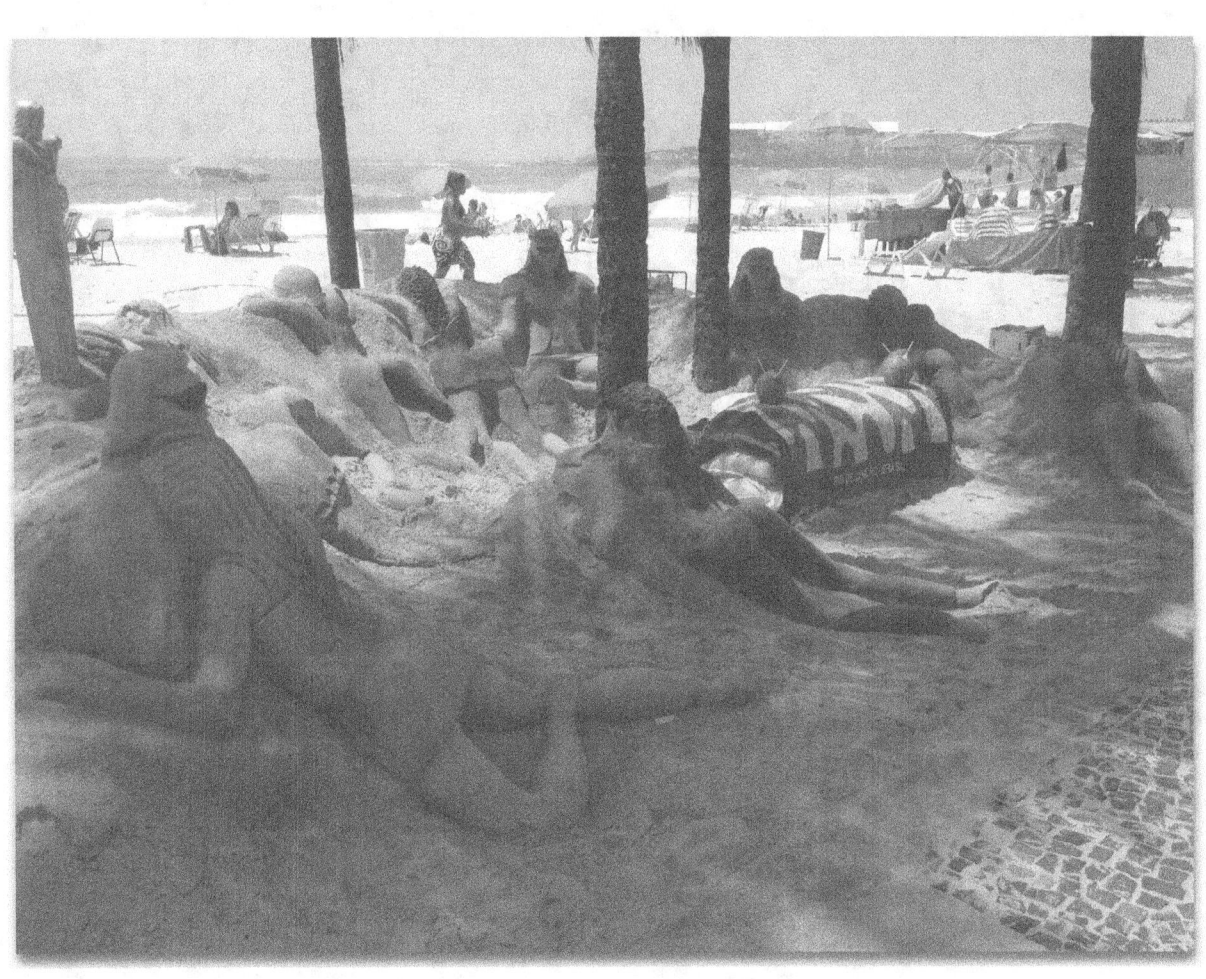

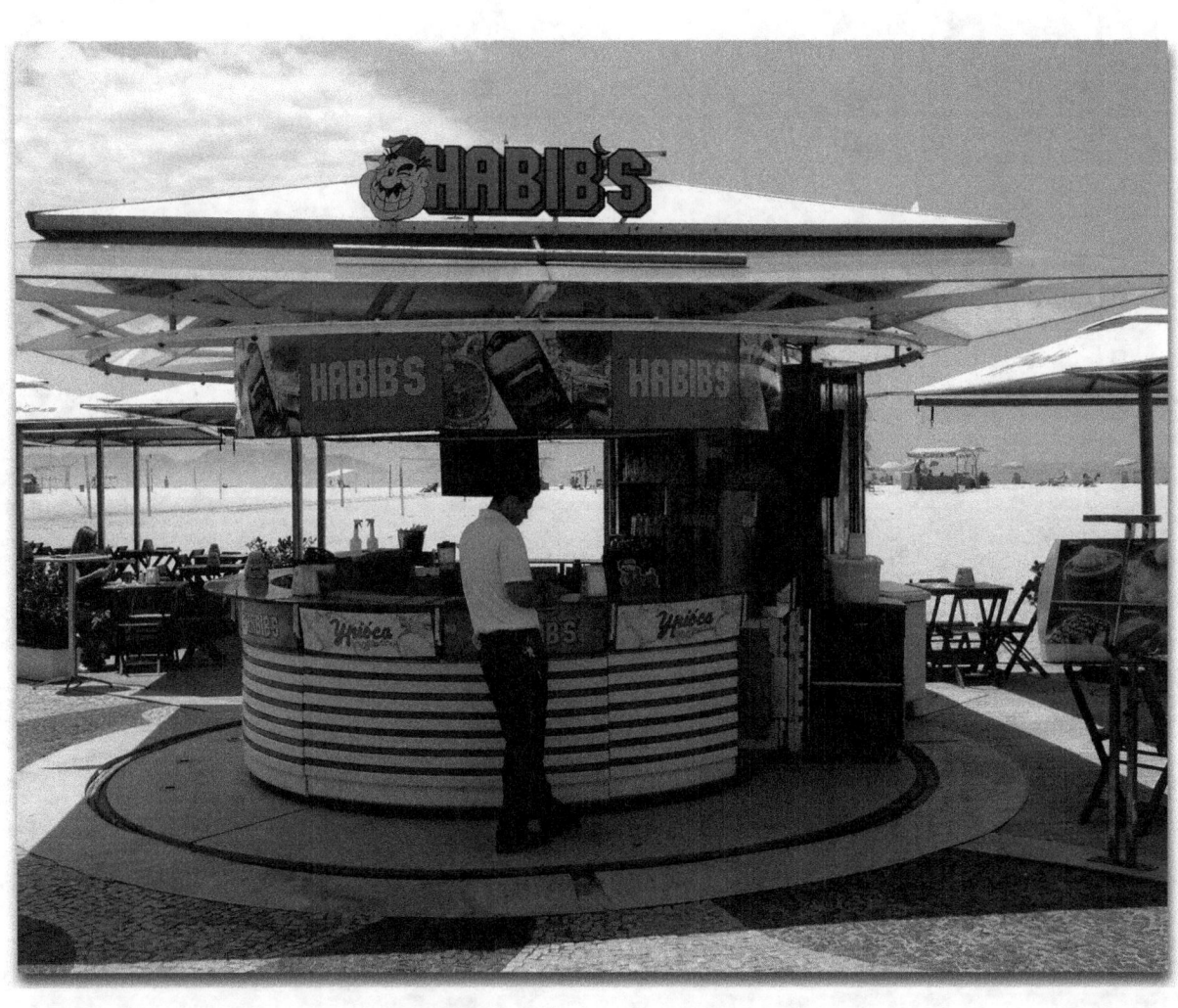

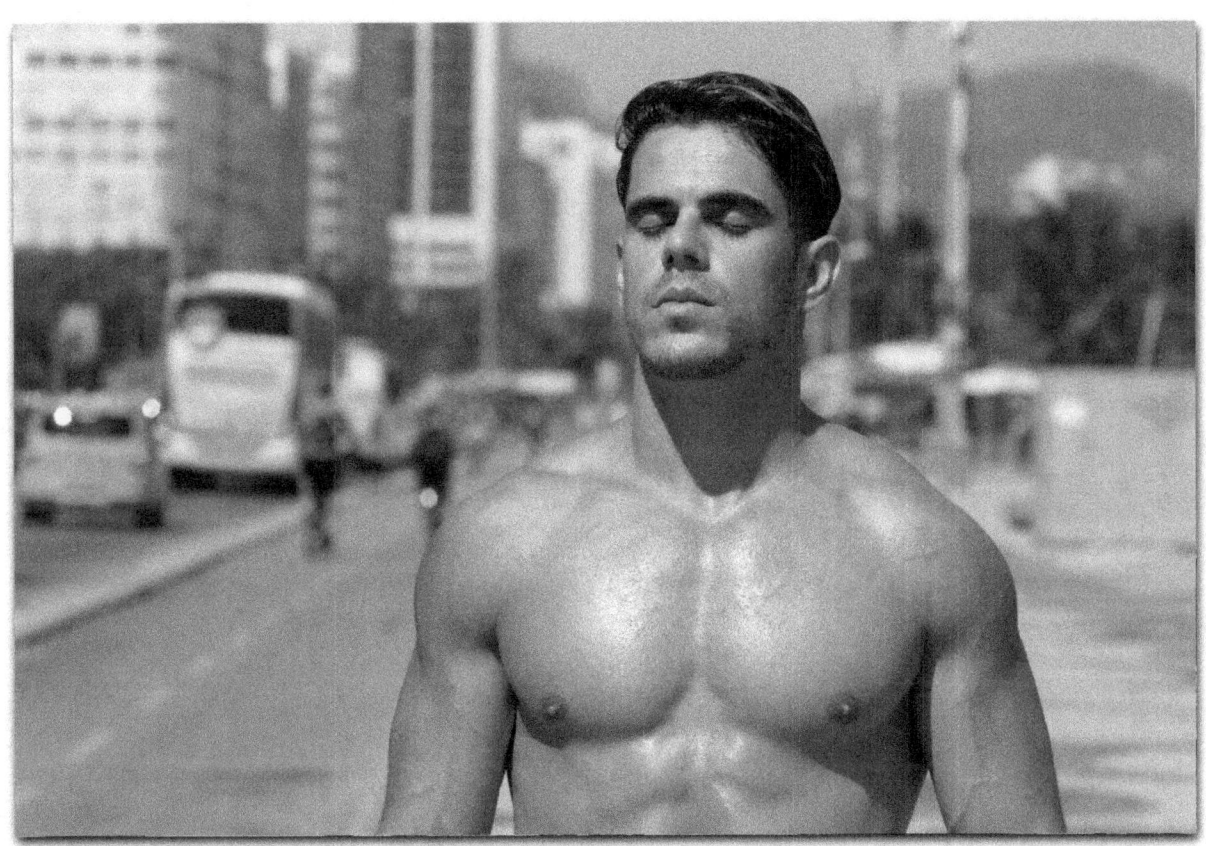

Leo communing with the sun on Avenida Atlântica.

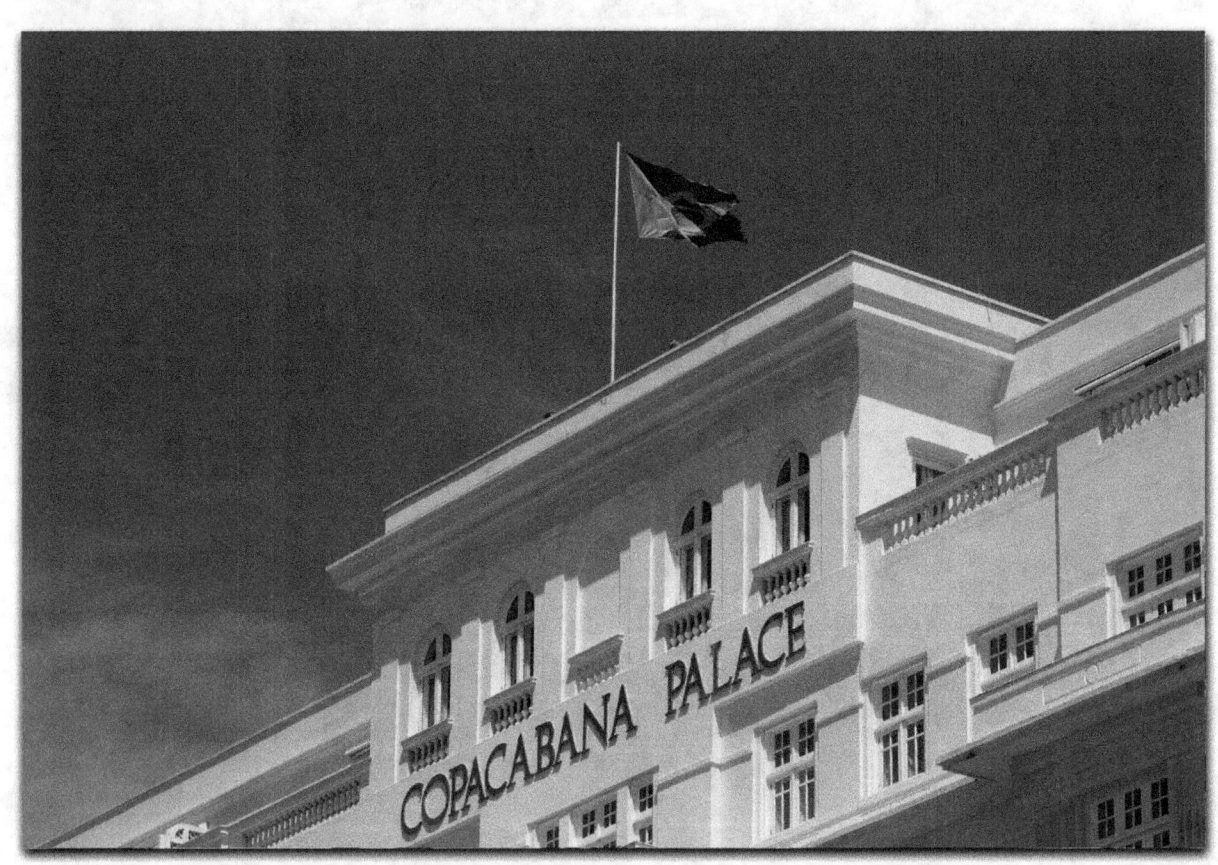

Luxury on **Avenida Atlântica**: One of the high-end properties on this avenue, Copacabana Palace.

The Most Expensive Street

Properties on **Avenida Atlântica**, although without a doubt some of them are really most beautiful you will find anywhere in the world, are some of the most expensive in all of South America.

The street is lined with buildings that are generally eleven or twelve floors and house hotels, residential apartments, and on the lower part, usually street level, restaurants, bars, and few exclusive shops.

Because the dollar is currently three times more than the Brazilian real, these hotels on this avenue are not as expensive as they used to be. For example, at the famous **Royal Rio Palace** you could stay in the Presidential Suite for a 3-day weekend (staying January 22 – 25, 2016, booked on January 12th) for just $600.

You see, the hotels on this avenue change dramatically based on the dates. If you were to book, for example, one of the executive suites at **Porto Bay Rio Internacional**, a four-star property just down the road from Royal Rio Palace, for a 3-day weekend during the Carnival, you would be paying a nice sum of $6,000. For the same suite at this property, booked on the same dates as the Royal Rio Palace in January, would cost just $1,300.

Now, to give you comparison, the **Windsor Guanabara** in Centro (downtown), a four-star property, would cost you just $500 for the same dates in Carnival.

"You pay for the famous name," says Leo, who I photographed in this street, "The same quality somewhere else will cost maybe half if not lower."

In 2014 the famous architect Zaha Hadid announced plans to create her first property in South America on this avenue. That means, for sure, it will add more luxury to this area.

Watch this video about the **Windsor Excelsior Hotel** in Copacabana:

https://youtu.be/MGDSy0gM8bQ

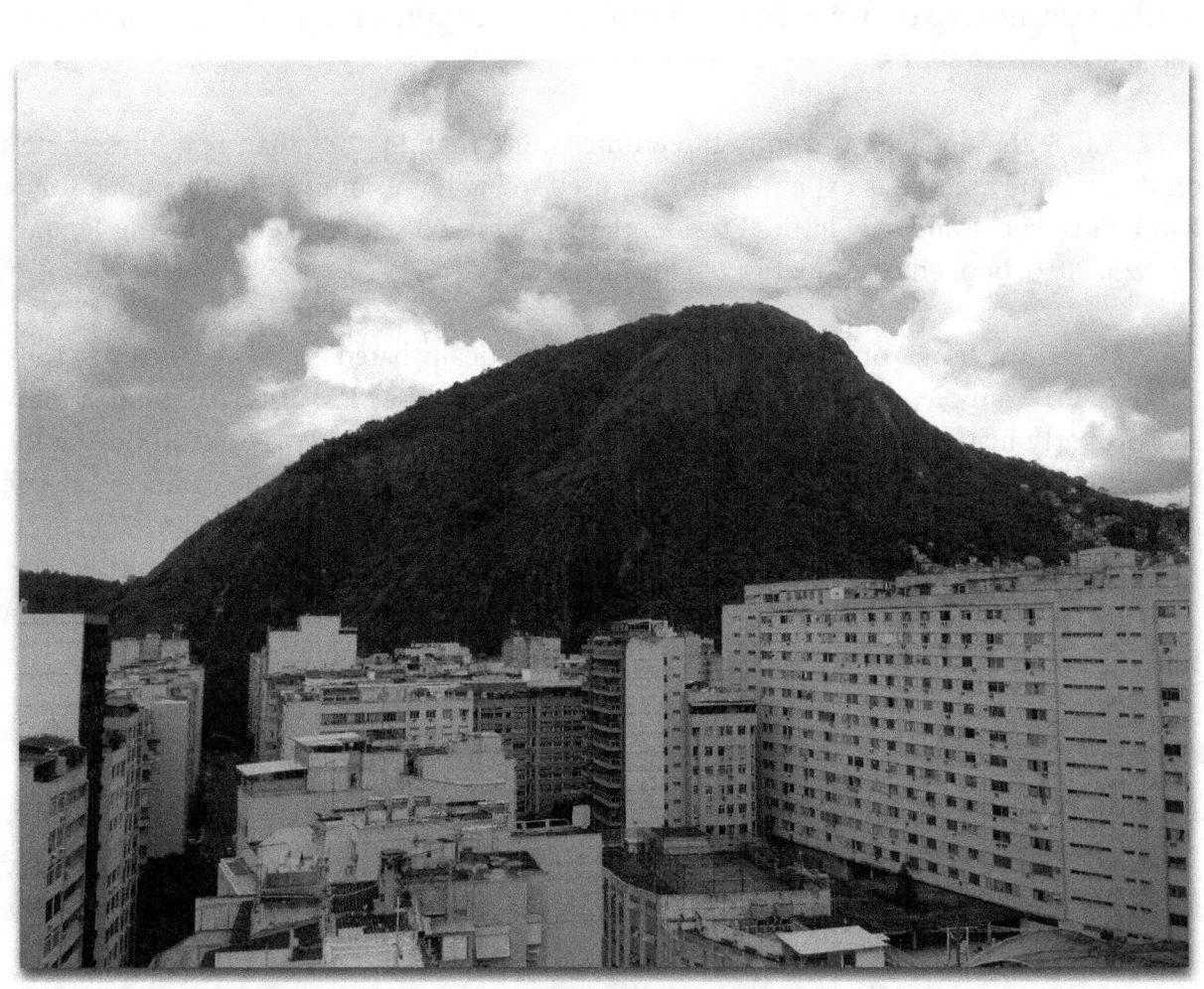

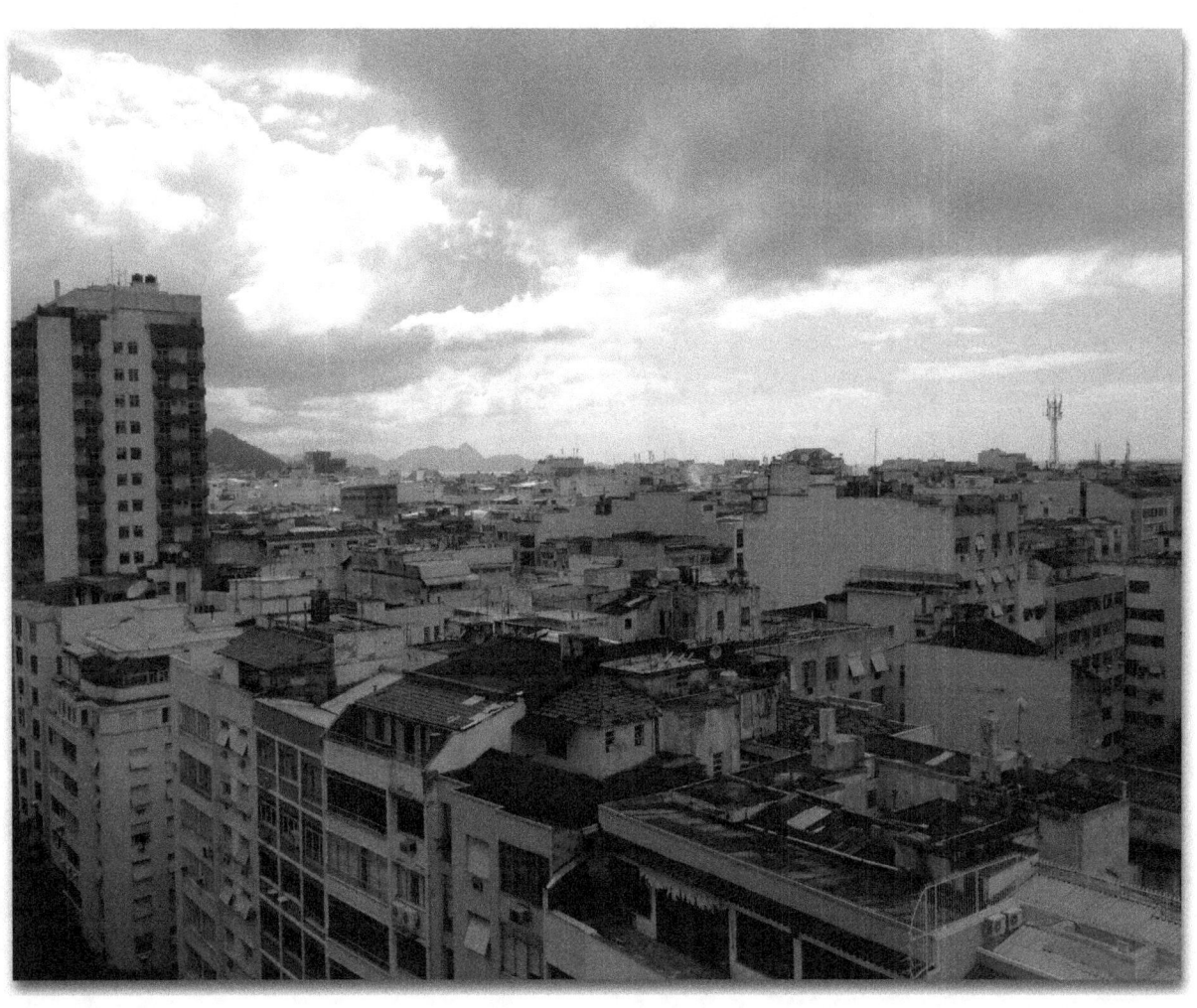

Botafogo

Botafogo is another beachfront neighborhood, situated between the Guanabara Bay, and the hills of Dona Morta, Mundo Novo, and São João. It is home to **Botafogo** football club and as such is famous nationally.

The popular **Botafogo Praia Shopping** and **Shopping Rio Sul** malls are located here. **Cemitério São João Batista** (John the Baptist Cemetry), which is home to many famous dead people and is the only cemetery in Latin America to be featured on Google Street View, is also located here.

Renato, a young man who lives in the northern part of the city but who works in a simple café in the neighborhood, said that for him the neighborhood is an interesting place to be.

"It's very nice and quiet. It's not so crazy like Ipanema or Copacabana," Gerson Couto, who lives in nearby Flamengo, agreed, as I took a photo of Renato's co-worker juicing organic oranges.

Marc Kruas, an artist I photographed and who lives in the neighborhood, says his neighborhood is booming with artistic flair.

With a young crowd, who enjoy the cute restaurants and bars, many locals are referring to this area as "BotaSoho" (check the hashtag on Twitter and Instagram, for example, to see cute photos from interesting neighborhood hangouts).

"I love living here because it's a bohemian chic neighborhood," said Marc, whose colorful body I photographed at home and in Lagoa nearby, adding, "I love it here because it's a very young neighborhood. There are a lot of good bars and restaurants, new art galleries, cinemas, good stores––all we need to live, simple and cozy place."

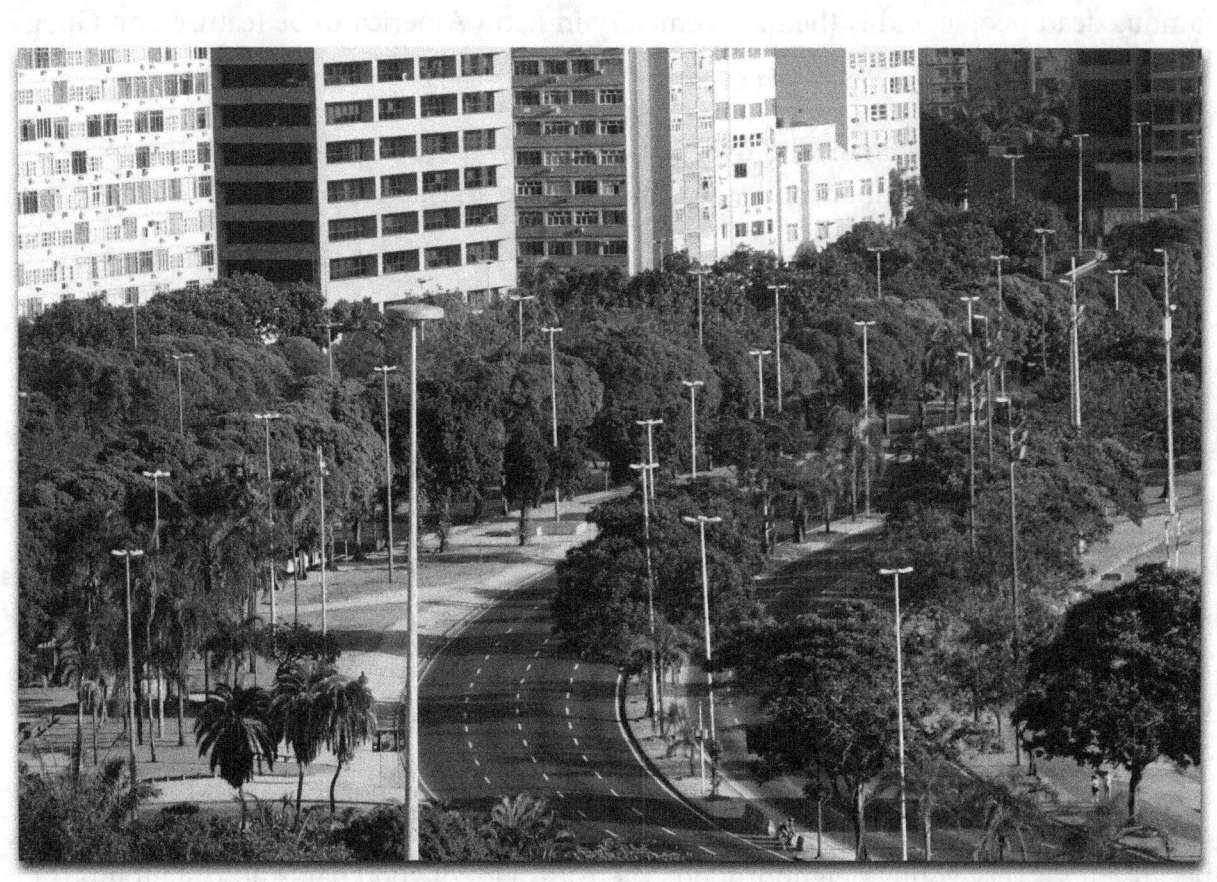

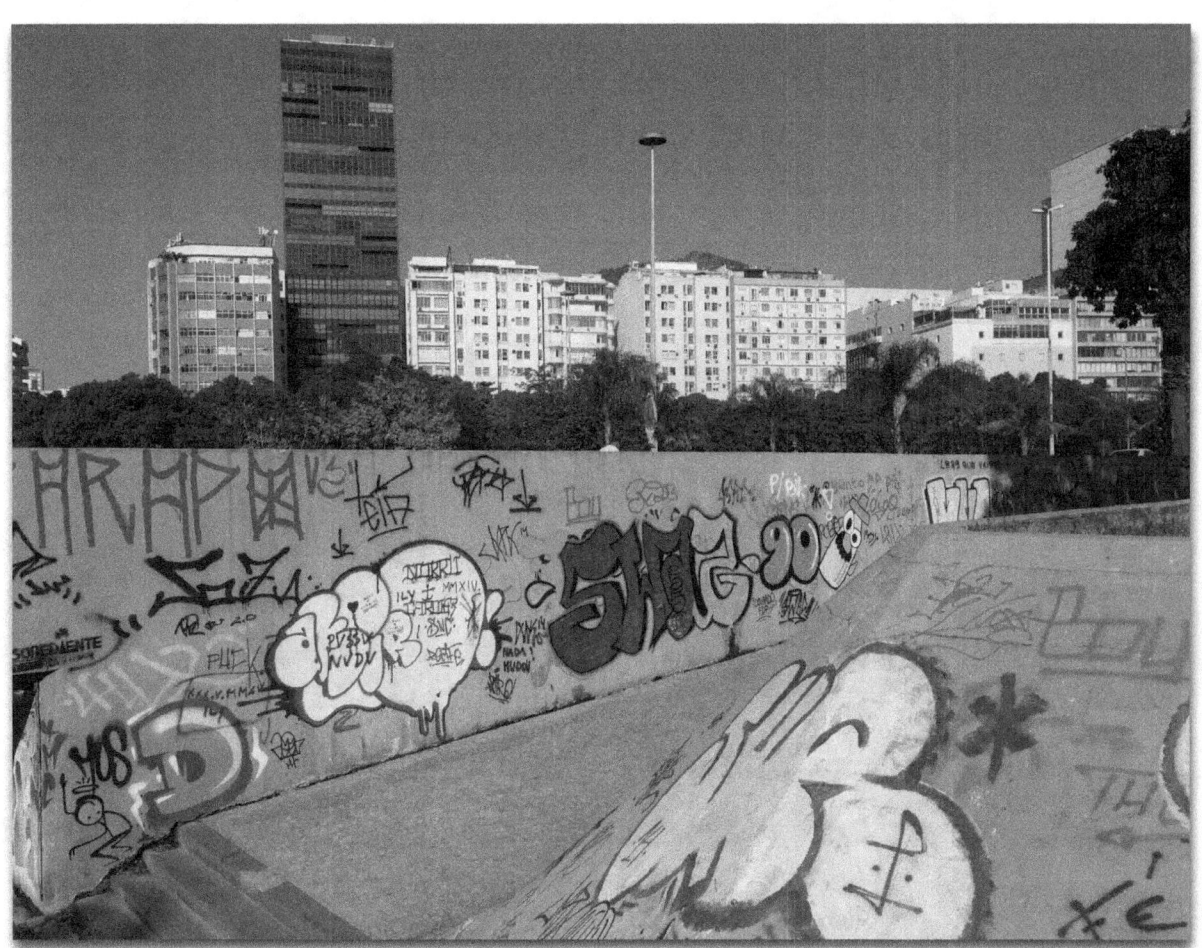

Colorful Underpass: Graffiti on the **Avenida das Nações Unidas** underpass.

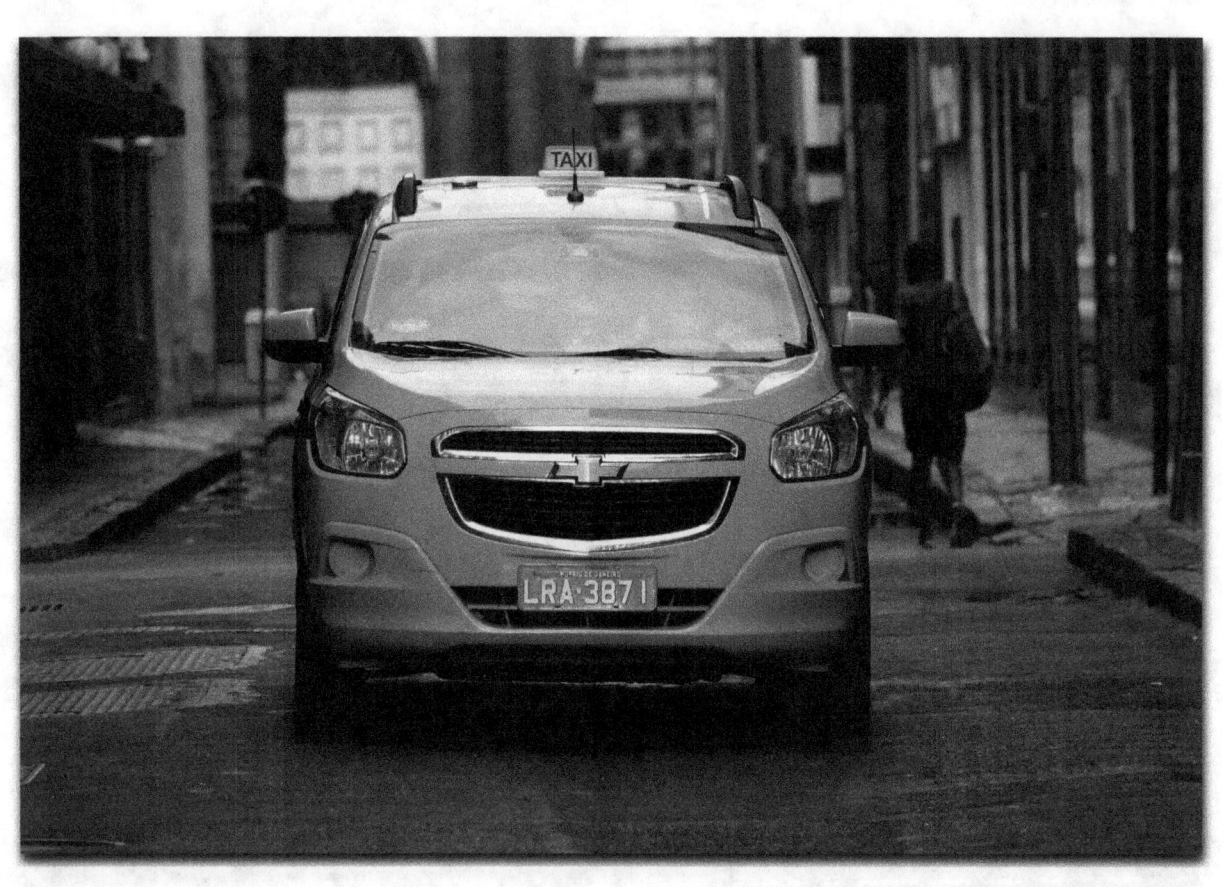

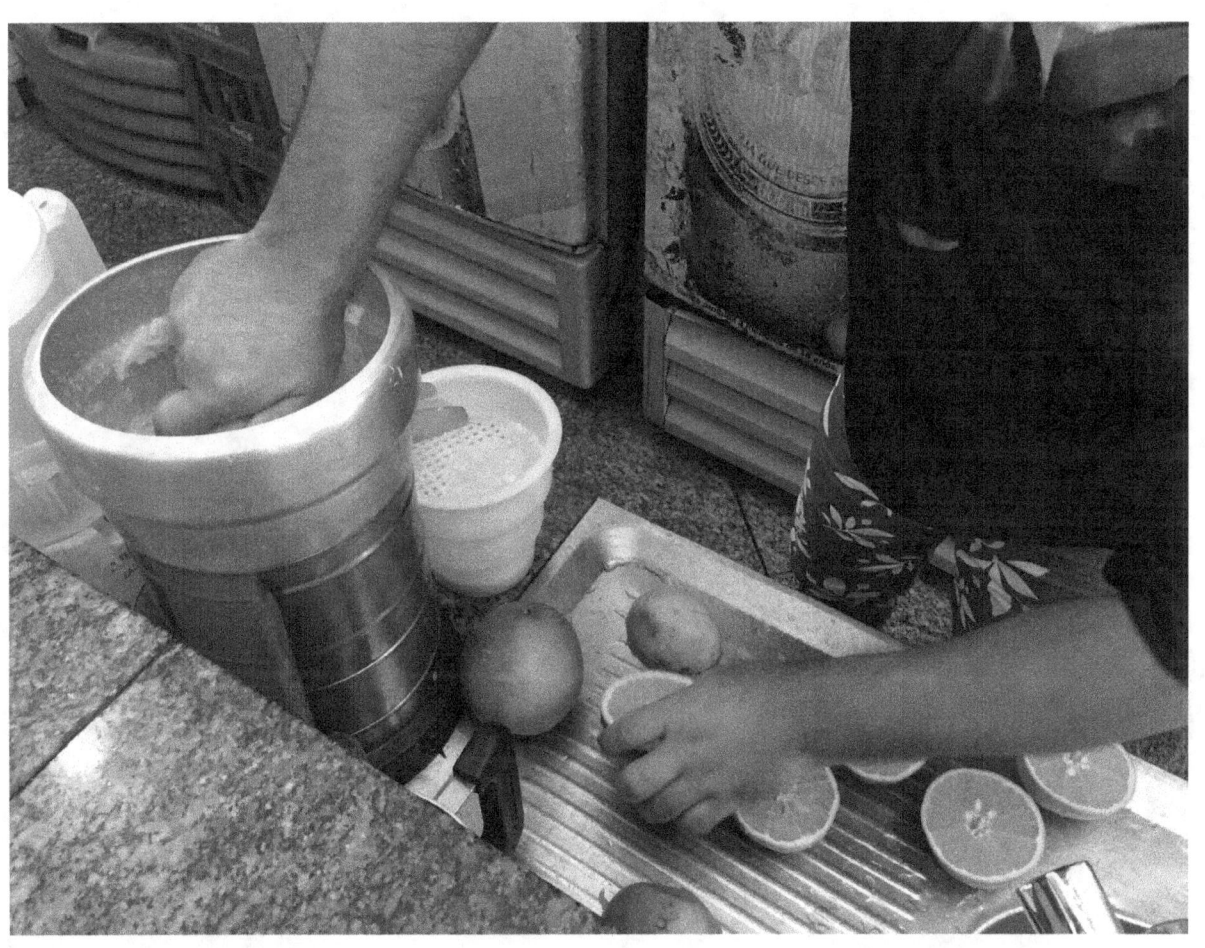

Flamengo

Olivier van Noort, the Dutch maritime explorer, tried to invade the area known today as Flamengo in the late 1500s.

At the time the Portuguese called the Dutch "Flamengo" or "Flemish," and they even had a "Belgian-Portuguese" dictionary in which, of course, the "Belgian" part actually meant Dutch.

This is because the Portuguese were familiar with the Flamengos do Faial, or the Flemish who settled in the Island of Faial in the archipelago of the Azores.

As such, this part of the city grew around the beach, **Praia do Flamengo**.

Of course, these days no one thinks of the Flemish or the Dutch. Instead, this neighborhood is popular thanks to the **Aterro do Flamengo** or the Flamengo Park, the largest public park within the city limits.

On Sundays, when the park and its streets are closed to the traffic, city residents flock there and enjoy this part of their city without the cars. The oceanfront avenues in Leblon, Ipanema, and Copacabana and the Aterro do Flamengo between Botafogo and Centro are closed to car traffic on Sundays.

"Life is great here," says Gustavo, who lives in the neighborhood and whom I photographed at the beach and park, "I like living here because it's the perfect place to be active."

Gustavo, whom I spotted skating through the park and graciously agreed to be photographed by me, says having Sundays without the traffic really adds a special feel. "You just feel like you're free."

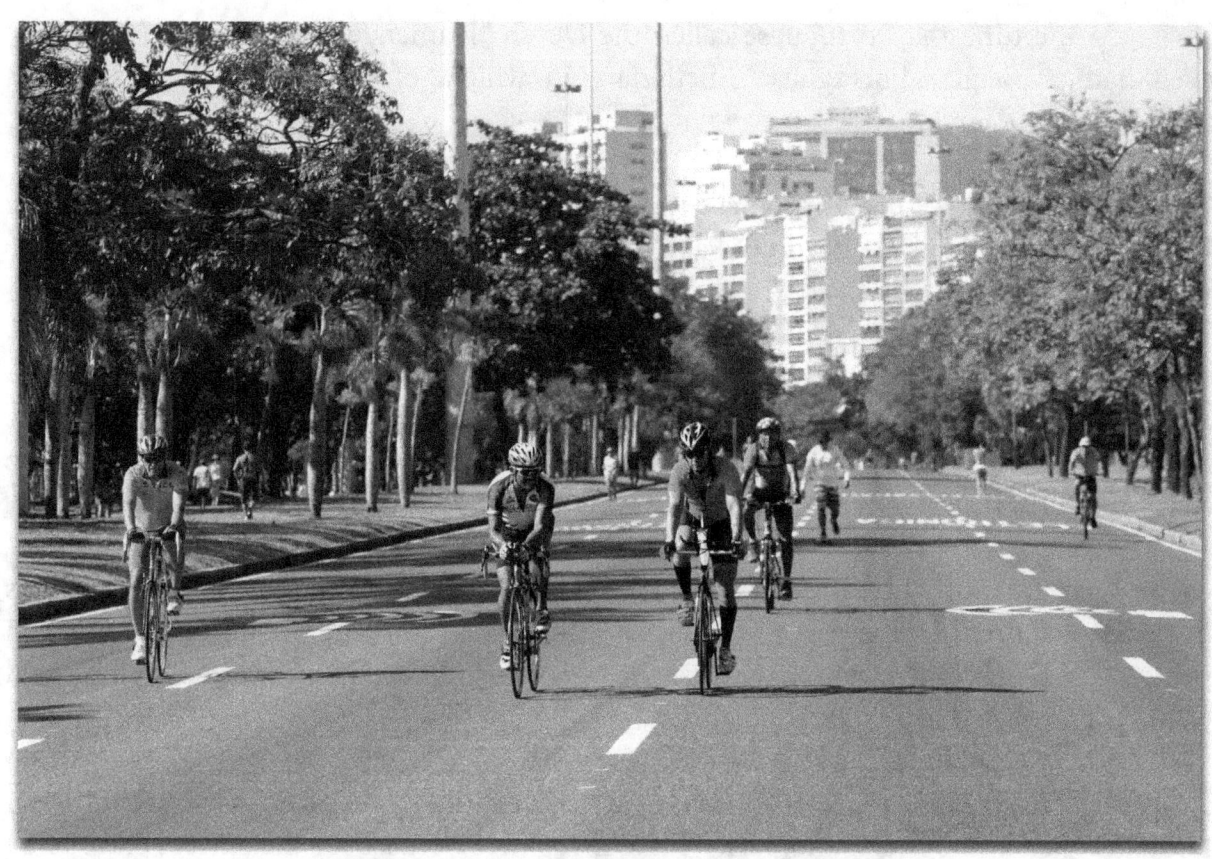

Sundays without Cars: Cyclists, skaters, and runners
enjoy **Avenida Infante Dom Henrique** in Flamengo Park.

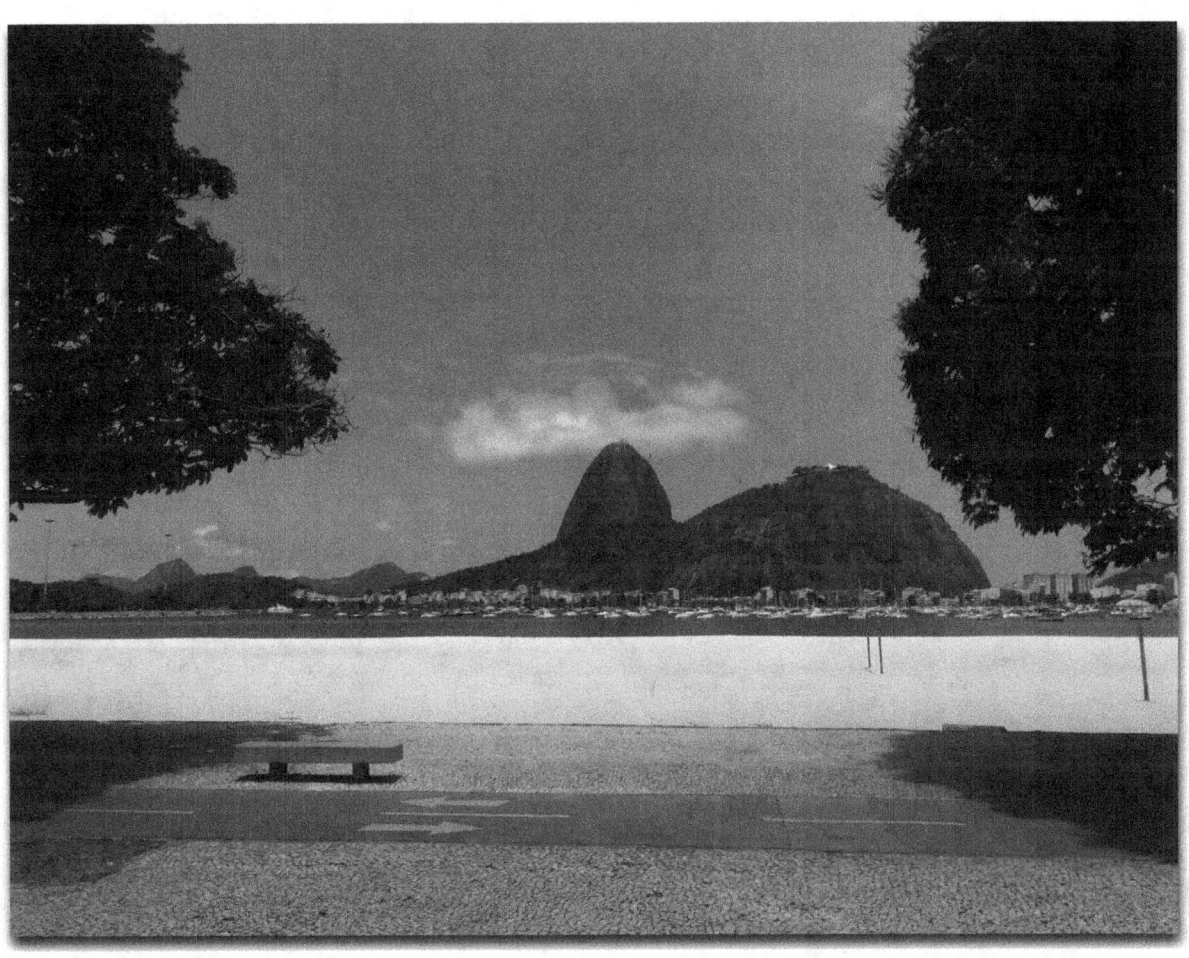

Flamengo Beach is a good place to sit and take in **Pão de Açúcar** (Sugarloaf Mountain).

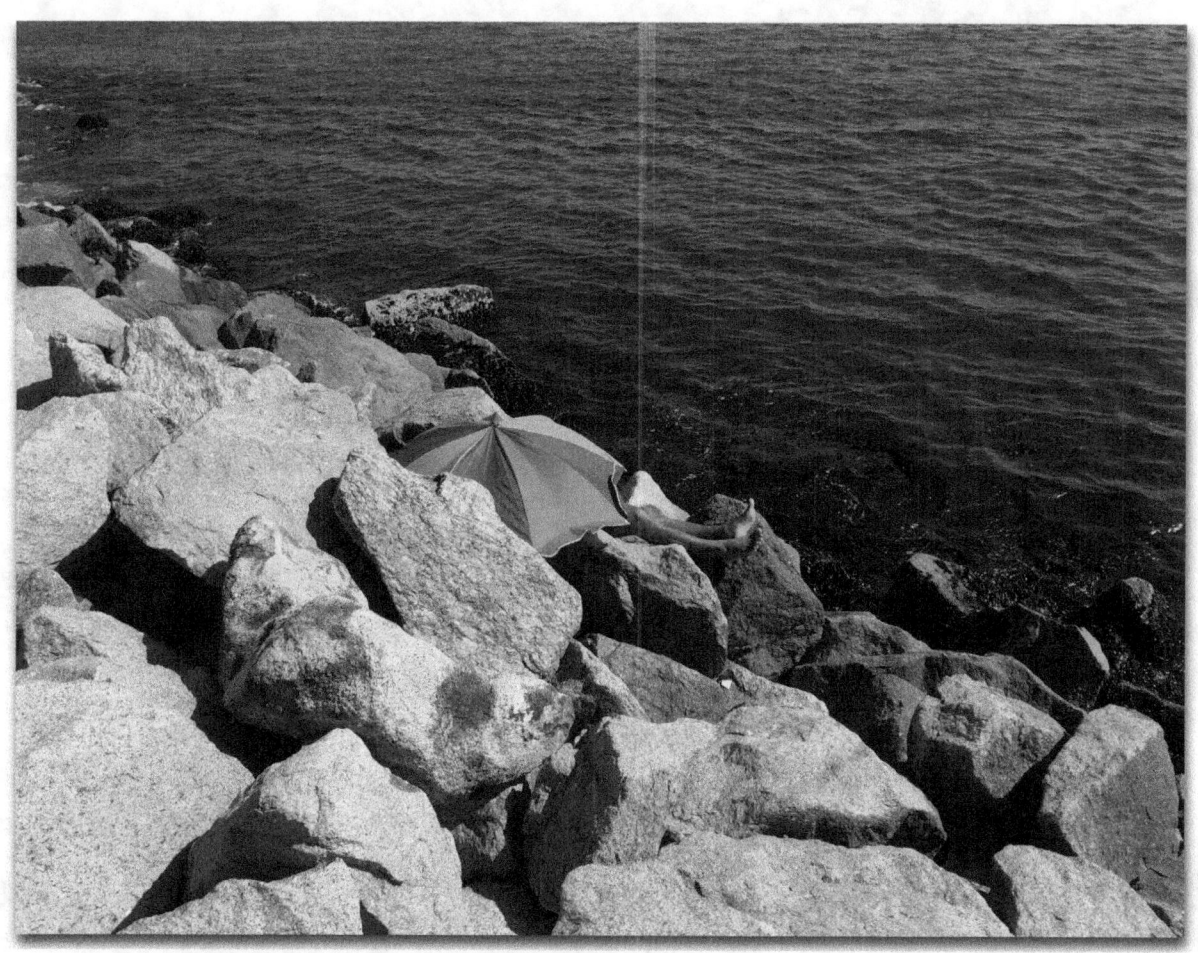

A woman having a nap on the rocks just before Flamengo Beach.

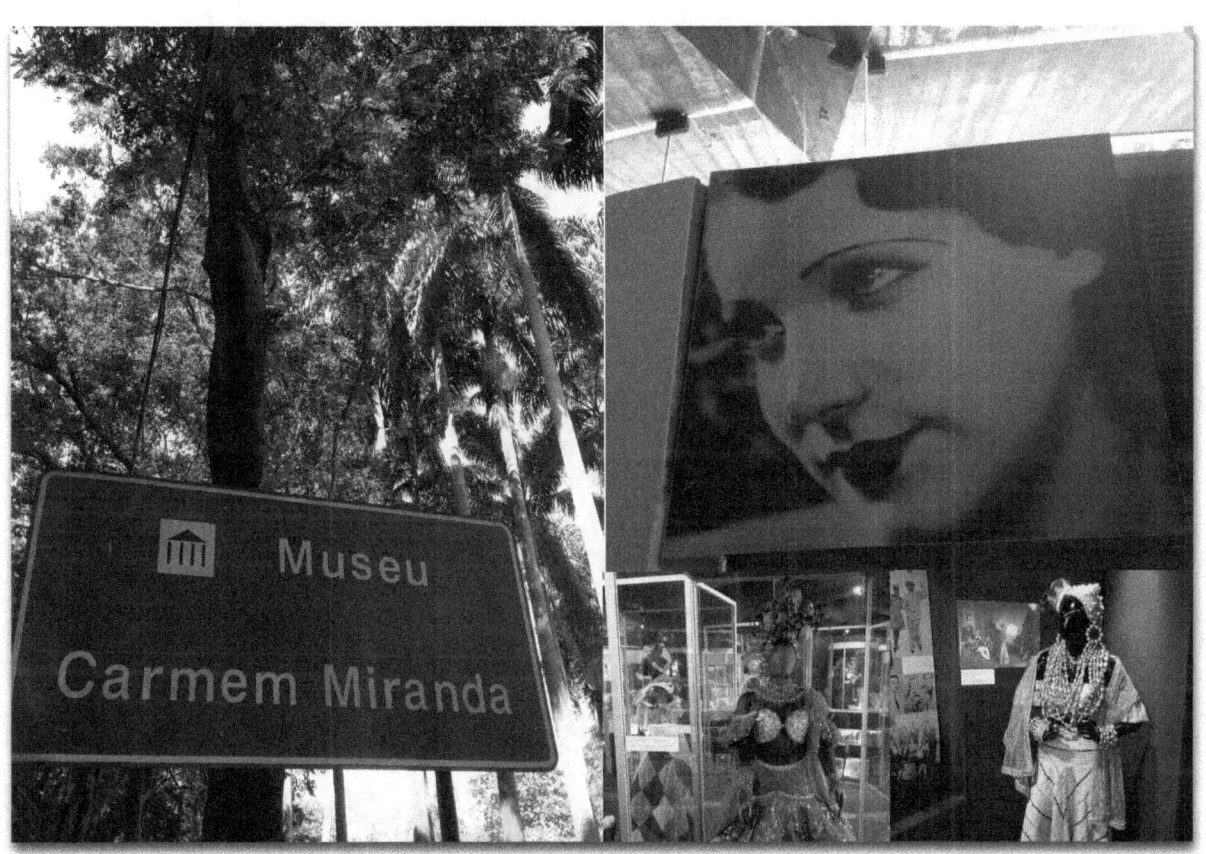

The **Carmen Miranda Museum** at Flamengo Park.

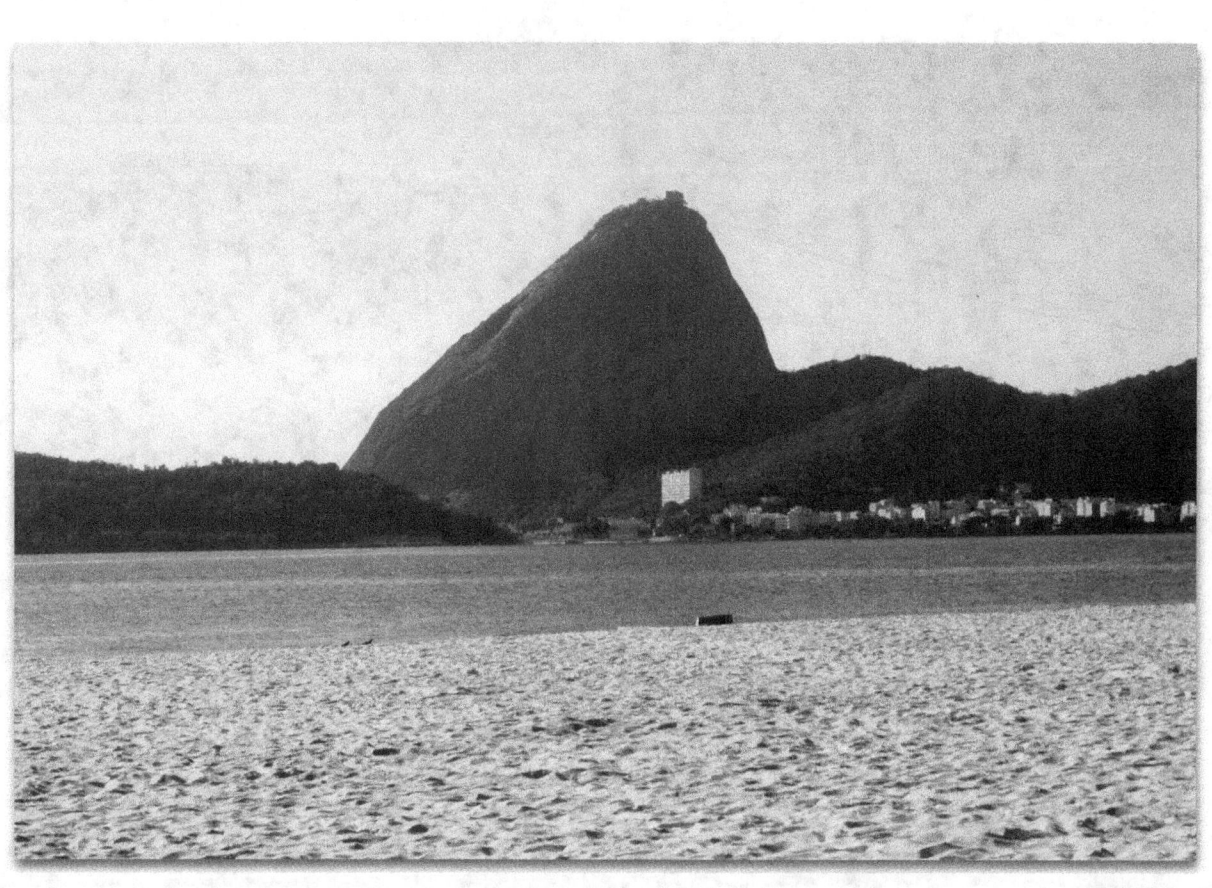

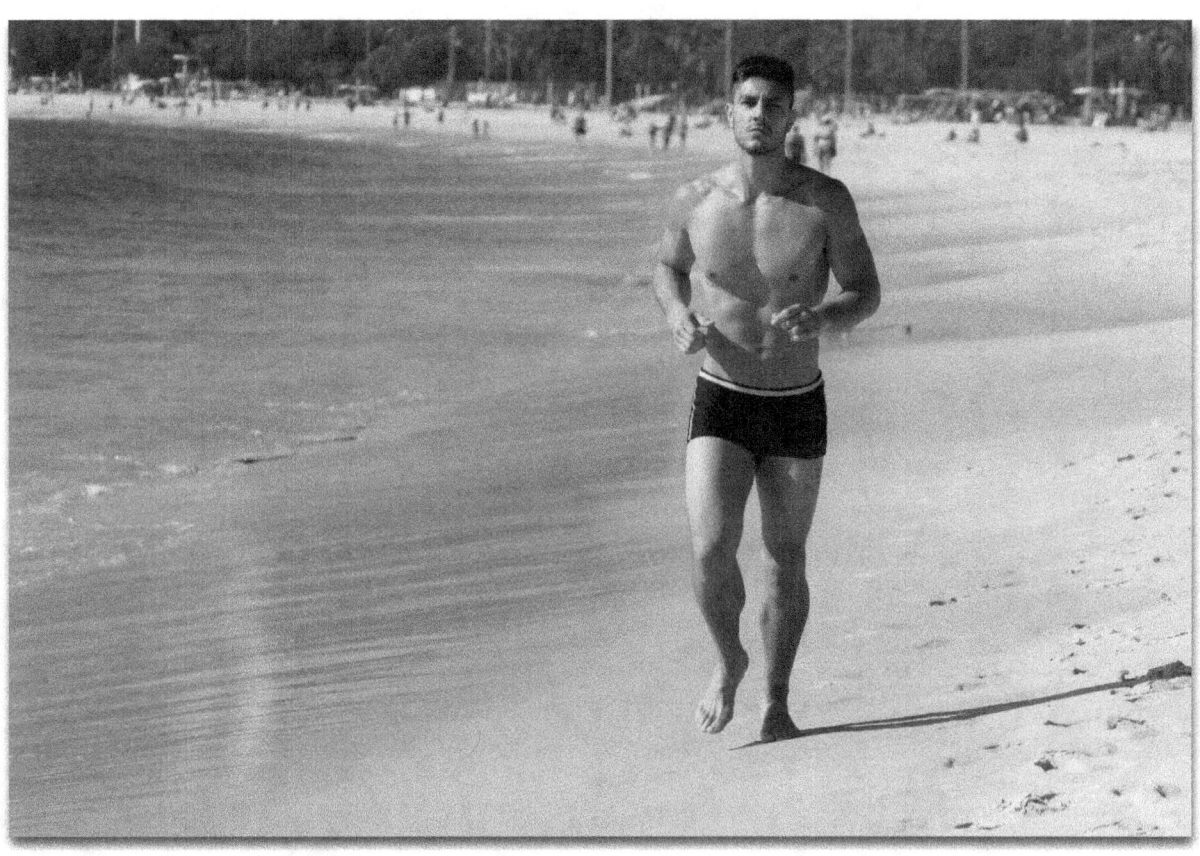

Gustavo runs along the shores of **Flamengo Beach**.

Glória

Believe it or not but this is the area of town from which the name *carioca*, the modern demonym of the city, comes from. Before the **Nossa Senhora da Glória do Outeiro** (Our Lady of the Glory of the Hill), the church that was built in the 17th century, the area was home to a village occupied by the Tupí people called Karioca.

Since the church, however, the area is known as Glória.

Today Glória is home to **Marina da Glória**, the popular **Feira da Glória** Sunday market, the famous church, and **Praça Pistóia**, a park where important World War II memorial monument is located.

"Glória is an incredible neighborhood," says Gerson Couto, who lives in the nearby Flamengo, "I love the Marina and the Sunday market," he adds, as we walked through a boat on the Marina for a shoot, "I love to come here because I think the Marina gives me the feeling I could sail away any time. I love to be free."

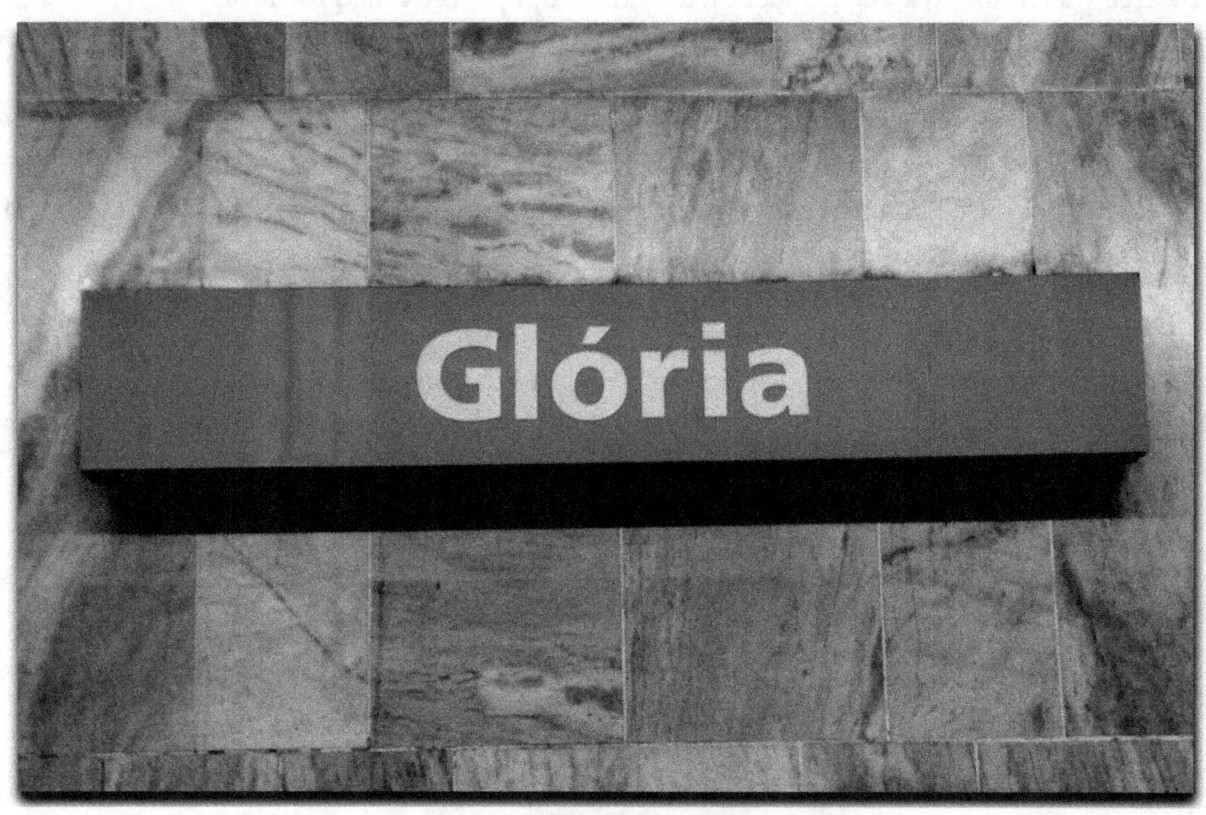

Glória's **Metrô Rio** station.

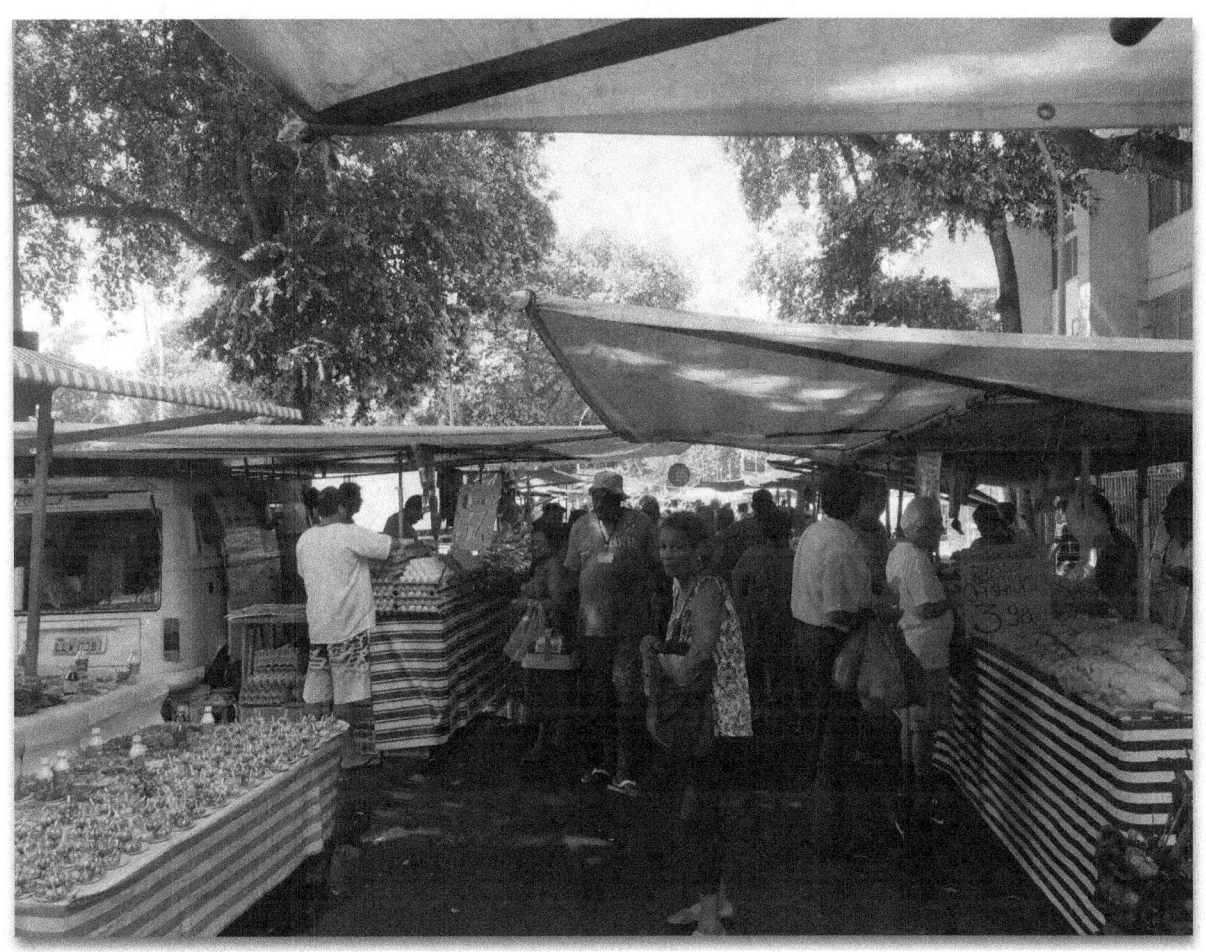

Sunday Market: **Feira da Glória** is a popular farmer's market.

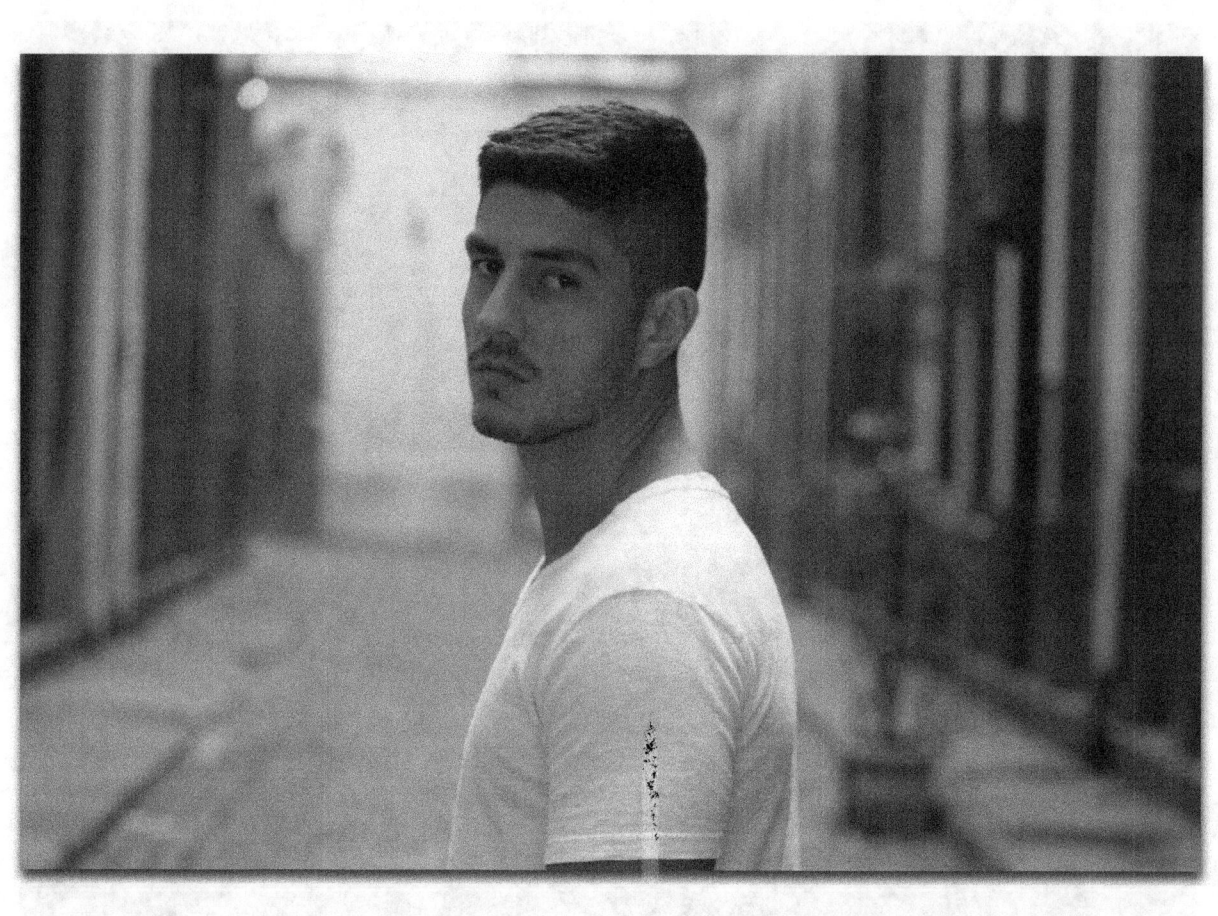

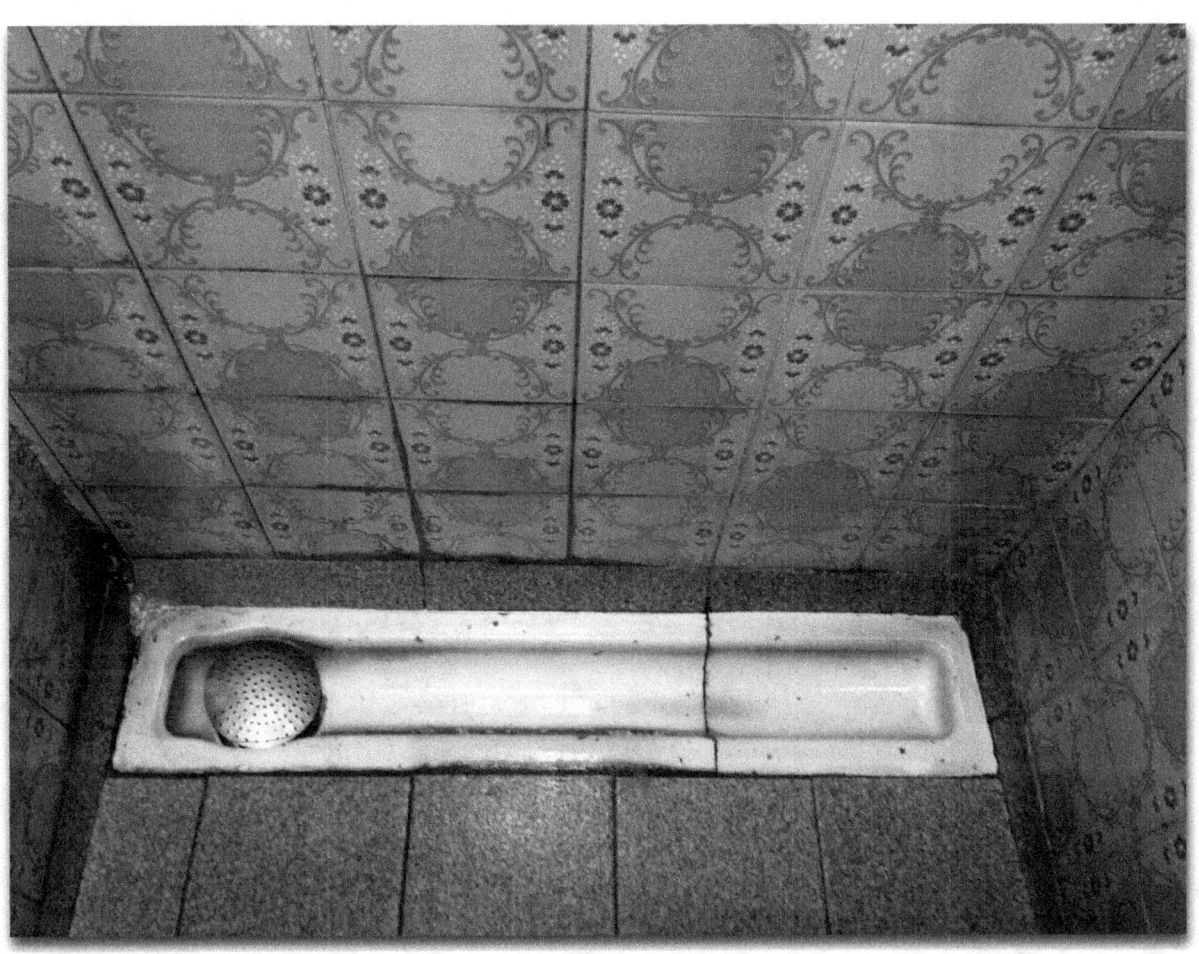

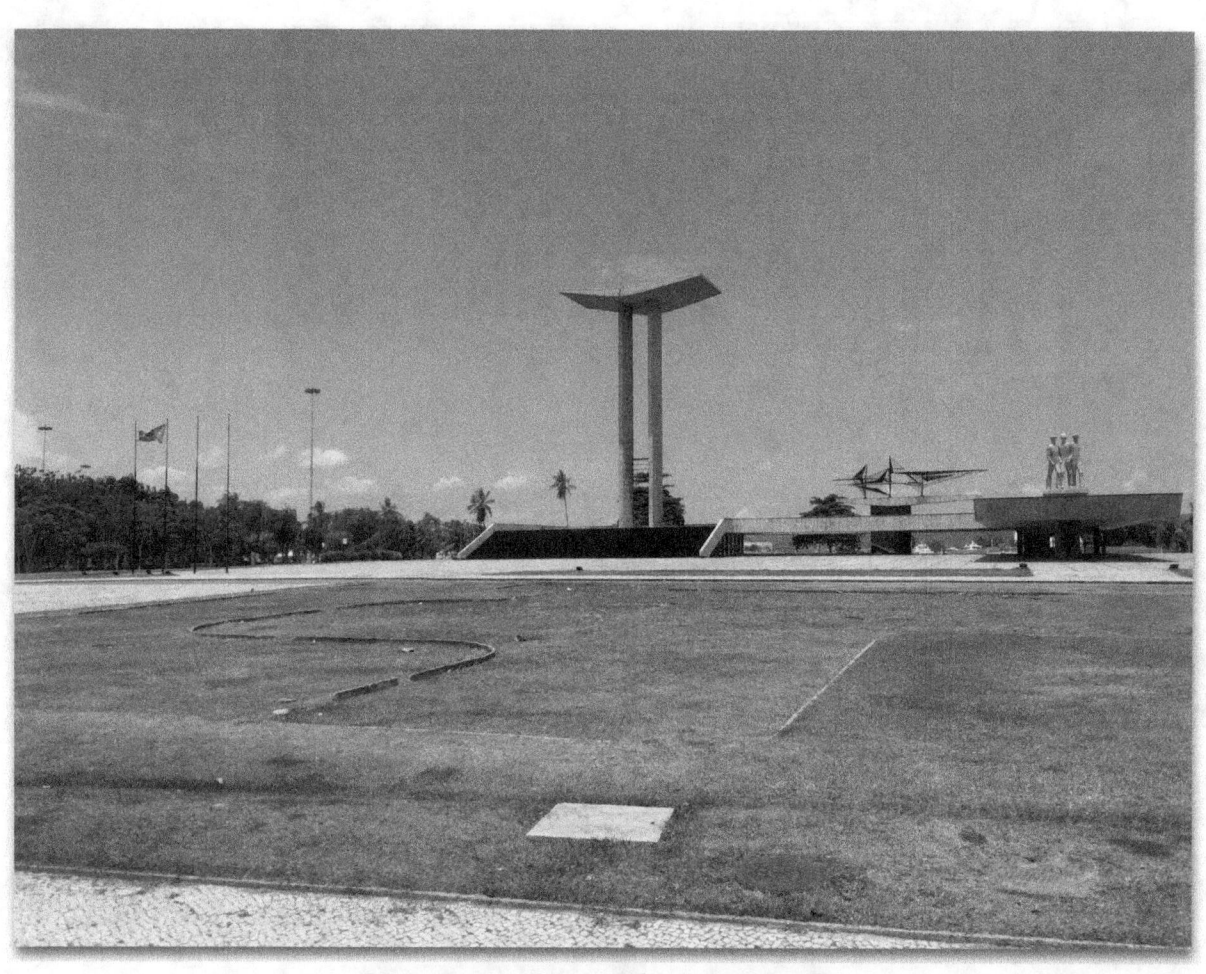

**Monumento Nacional aos Mortos da
Segunda Guerra Mundial** (World War II Monument).

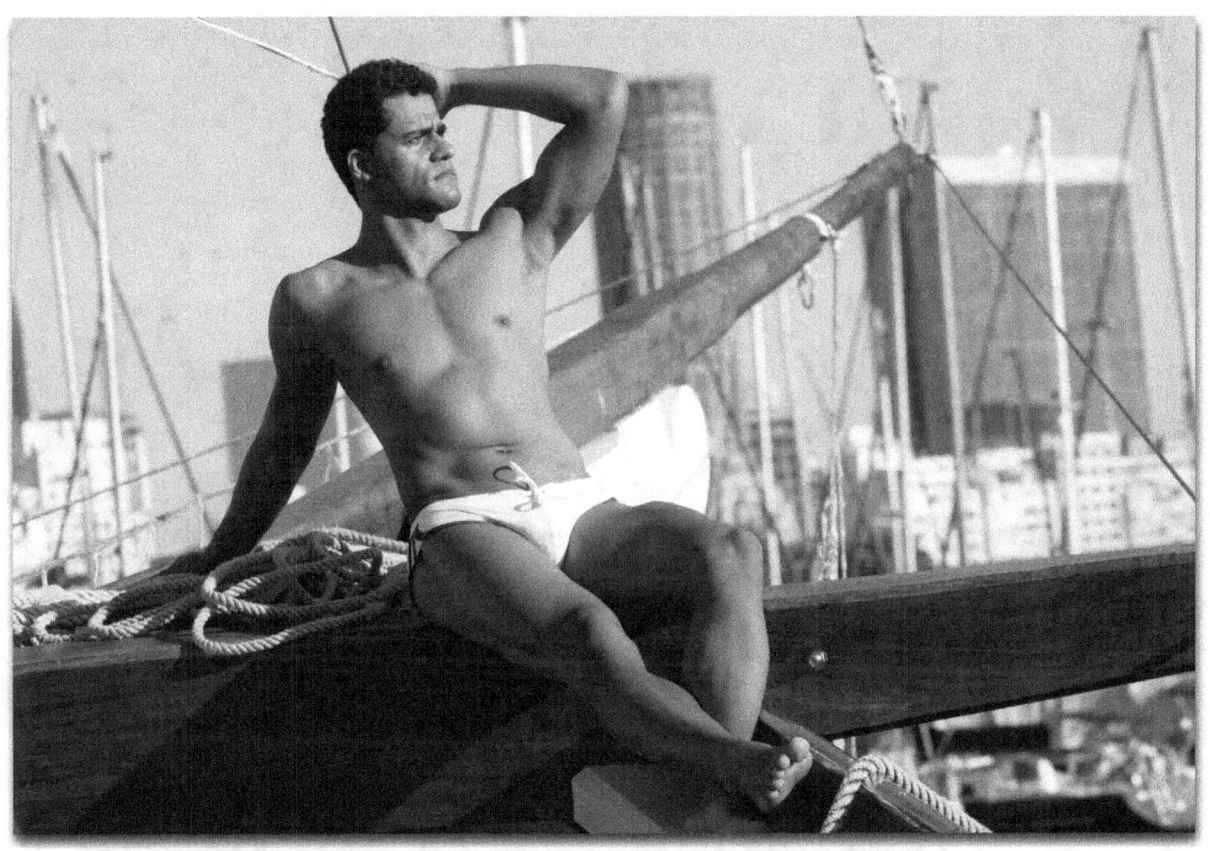

Boats on the Water: **Marina da Glória** is the most accessible to Rio.

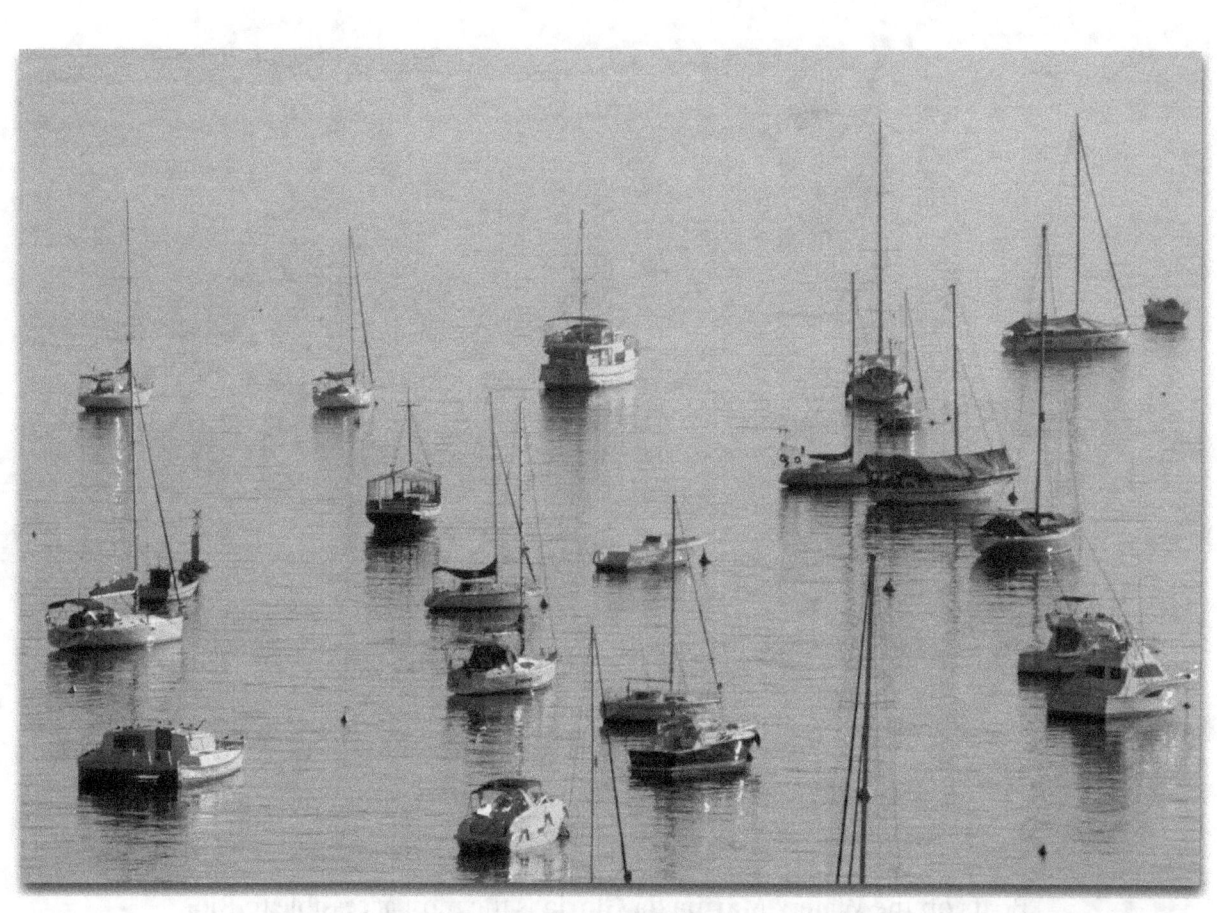

Santa Teresa

Santa Teresa is a neighborhood that seems to be beautifully straddled in the past and the present at the same time.

The **Escadaria Selarón**, the world-famous colorful stairs that the neighborhood shares with Lapa, the work of the late Chilean-born artist Jorge Selarón, is certainly a modern part of the area.

However, there are many historical mansions, such as the one that is part of the **Parque Das Ruínas**, which once belonged to heiress and important socialite Laurinda Santos Lobo, that are in ruins.

At the same time, Santa Teresa is home to the most authentic colonial feel of the city. When you walk around its streets, you can almost hear the ghosts of colonial past.

The **Largo do Guimarães**, a popular square in the heart of the neighborhood, leaves you feeling like you're somewhere in Portugal.

"This, to me," smiled Ryan, a tourist, "Is what Santa Teresa is all about."

With Rua Paschoal Carlos Magno, Rua Carlos Brant, and two small hill roads all merging into Rua Almirante Alexandrino, you understand that this part of the city really retained its European past.

For the ones who live here, like a young man named Felipe, Santa Teresa is simply a diverse neighborhood.

"There are the poor, the rich, and the in-between," he says, "I wake up and I see a favela on the other side of the hill," Felipe continues, "I love that because it reminds me there are people who are less fortunate than I am."

Although the mansions of Santa Teresa are not as kept as they were back in their heyday they are very charming, and this neighborhood attracts a lot of tourists.

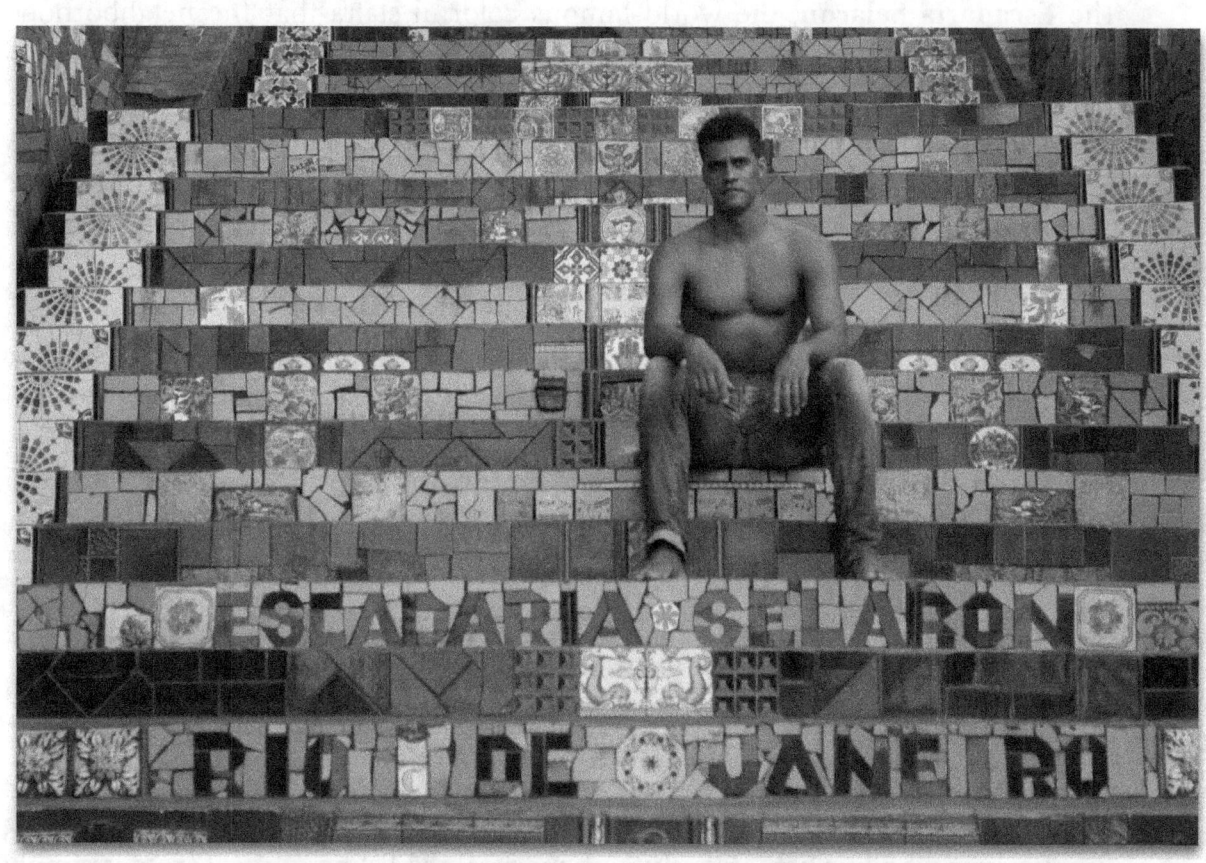

Gerson Couto sitting on the famous **Escadaria Selarón**.

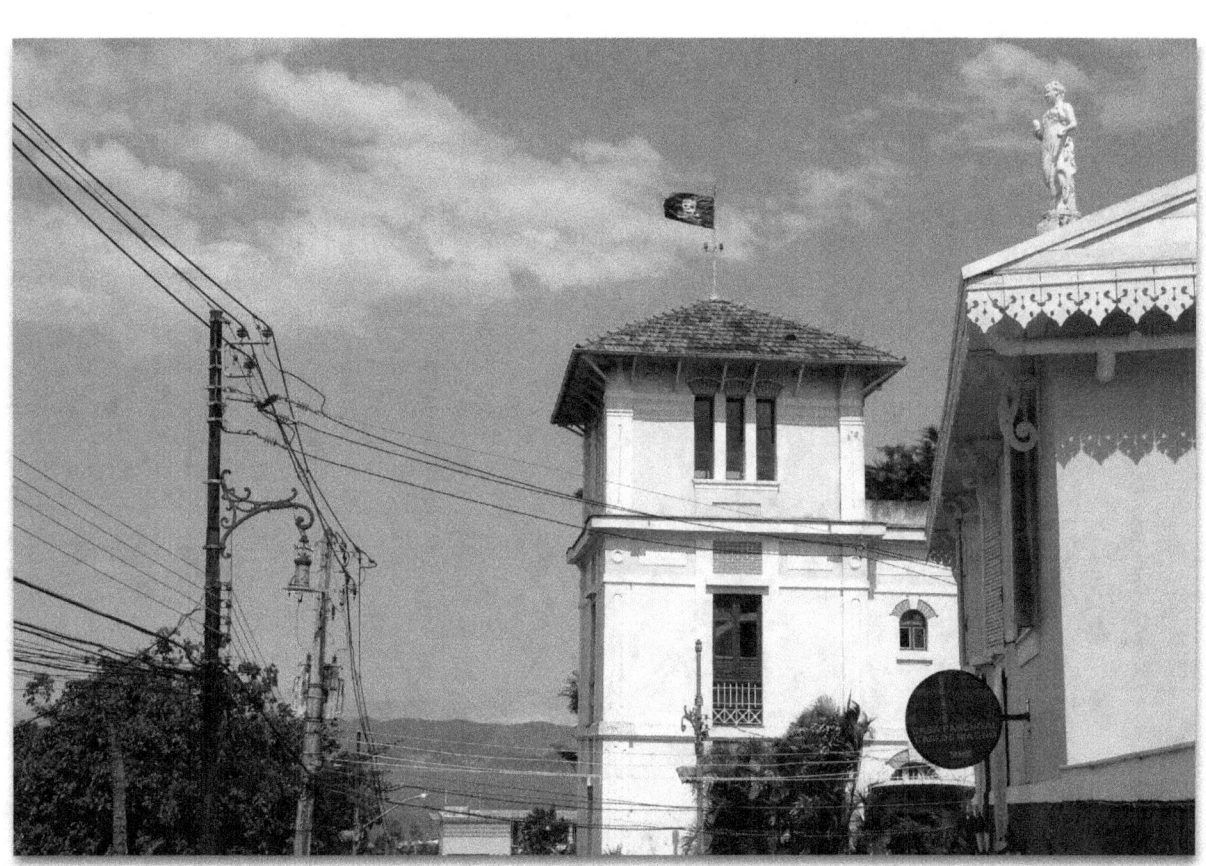

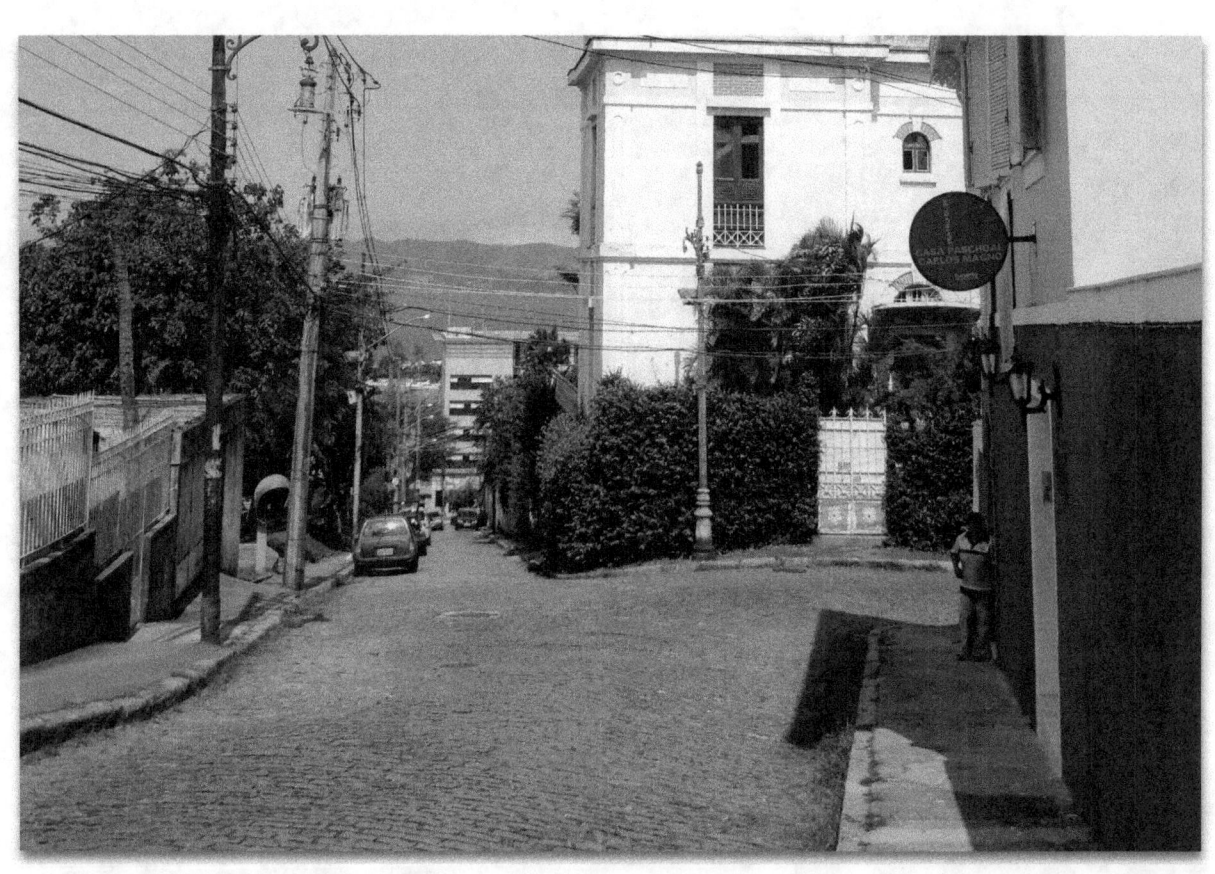

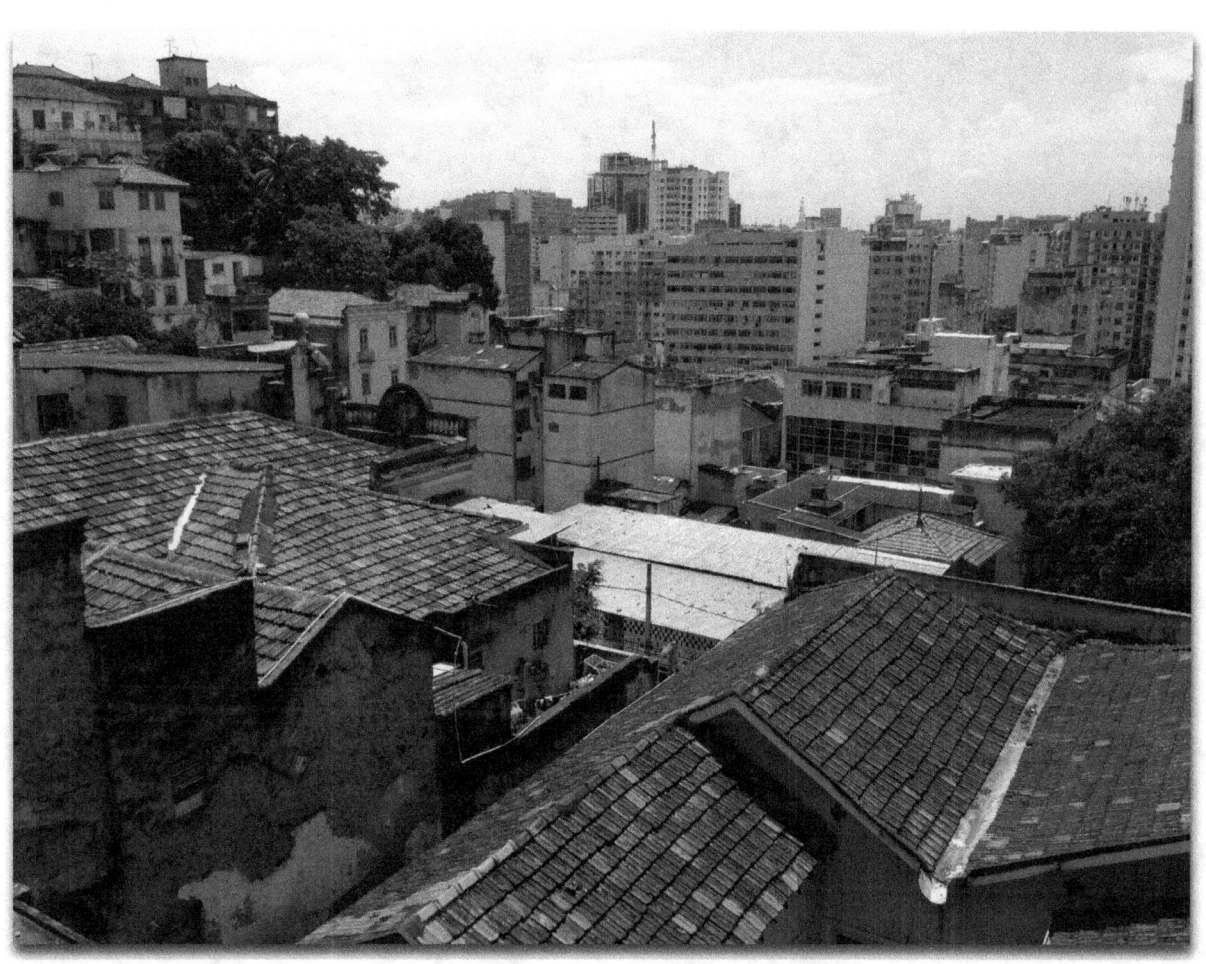

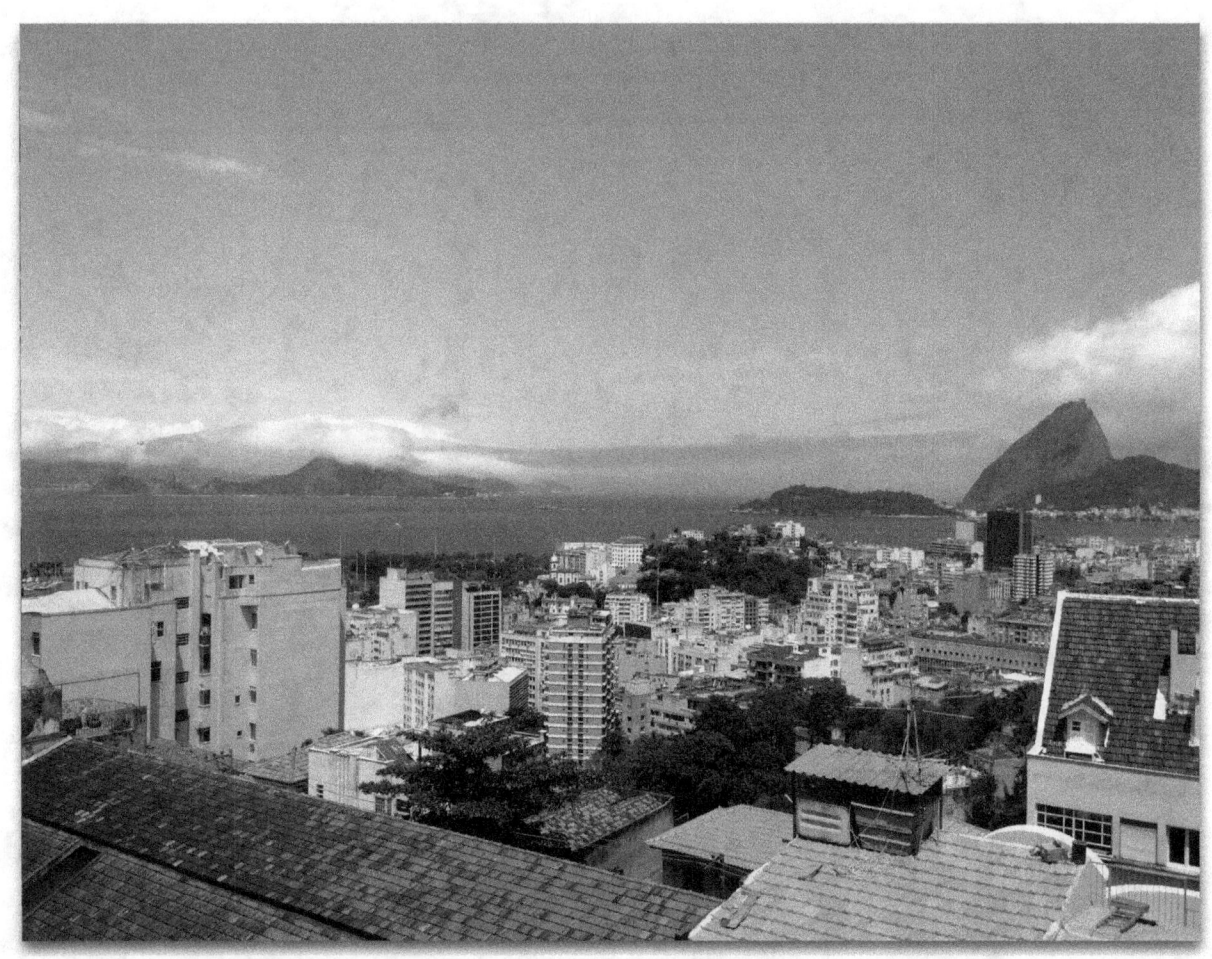

The **Parque Das Ruínas** at the top of the hill offers unmatched views.

Centro

The "center" or "downtown" of Rio is mostly commercial.

There are offices, hotels, restaurants, et cetera. It is booming during business hours, 8am to 6pm, Monday to Friday.

Truly, it's one of the busiest parts of the city. There are thousands and thousands of people on the streets. There are business people, the insane world around them, and the communities who rely on both.

There are also many people who live in this neighborhood, such as those who live in **Castelo** area, but they are sucked in by the commercial atmosphere of the area and generally tend to go elsewhere for everyday life.

"You get fed up with all that happens here in the day," said Rafael, who added that he and his girlfriend generally end up going to the areas in Zona Sul (Ipanema, Copacabana, et cetera).

On the weekends Centro is very quiet. There are streets that are like ghost towns, where all the businesses such as stores and restaurants use rolling gates to keep the street artists from spraying on their doors. Therefore you will see many rolling gates full of colorful street art.

"Centro is the heart of Rio," told me an official of the city who wanted to remain anonymous, "I would say this neighborhood brings more to this city than anywhere else, financially speaking."

Companies like Petrobras, Eletrobras, BNDES and Vale, which are all some of the biggest companies in Brazil, are headquartered here.

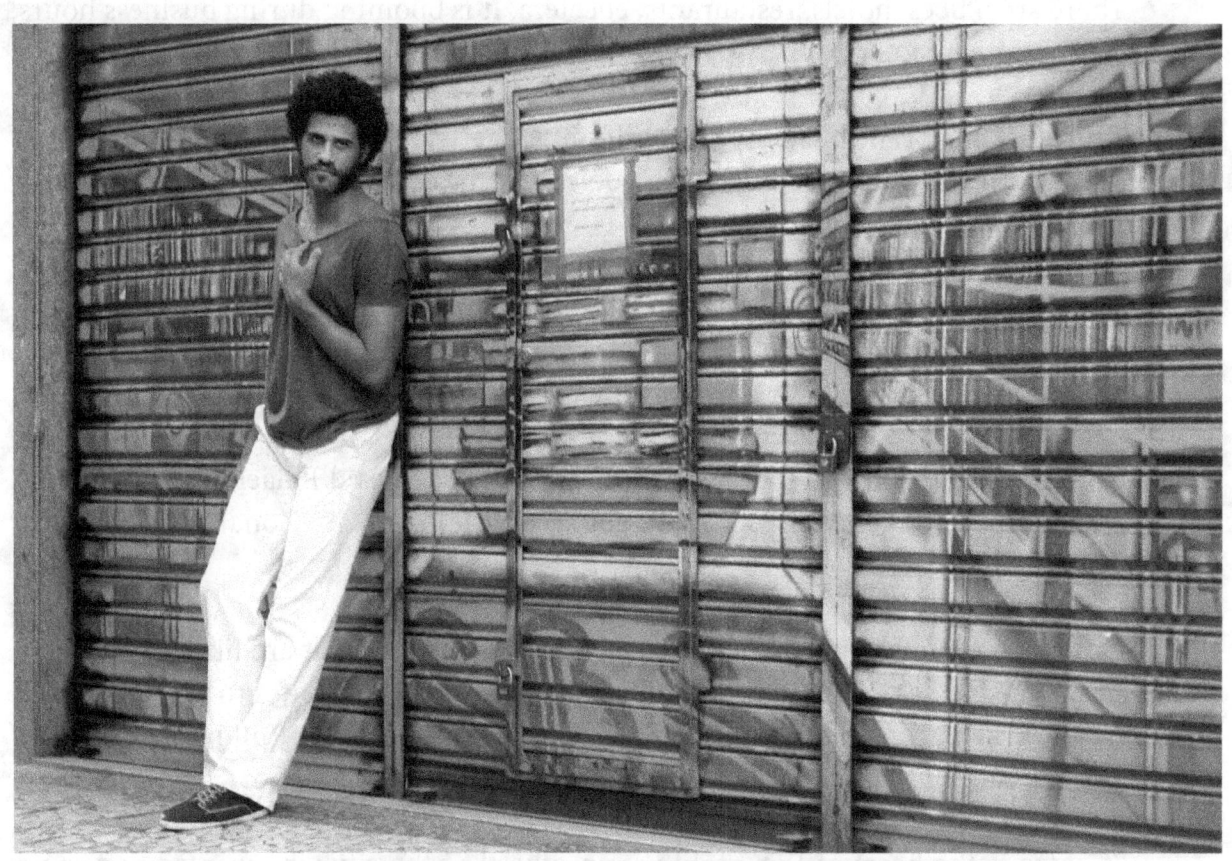

Gerson Couto in front of a café with a rolling gate.

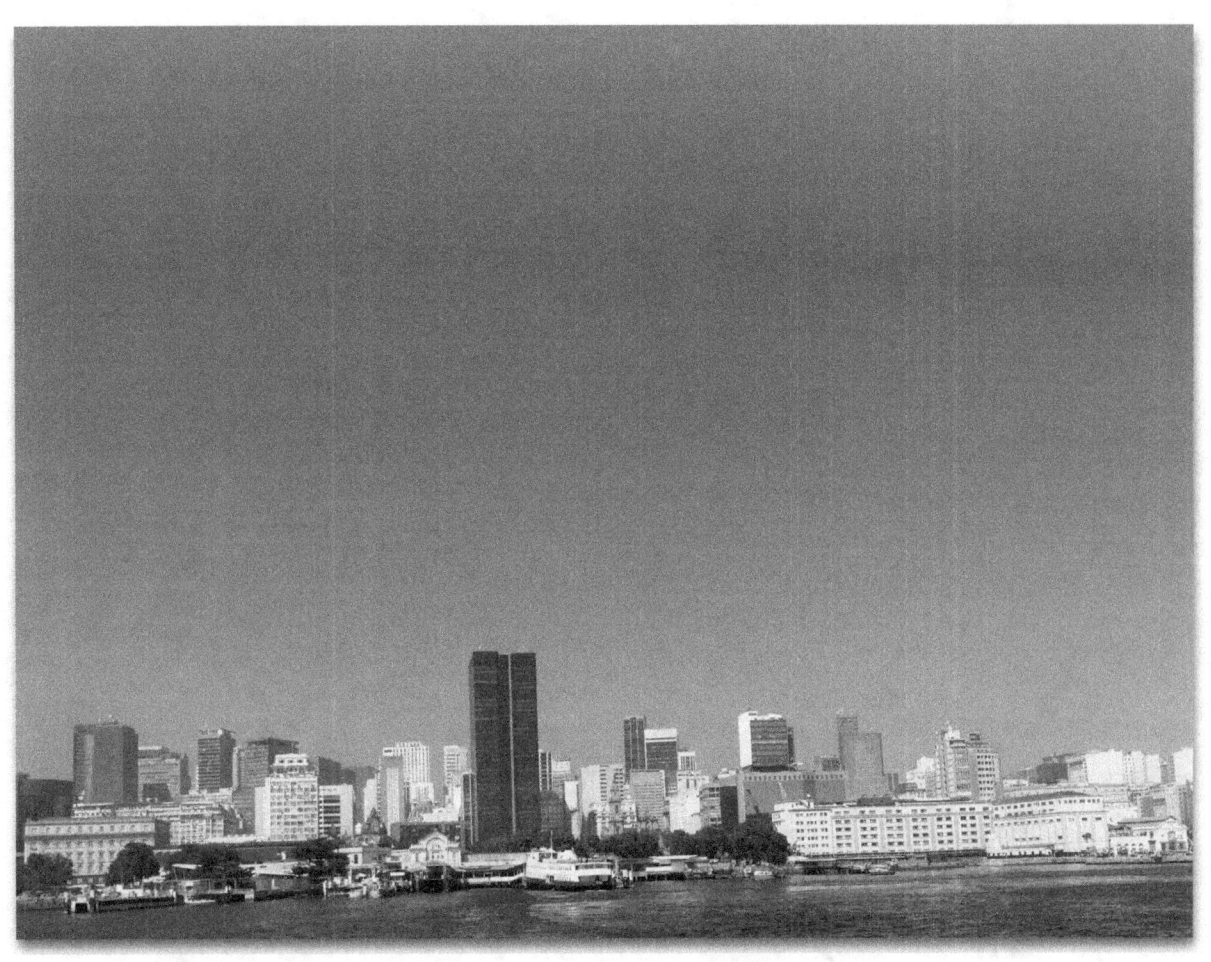

Centro as viewed from **Guanabara Bay**.

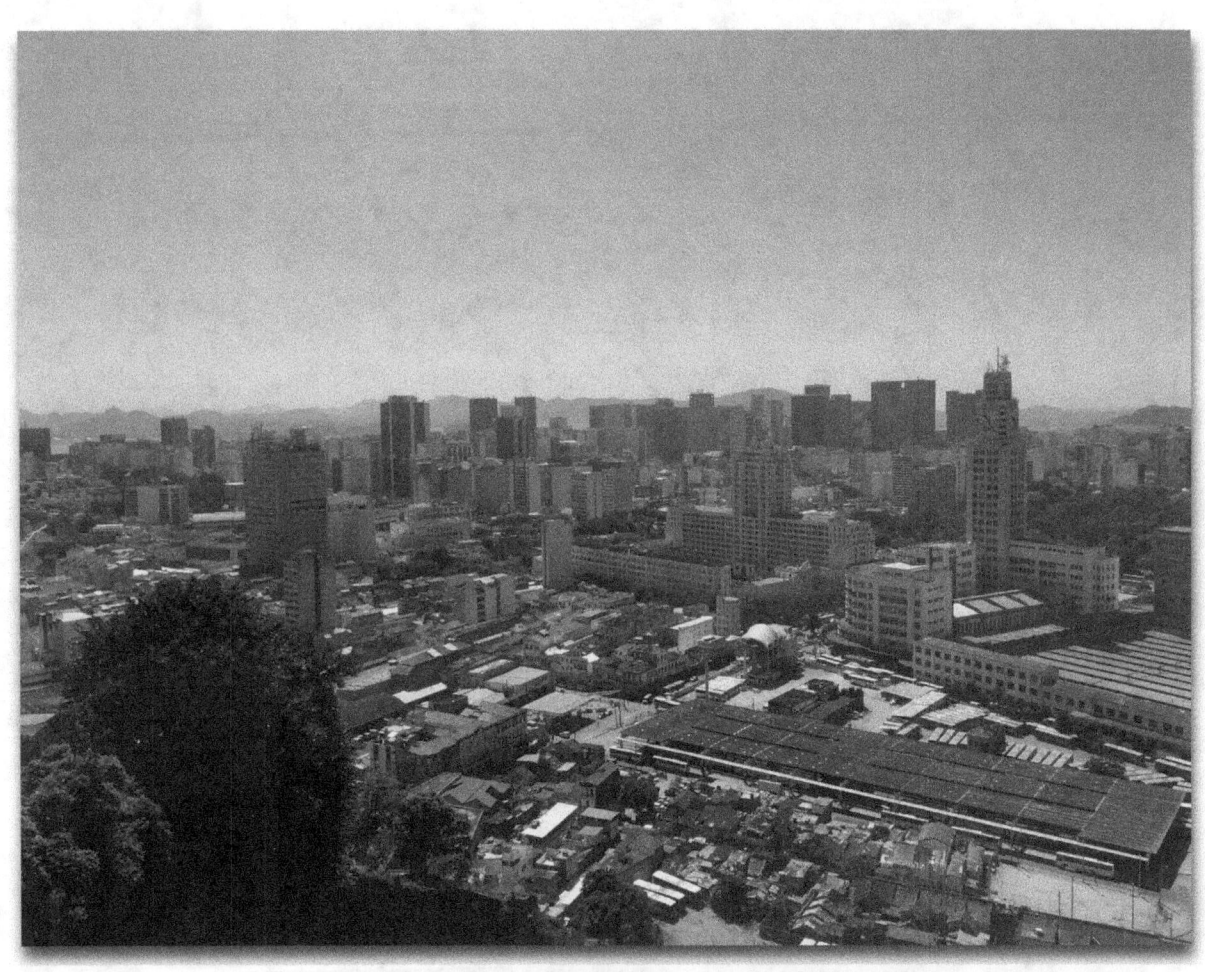

Centro as viewed from the **Morro da Providência** favela.

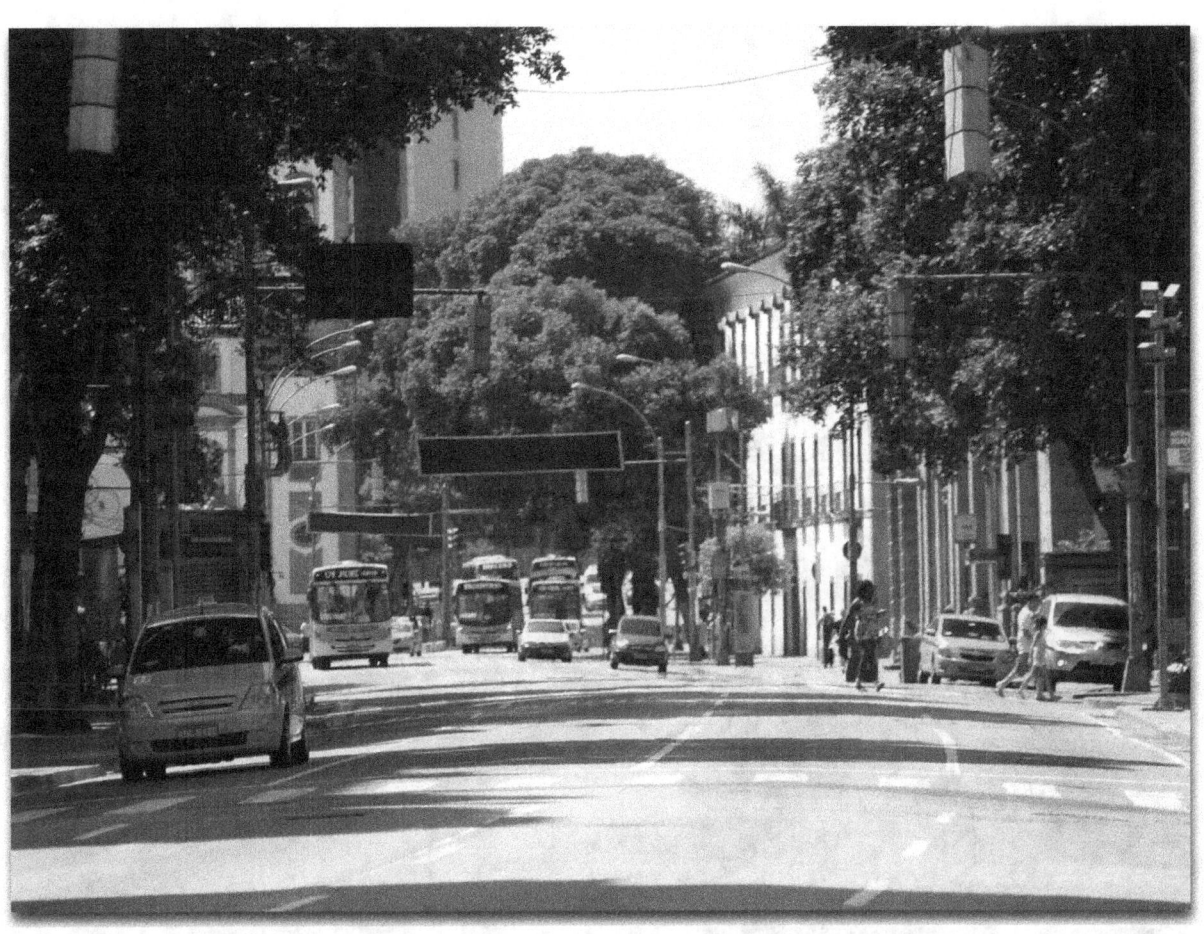

Busy **Rua Primeiro de Março** near Praça Quinze de Novembro.

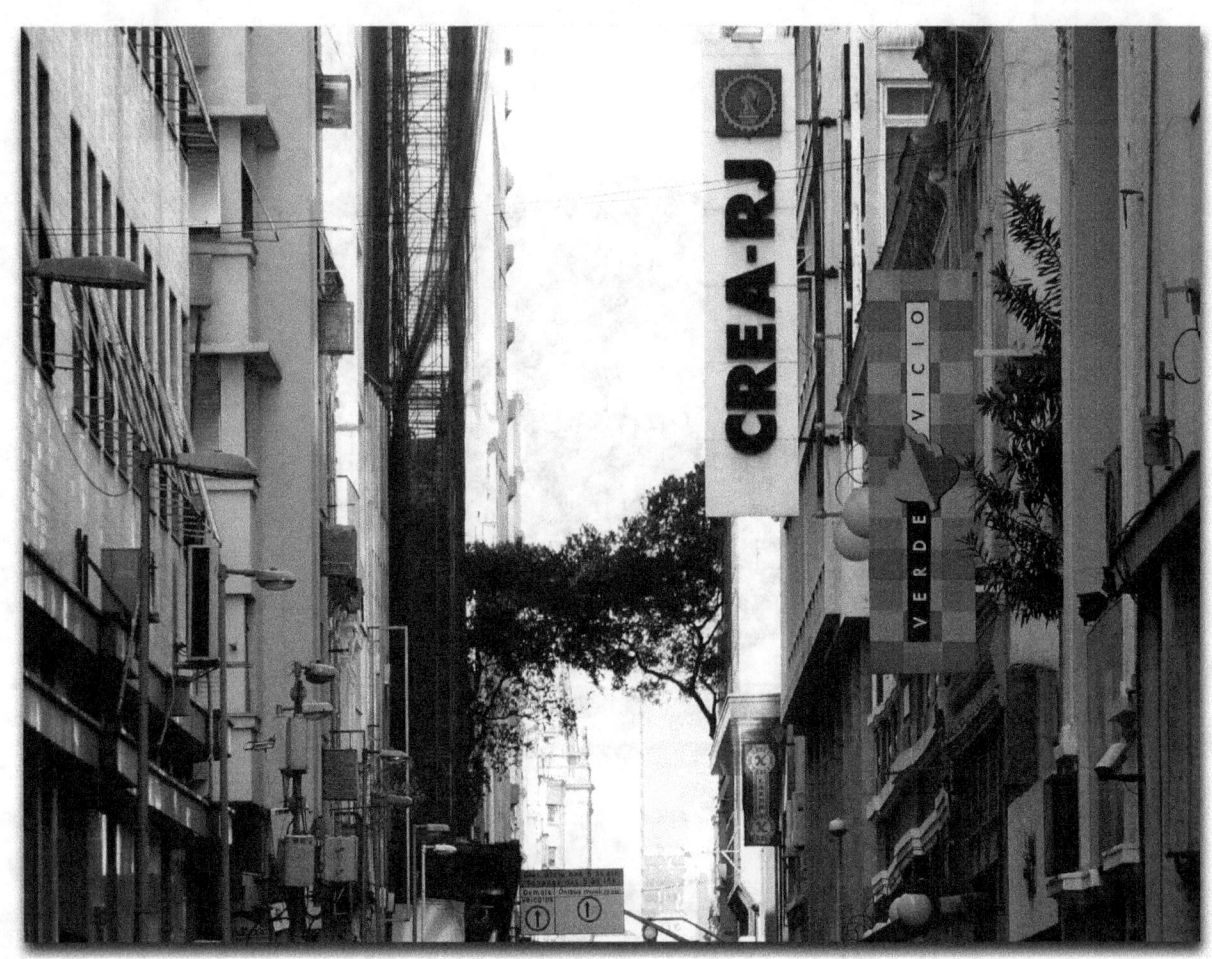

Typical street in Centro.

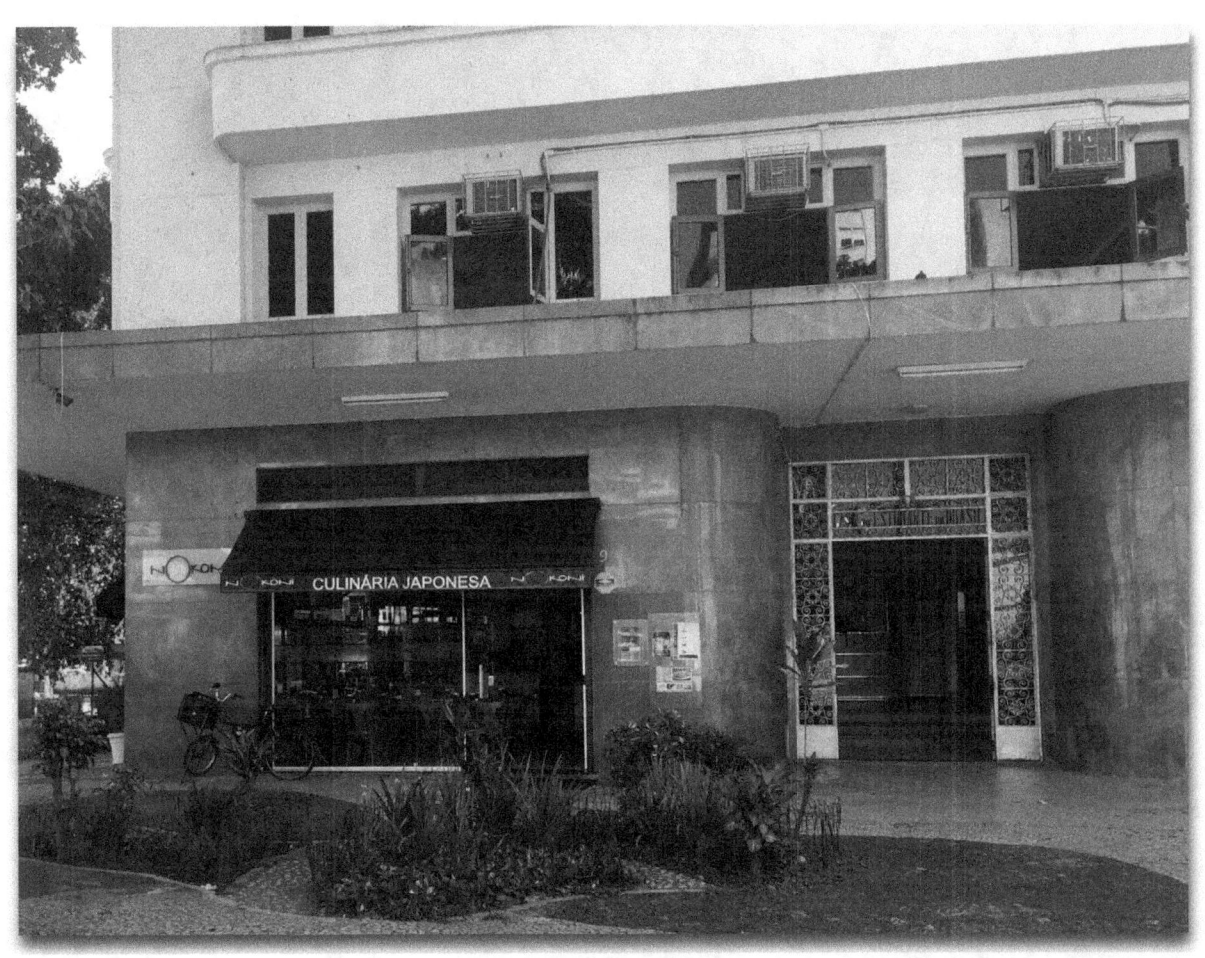

A Japanese restaurant.

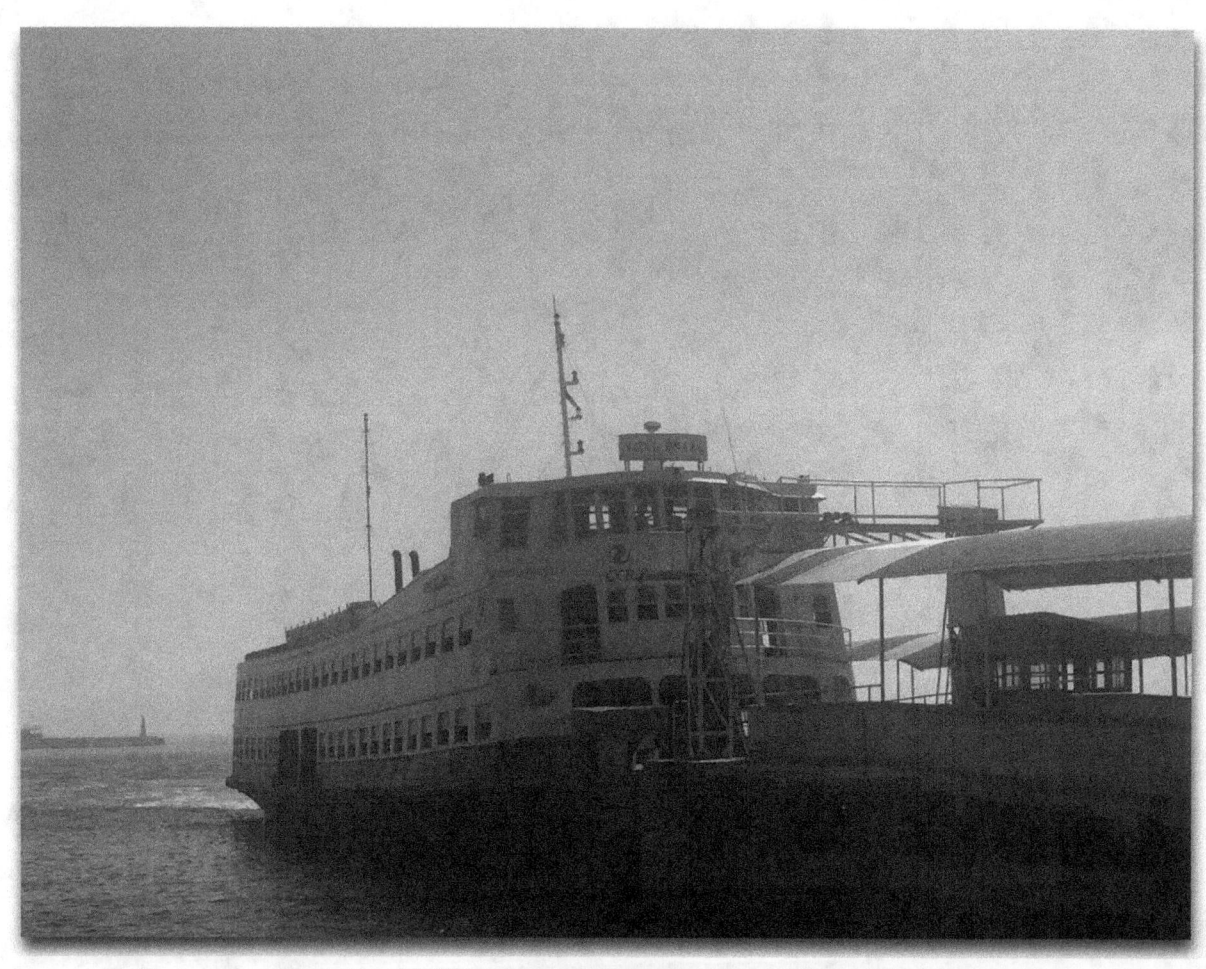

Ferryboat sits at **Barcas Transportes Marítimos** waiting to take passengers.

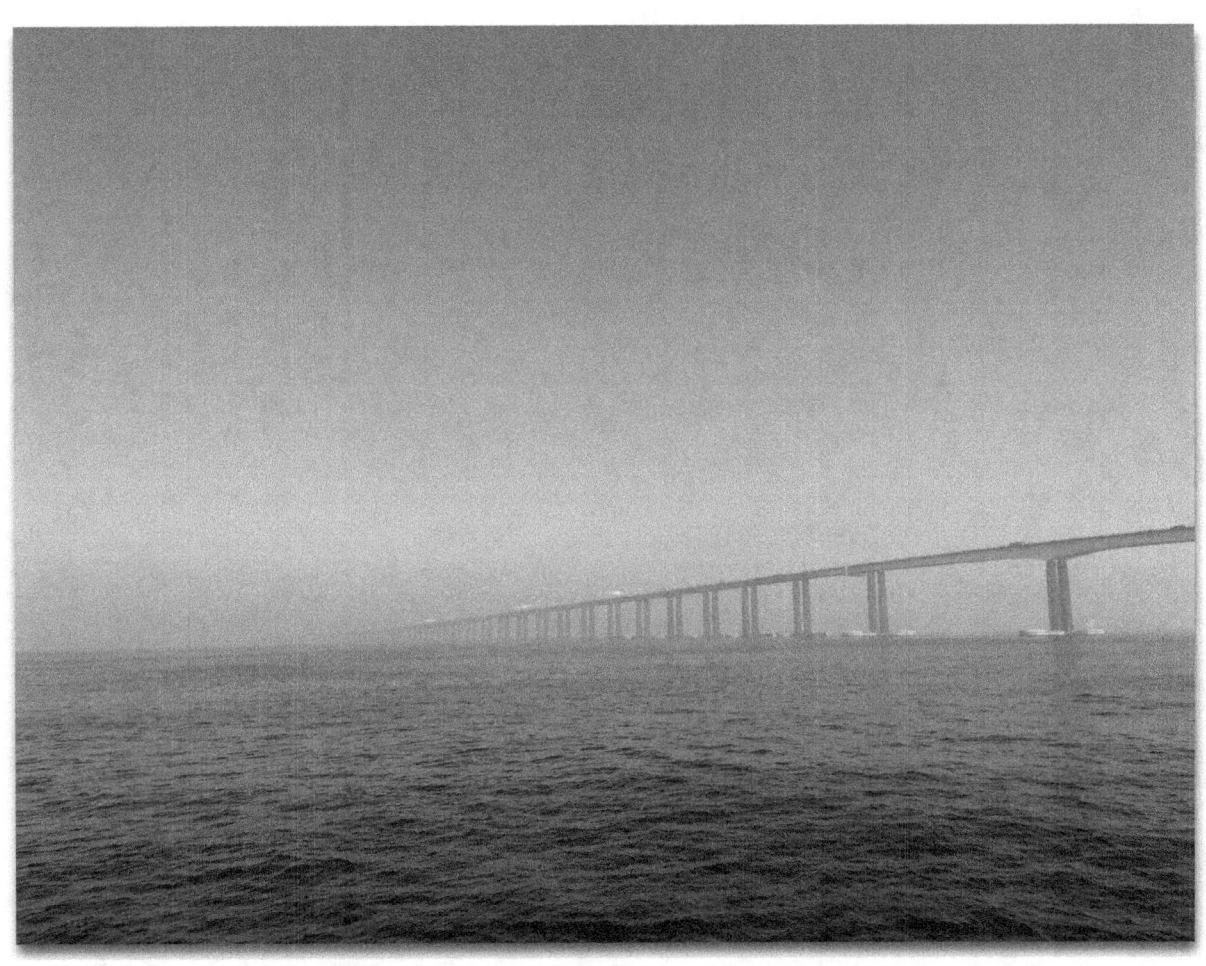

The **Ponte Presidente Costa e Silva** known as Rio–Niterói Bridge.

Paquetá Island

One of my favorite areas of Rio is definitely Paquetá, which, belive it or not, is part of the city of Rio.

Just because it is one hour away on a ferryboat, even if it feels a lot further, doesn't mean it's not part of the city.

In Tupí language the name means "many pacas," referring to probably a time in the past when the island had many of these interesting animals.

The history of Paquetá tells the changing hands of the French and Portuguese, and the local natives who took the sides of each colonial powers, and the influences the experience has had on its natural history, architecture, and culture.

These days its beautiful green scenery, historical homes, and the fact that it is the only part of Rio that is 100% auto-free characterize Paquetá.

"I love to come here," said Gerson Couto, whom I photographed on the island, "I love the nature and the calm lifestyle of the locals. The beaches are incredibly beautiful."

Many residents of Rio mainland go to the island on the weekends. During the week, when hardly any tourists are hanging out, it offers a calmer experience.

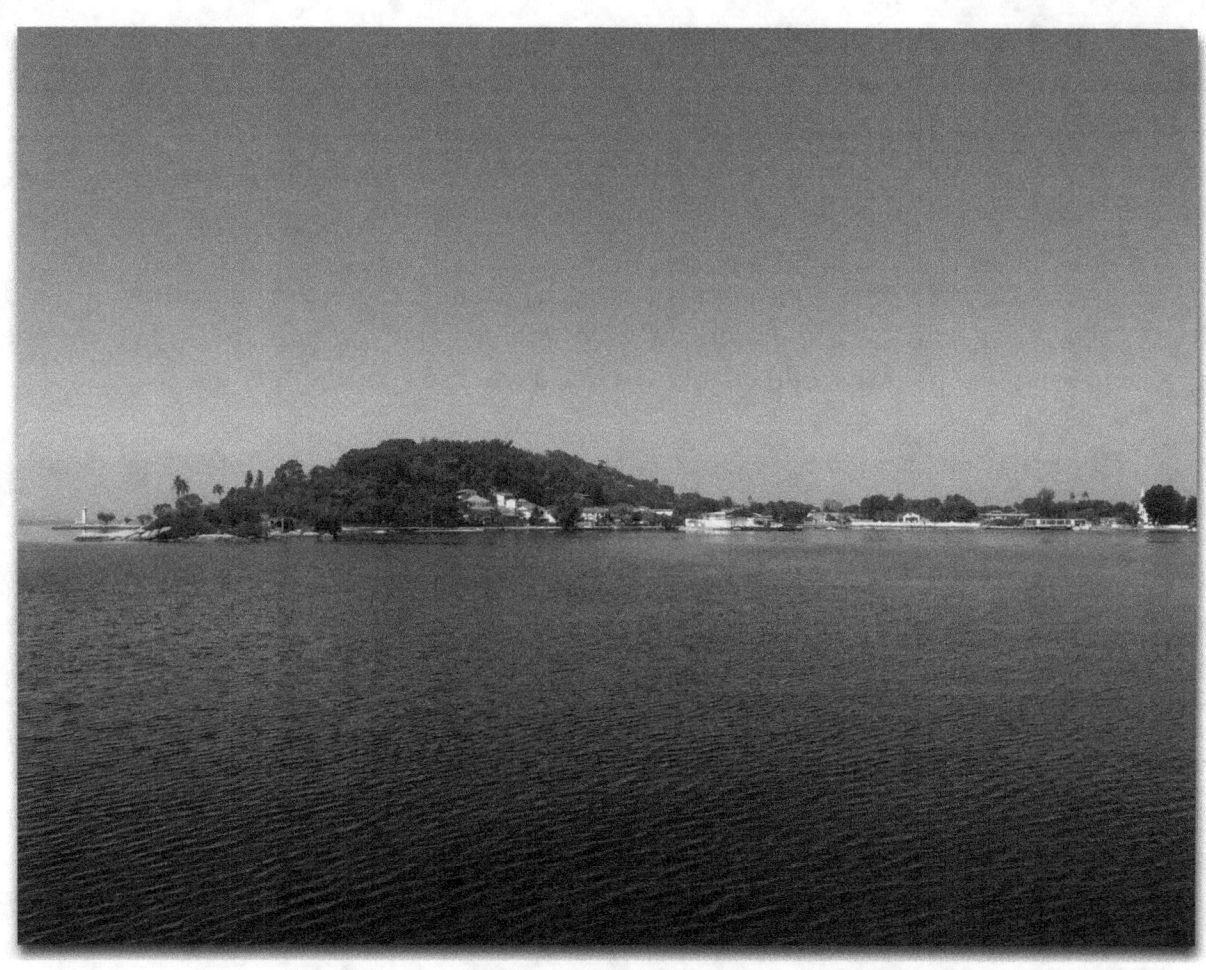

The island sits in the middle of the **Guanabara Bay**.

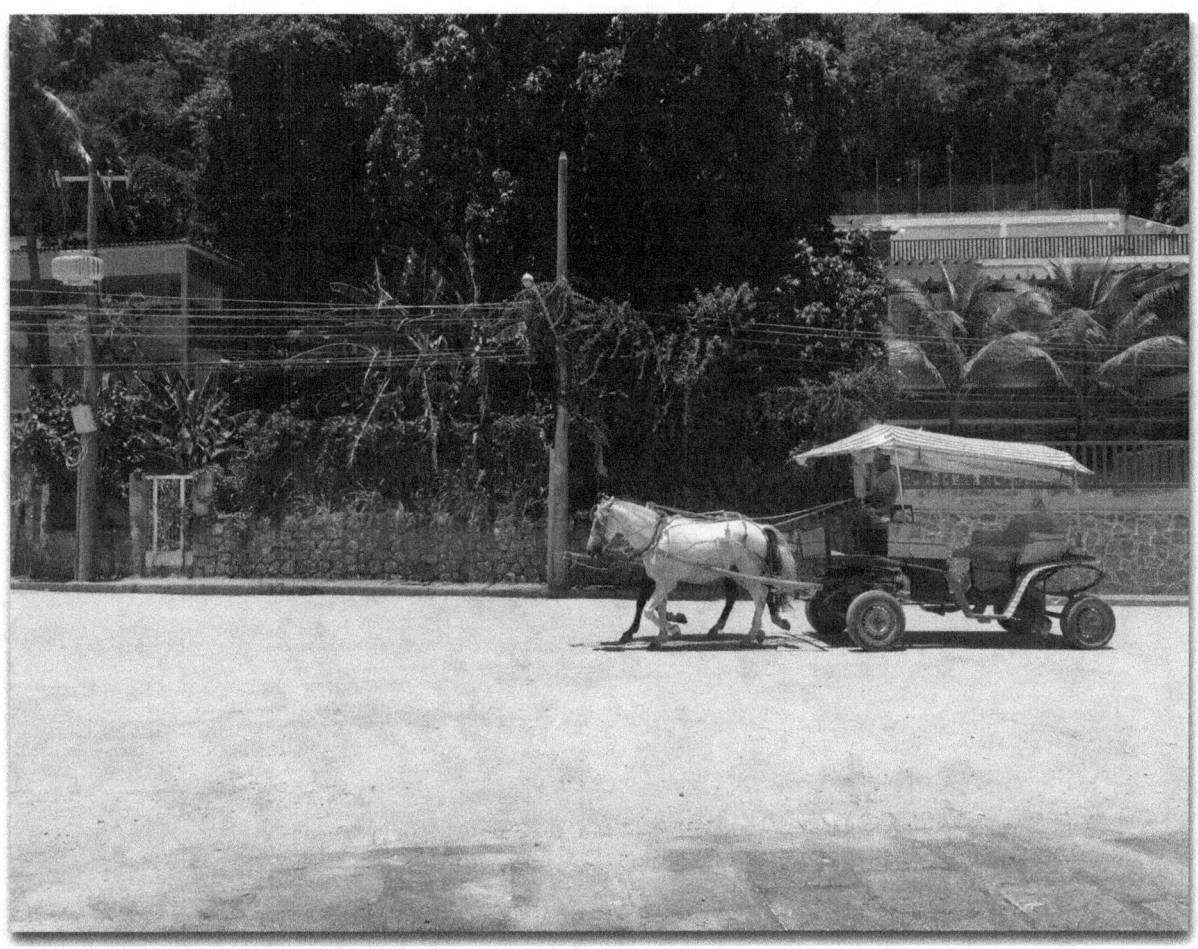

Horse carriages and bicycles constitute the main transportation of the island.

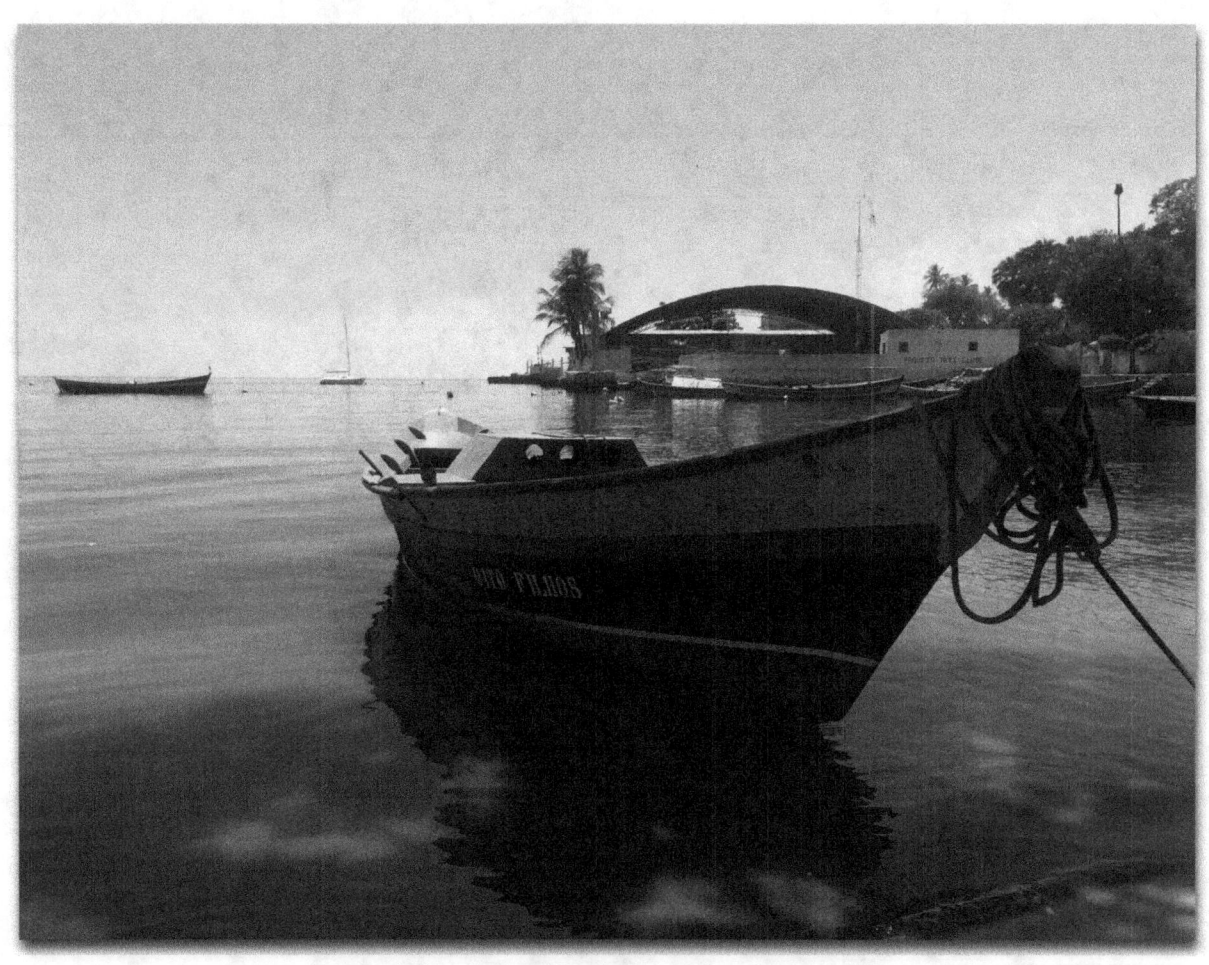

Calm lifestyle is what the island is famous for.

Cariocas

Simply put "carioca" is anyone from Rio.

In Tupí language "carioca" means "white man's house."

I have met Cariocas whose families have been in the area for generations.

Of course, as the second largest city in the country, and being the cultural capital of the country, Rio sees many people migrating from other parts of Brazil.

Cariocas, therefore, are ethnically diverse group of people.

Thanks to **Rede Globo**, which is based in the city and is the largest television network in Latin America, the carioca accent, locally known as *sotaque*, has taken a national prominence.

Cariocas have also introduced to Brazil awesome things like *Futevólei* (mixture of football and volleyball) and *Bossa Nova* (mixture of Samba and jazz).

"Being a carioca makes me most fun in Brazil," said João proudly, laughing, "We are the heart of this country. You go anywhere in Brazil and people have no problem with your accent," he added, telling me his trip to the northeast with family when he was twelve, "I thought no one will understand me when I went to Salvador and Recife, but everyone understood me perfectly!"

João says his family has lived in Rio for nearly 300 years.

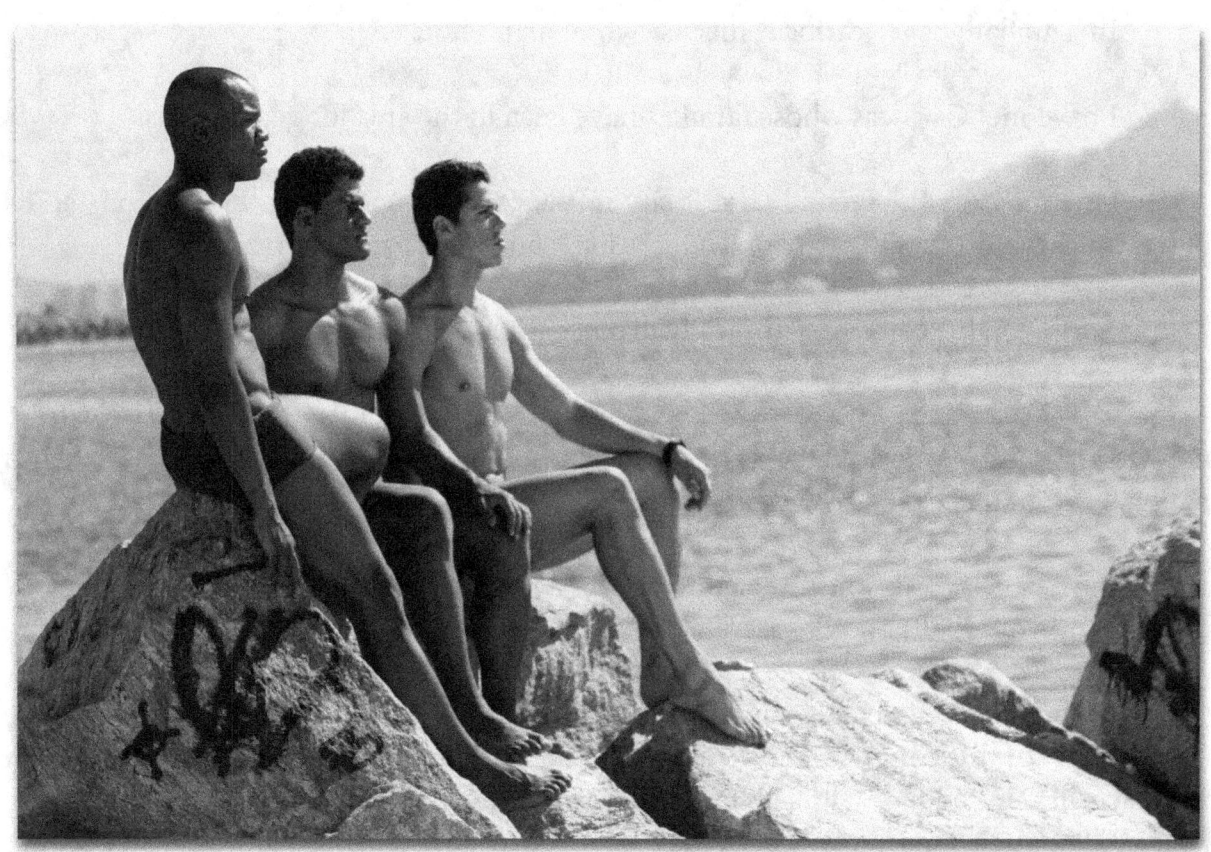

Matheus, Gerson, and **Thiago** at the rocks at the end of Flamengo Beach.

Gustavo

I had just finished a photo shoot when I met Gustavo at Flamengo Park skating, which piqued my interest.

I walked up to him and asked if he would let me photograph him, and he did. We had a test shoot on the spot... and met a few days later for a longer, more planned shoot.

I found Gustavo to be very interesting.

We talked about his neighborhood of Flamengo and he told me he loved living there. He is really into sports and he said it is a nice place for someone like him who lives an active life.

"I like being active at the beach, being in the water, doing fun things like skating," he told me.

Gustavo, who worked at the time at the Rio Sul mall in Botafogo and being a Muay Thai instructor in Copacabana, said living in his neighborhood made him feel free.

"It's a neighborhood where you can do what you want."

Gustavo was born and raised in Rio.

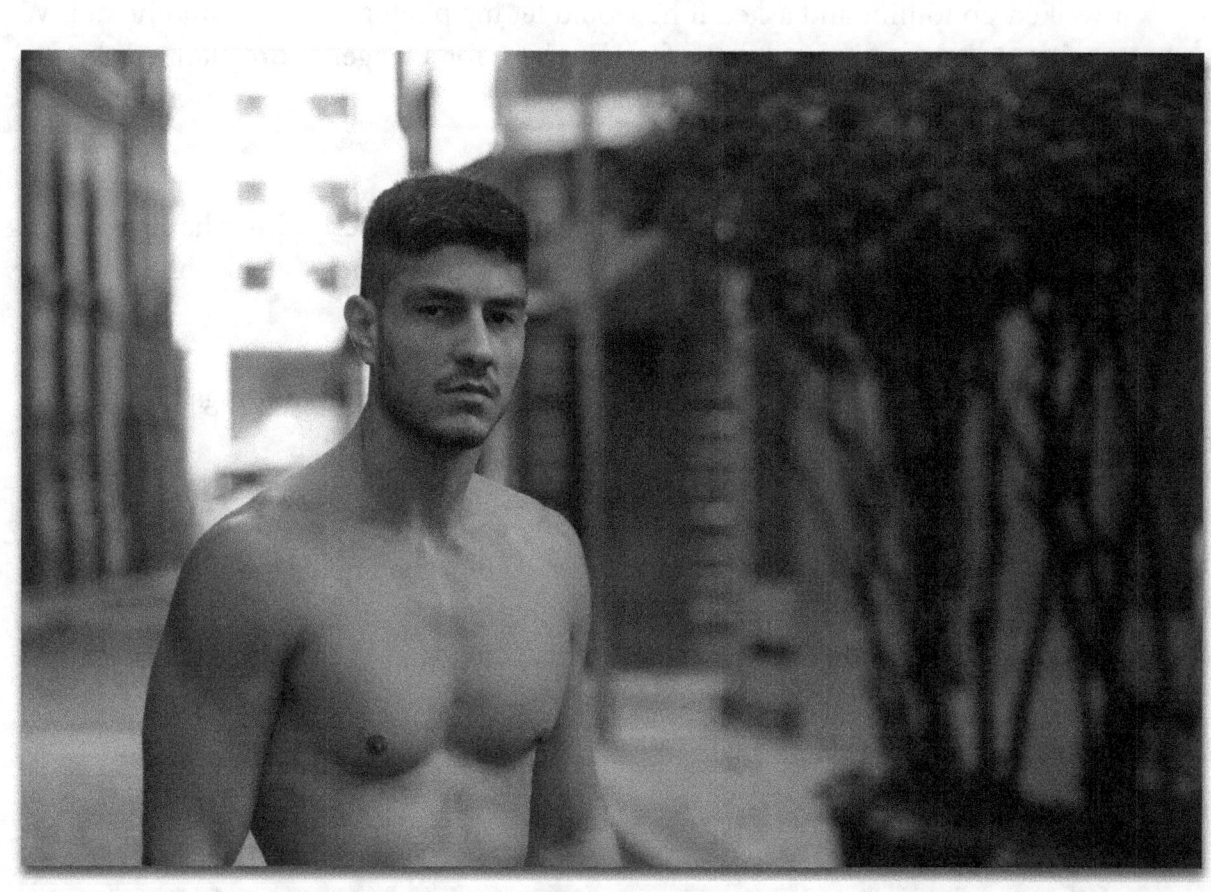

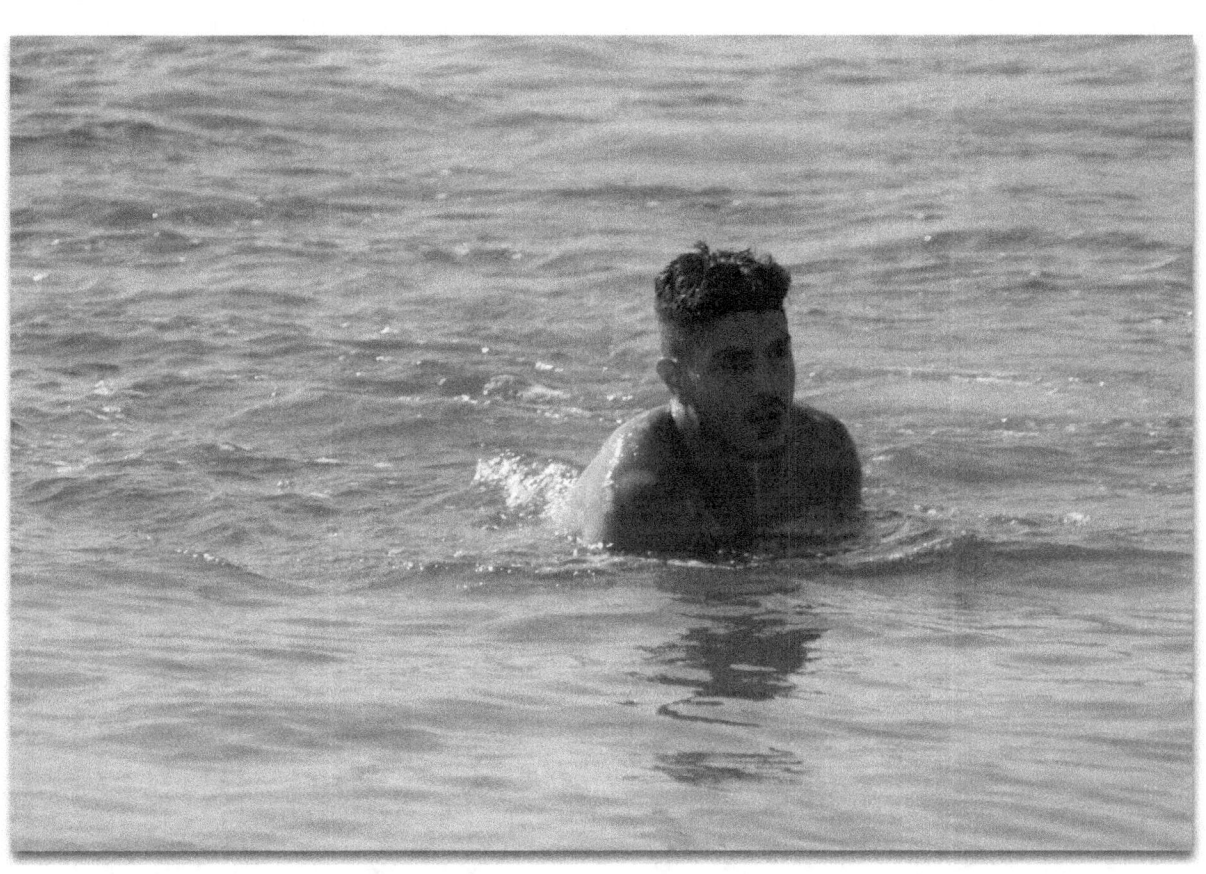

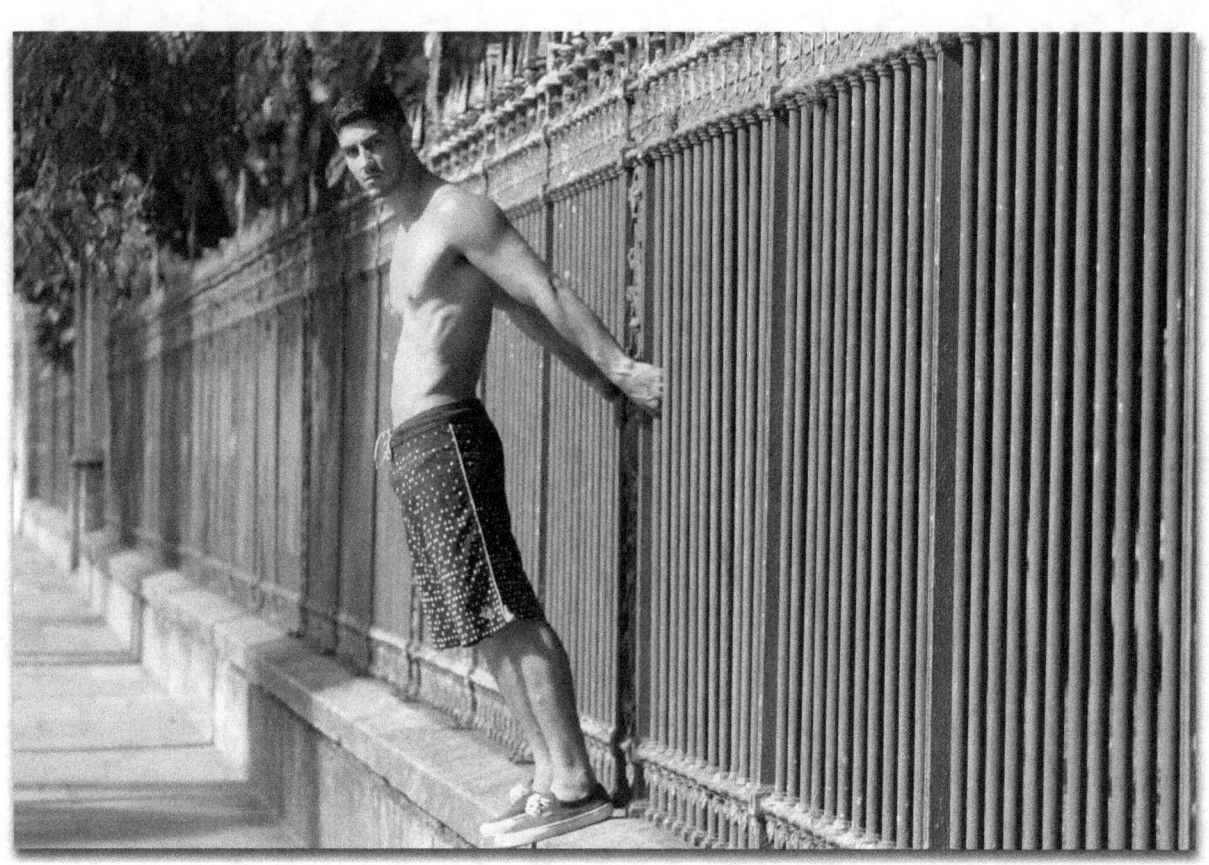

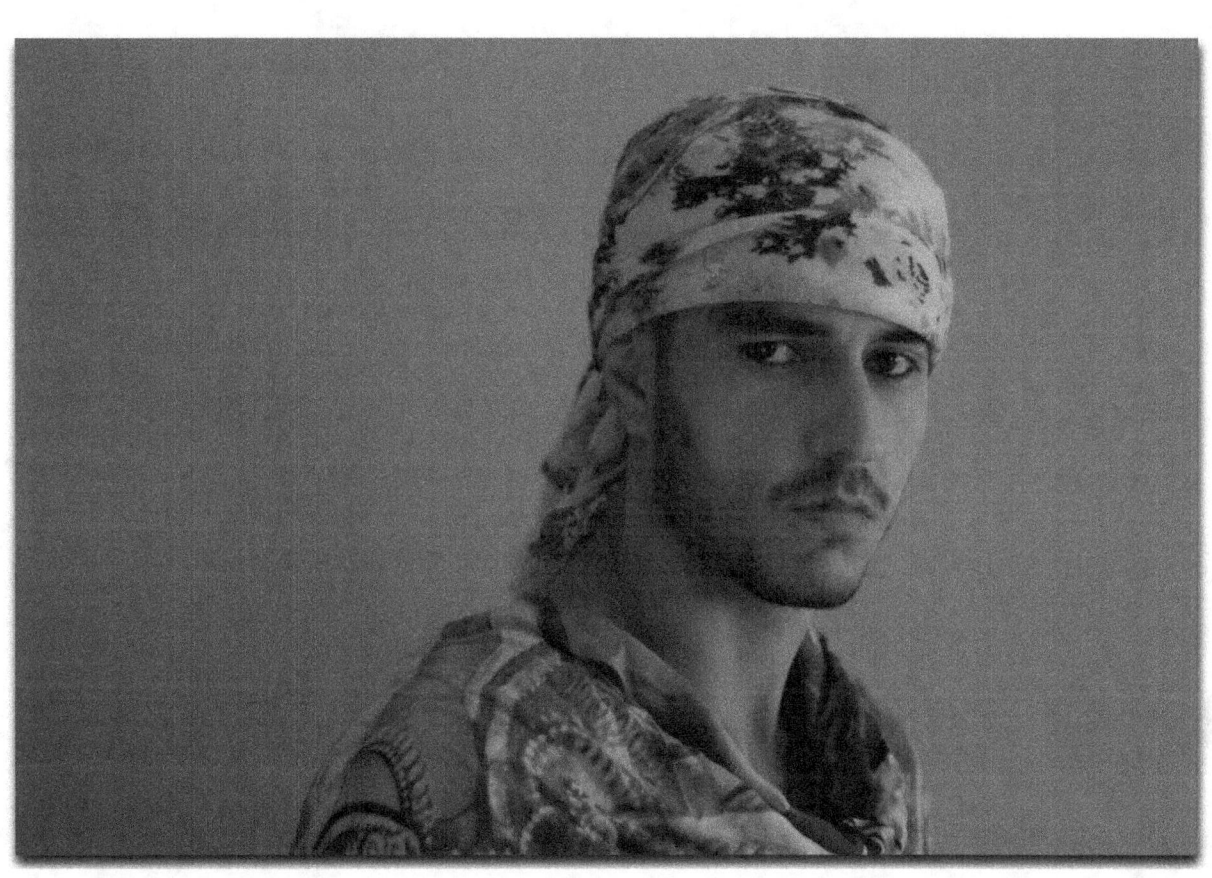

Lucio

When I first talked to Lucio we were both in New York City.

It was sad because we talked just the night before he was leaving. We even tried to shoot the next day but it was raining.

"We will shoot when you are in Rio," he told me, knowing I was going to be there a few months later.

Sure enough months later I was in Rio and we had our shoot. Lucio lives in the northern part of the city, but he came down to Zona Sul and we had our shoot in Ipanema, Copacabana, and Centro.

Lucio is a dreamer. He dreams of working for an international company and traveling all over the world. He loves traveling so much he actually now works for Rio's international airport.

He was only 20 when I photographed him, so of course he likes to party. Nevertheless, you get the sense of talking to an old soul when in discussion with Lucio.

He was born in Belo Horizonte and his family moved to Rio when he was just two. As such, he considers himself a carioca.

"I'm totally carioca," he told me, as we enjoyed coxinhas in Ipanema.

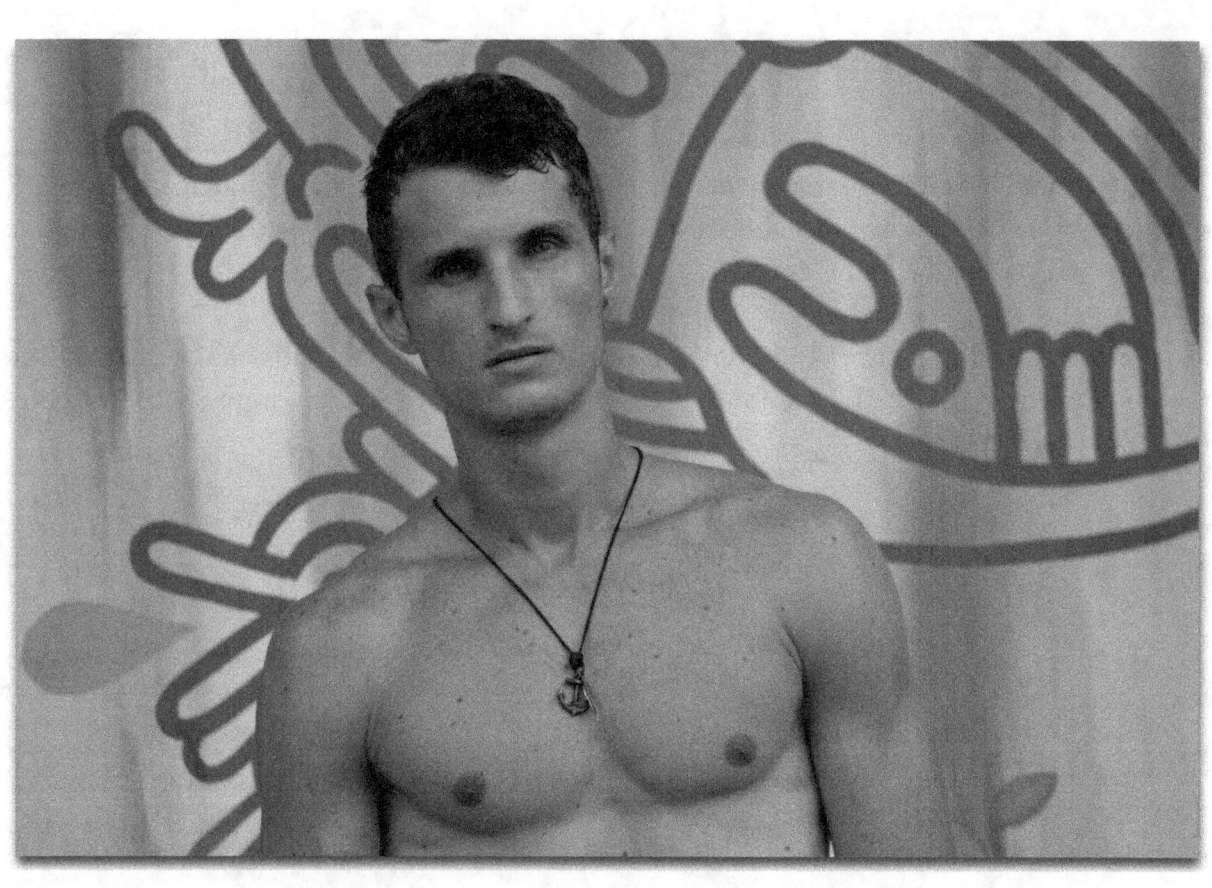

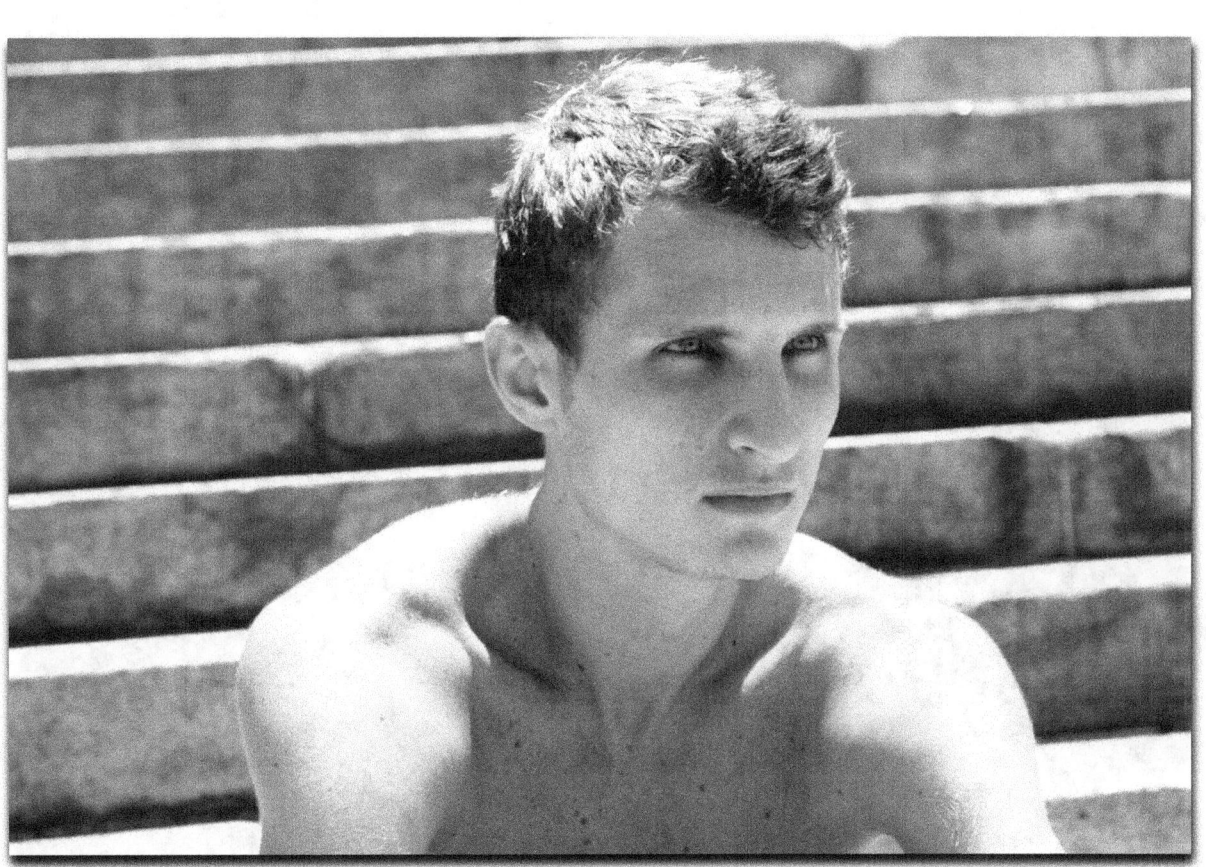

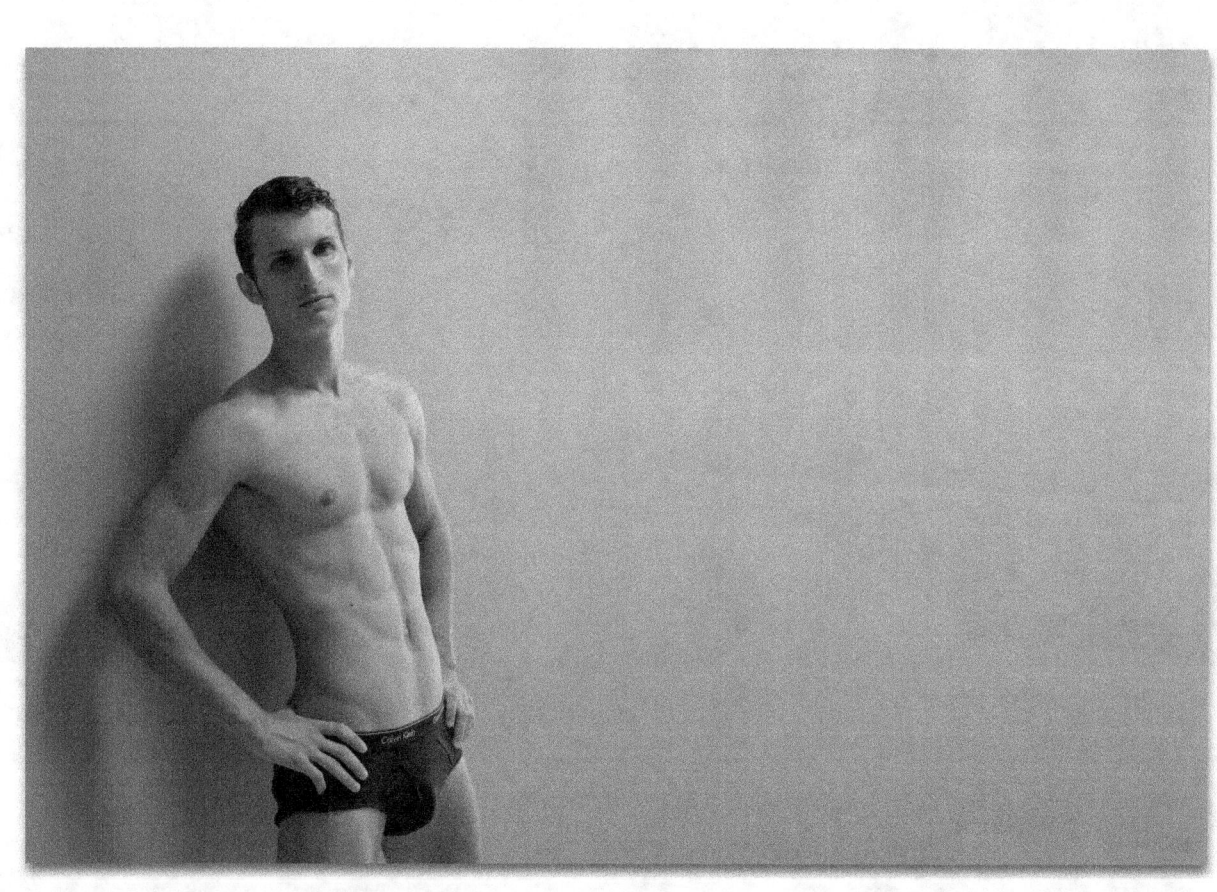

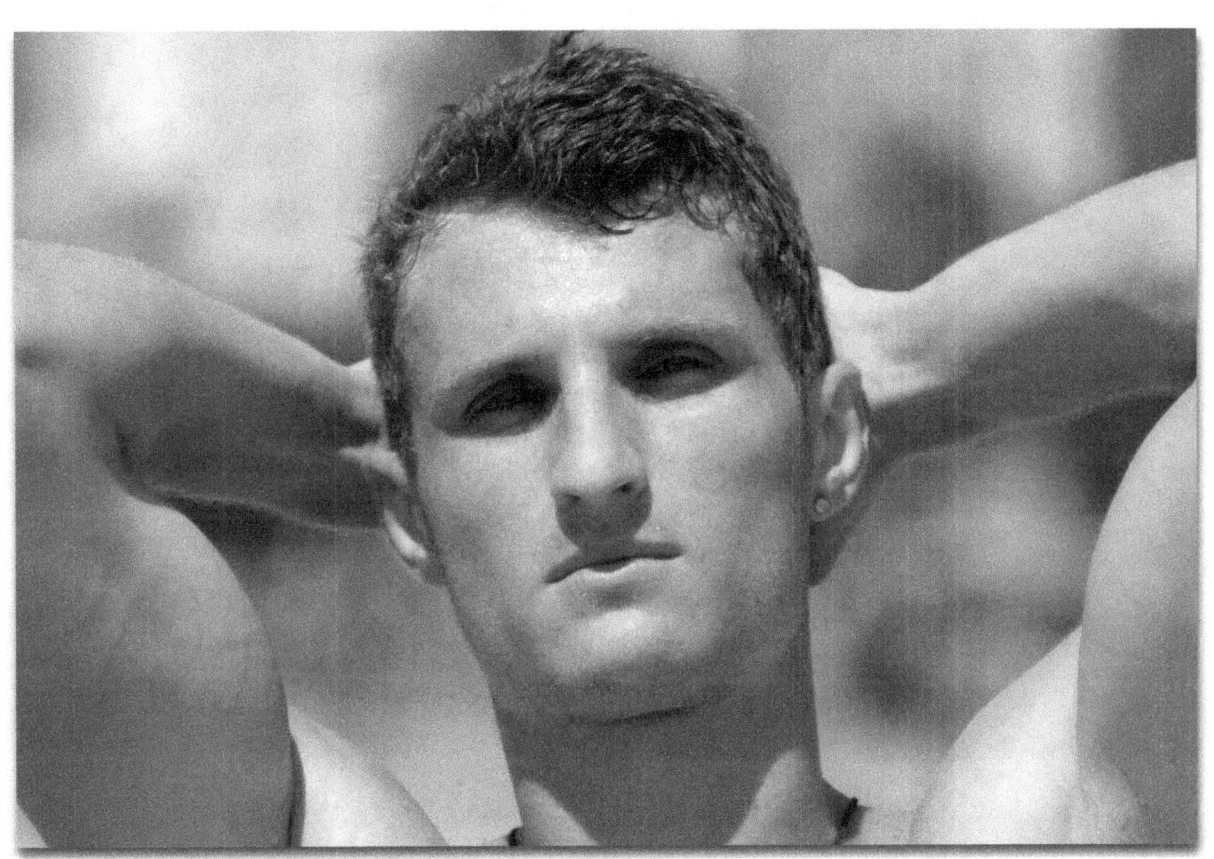

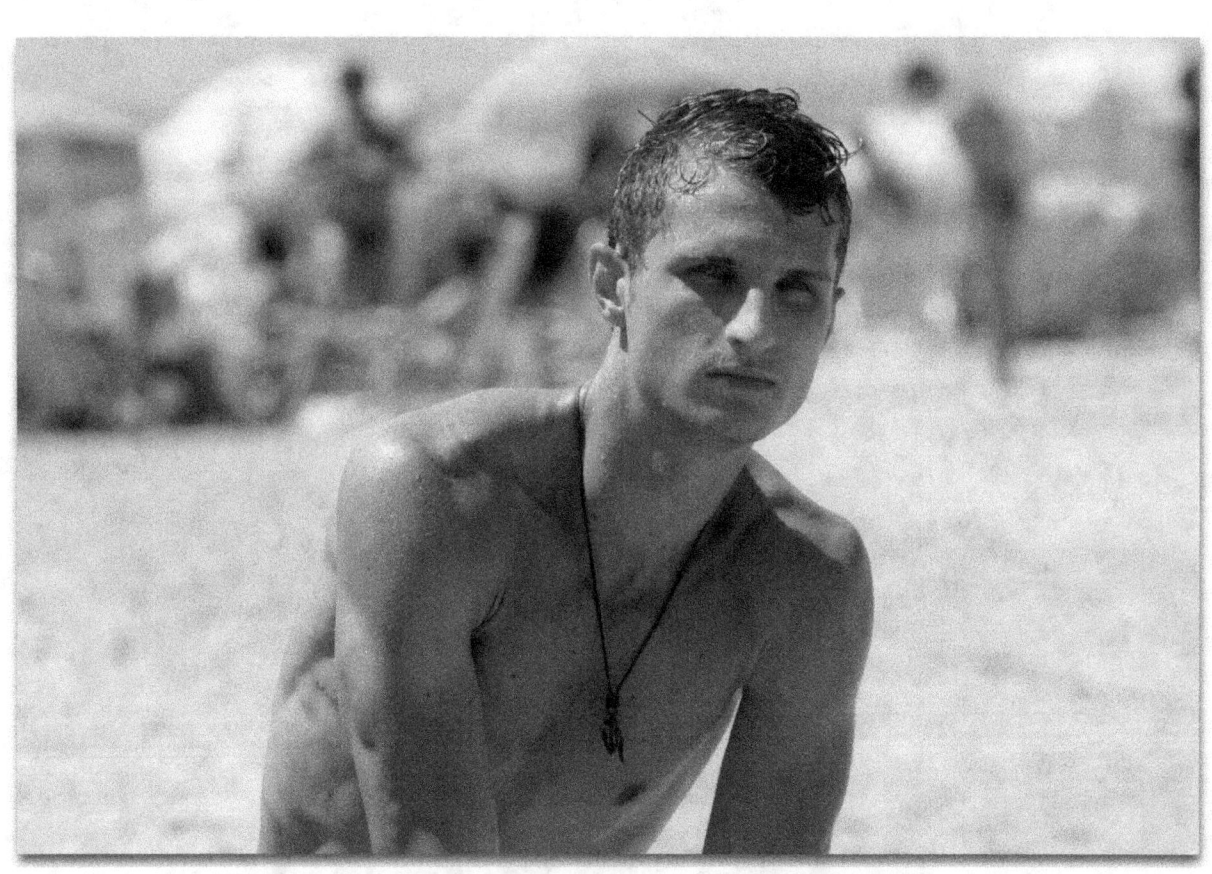

Italo

Italo is a really cool guy.

He was born and raised in Rio. I have heard about him through a mutual friend. One day, by coincidence, I met him in Lagoa during a photo shoot.

He was charming and very nice, and I told our mutual friend that I wanted to photograph him.

A week later we were shooting in Copacabana.

"I haven't been in the water in eight years," Italo told me, after he had just returned from a dip for our shoot. "I come here often, but I normally don't go in the water," he added, which really surprised me.

"In New York we think every Brazilian is hanging out in the water," I joked.

What I really liked most about Italo is his happy nature and willingness to do things unplanned. He was smiling most of our shoot, and I always like that because it puts everyone in a good mood.

At the end of our shoot I saw a couple of older men playing football. I asked him if he would play with them and he said yes, and later I asked them and they said yes, too (see that photo in the "Culture" section of this book).

Italo has several tattoos including a church, the image of an ex girlfriend, the name of a saint, and his neighborhood.

"I like tattoos," he said.

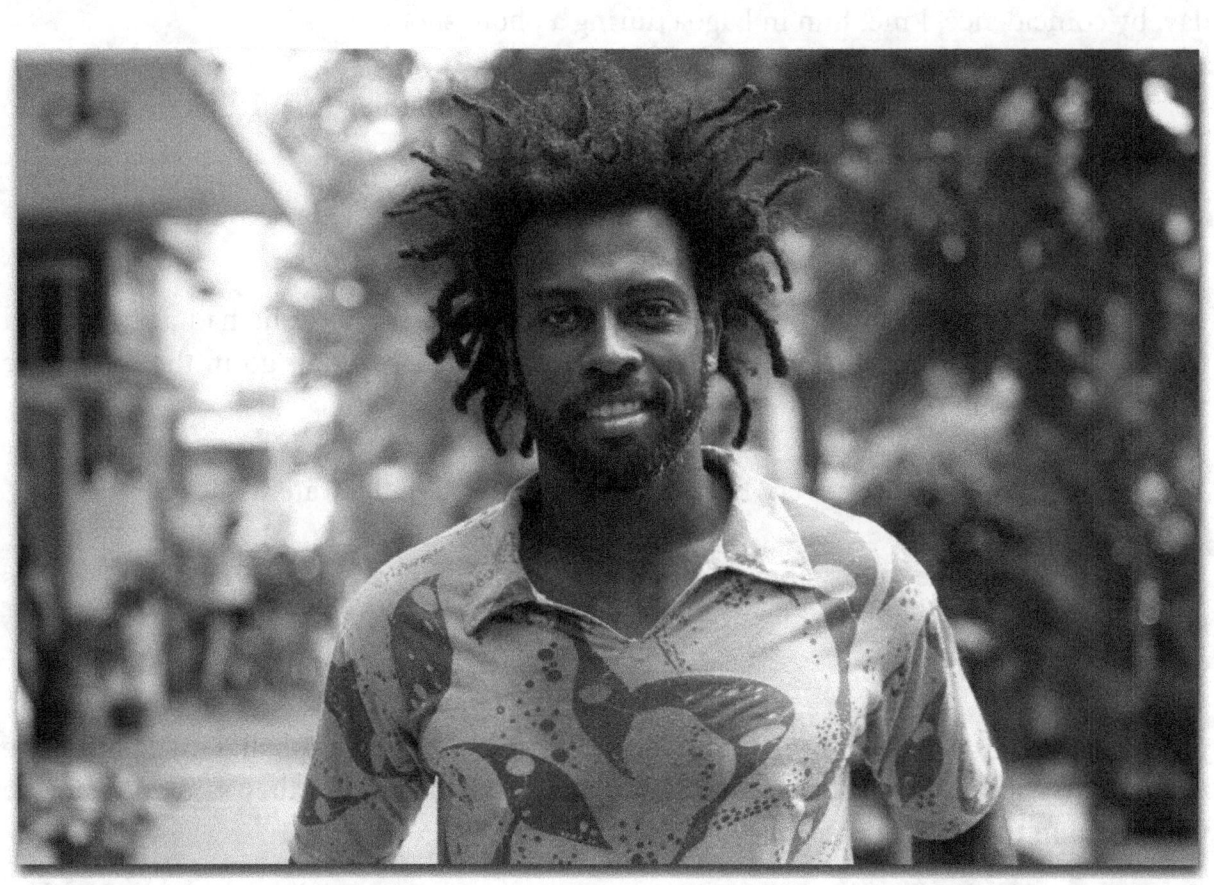

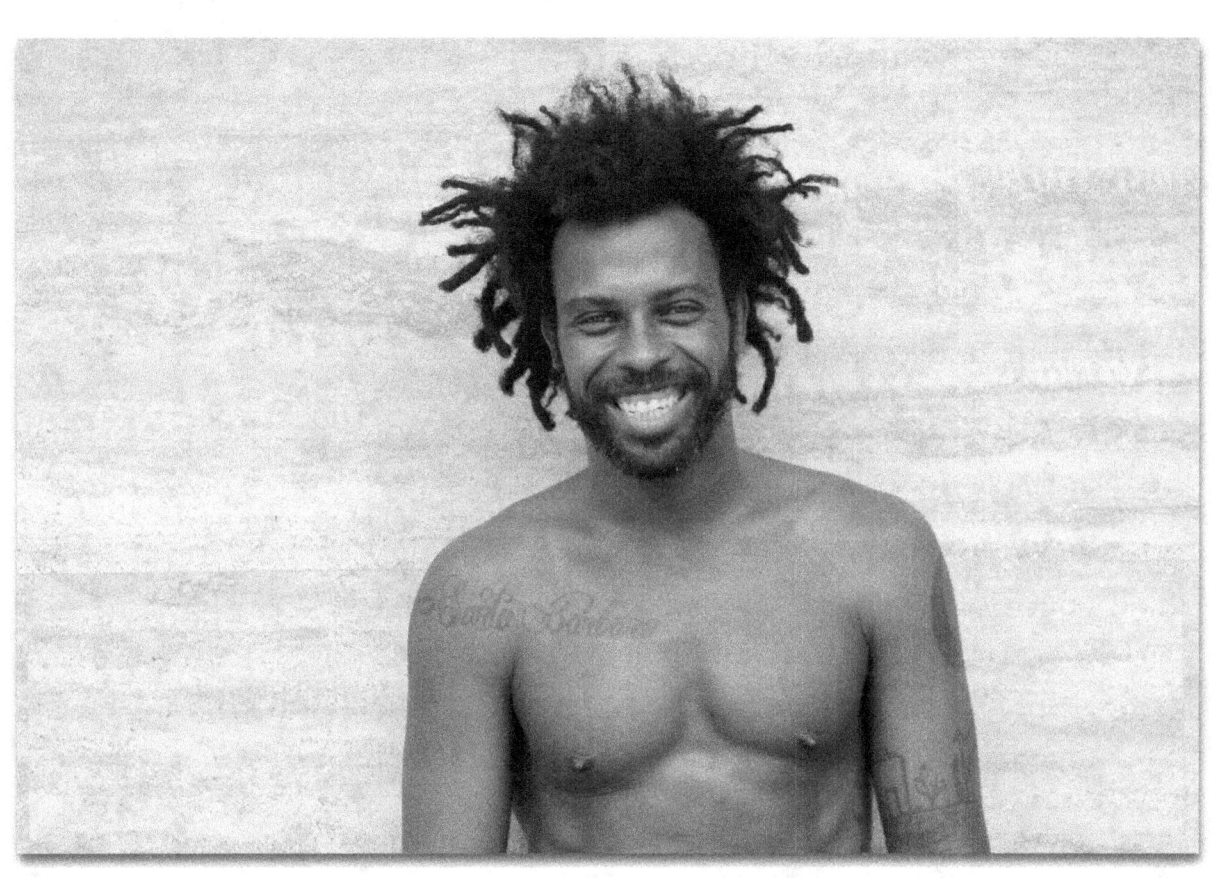

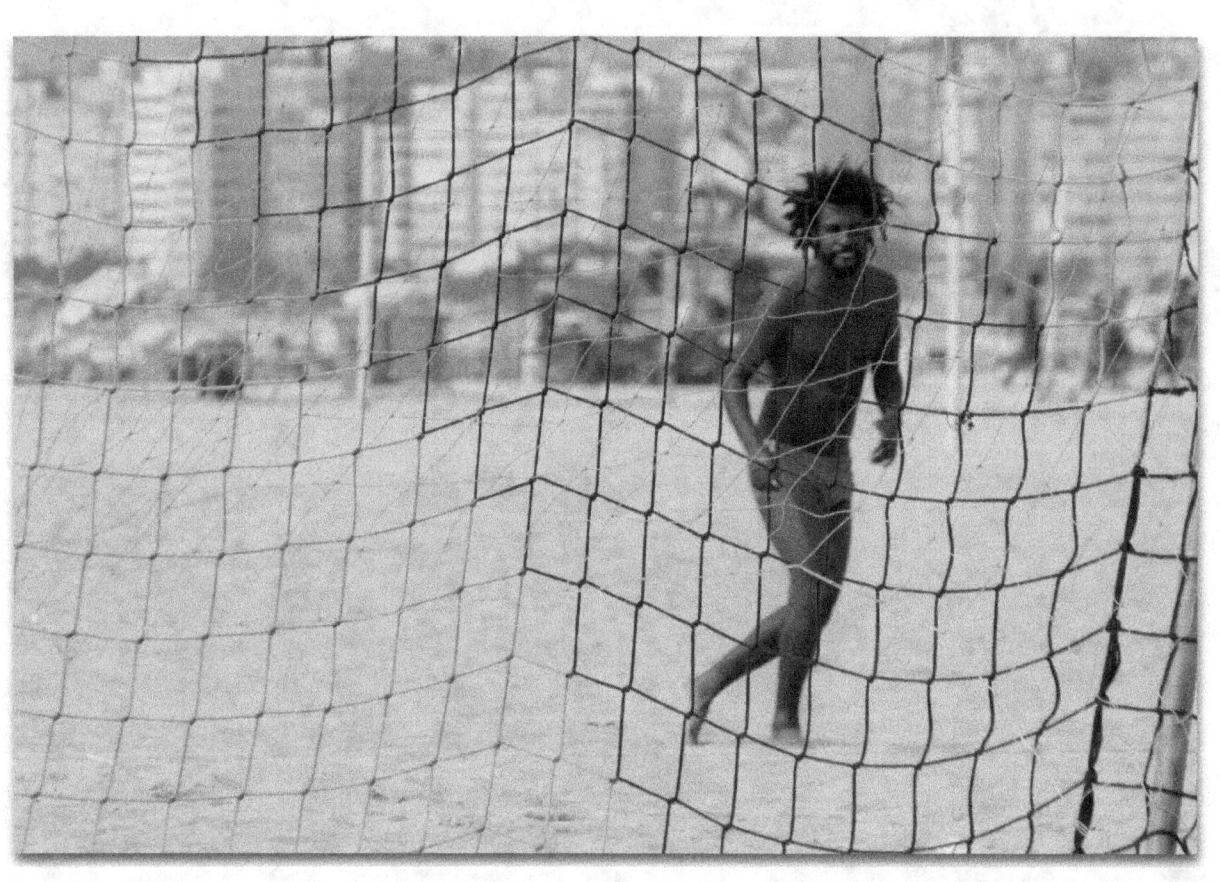

Leo

Leo moved to Rio de Janeiro to be a model.

Although he lives across the Bay in Niterói, with his partner of five years and their dogs, he spends most of his time in Rio. Aside from being a model, he is also a personal trainer and massage therapist.

"I love my work," he said to me, while we were shooting in Centro, "I like it because it gives me flexibility to do things like this photo shoot."

What I like best about Leo is his versatility.

We had shot some photos in which he played the cliché muscle guy, and we did some photo in which we showed a beautiful man (see the photo in the "Copacabana" section of this book). I understand now why brands work with him, because he can deliver anything that is needed.

"I like to put emotion in my photos," he told me.

He's good at it.

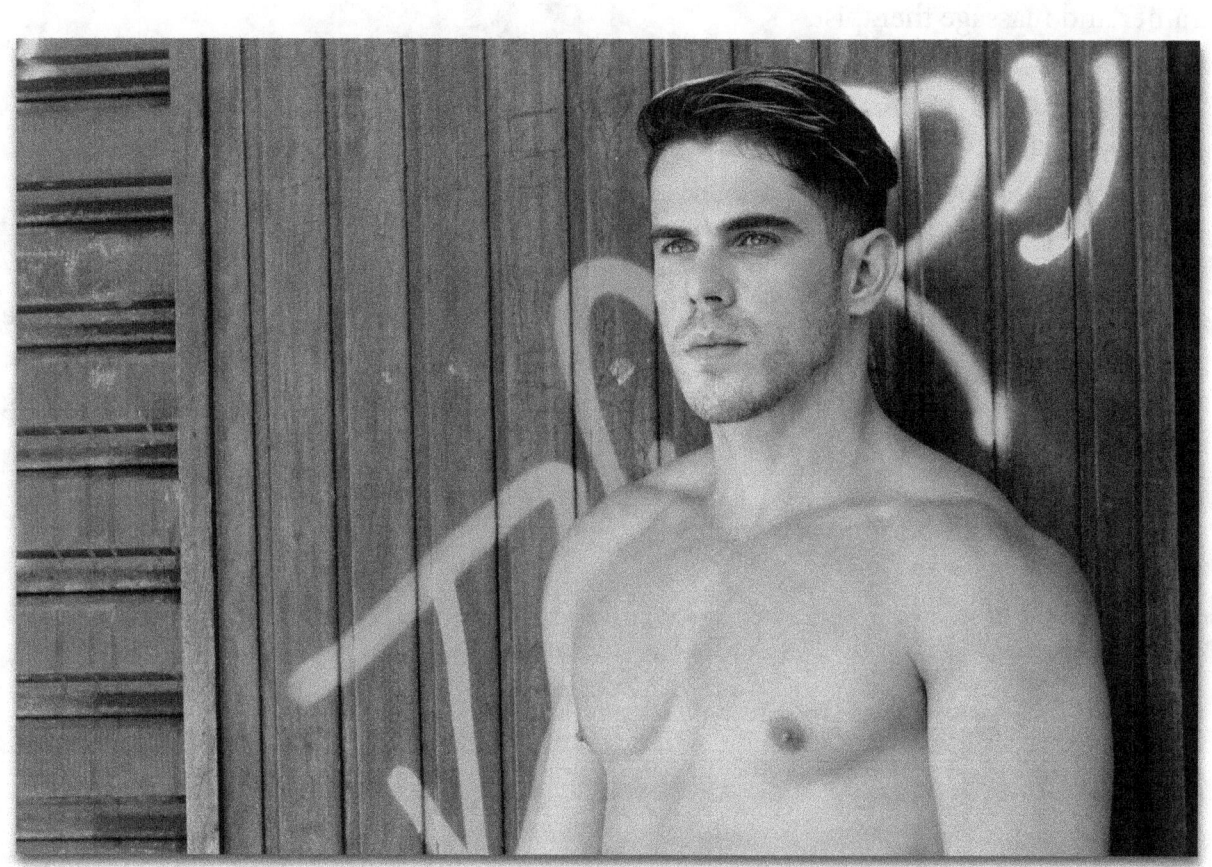

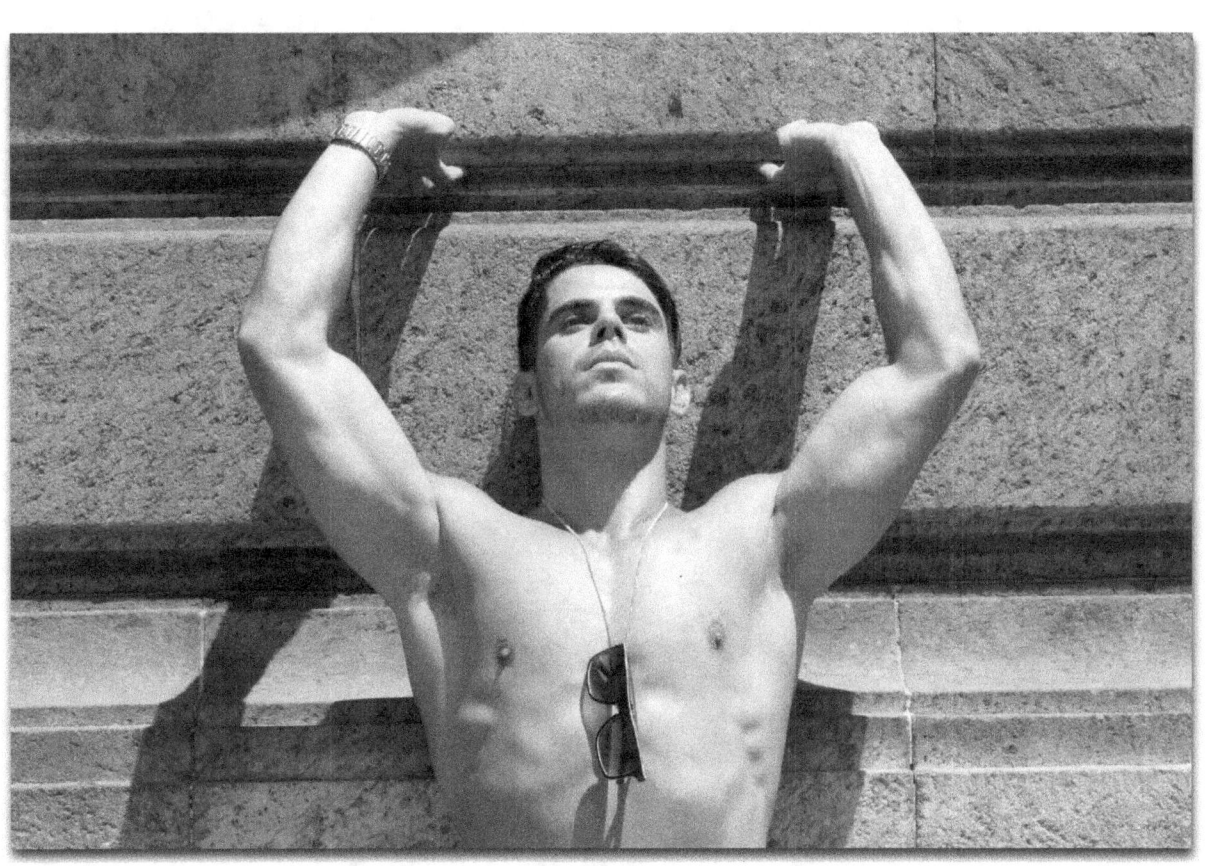

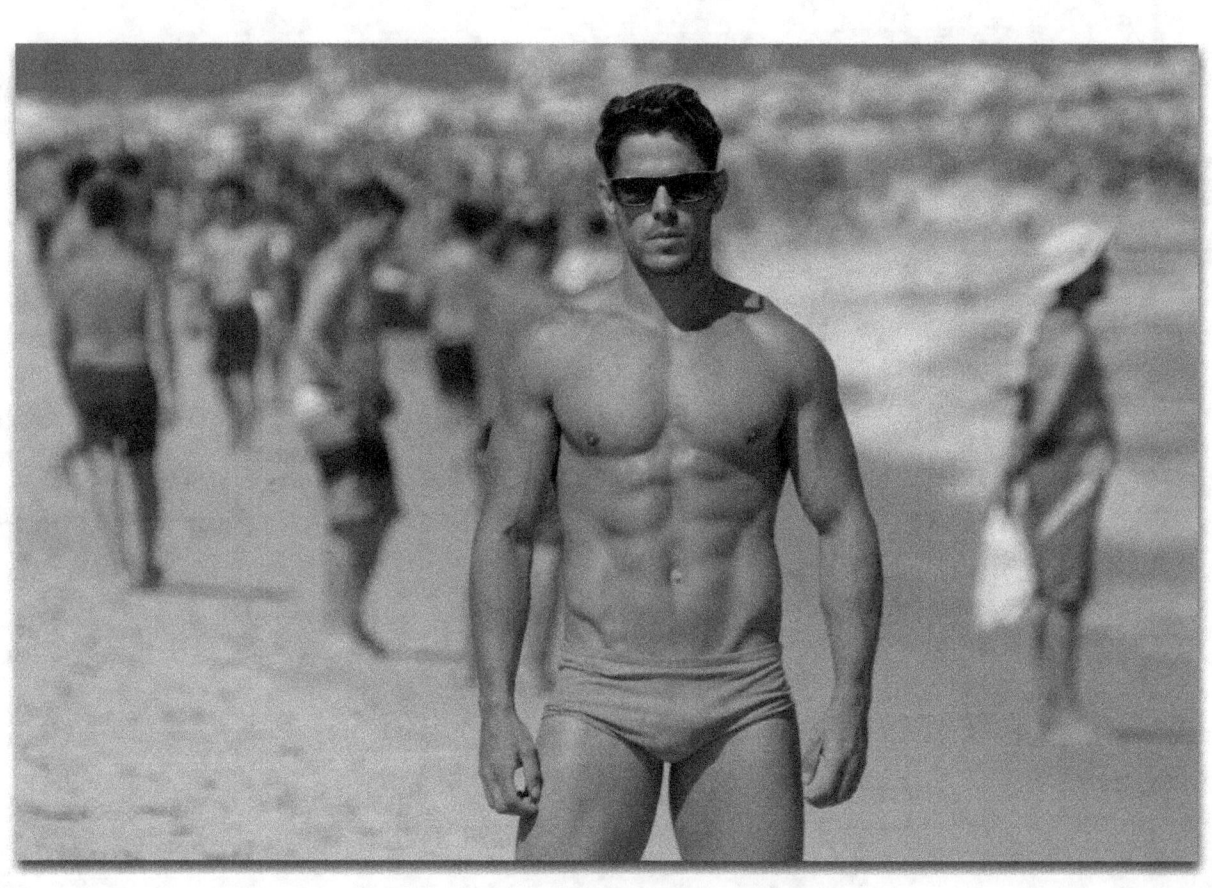

Marc

Marc was born 40 miles outside of Rio in Petrópolis.

He lives in the hip Botafogo neighborhood, which he compares to New York's Chelsea neighborhood. From the first moment you meet Marc you get the sense that you have met a real artist. No, really, he's a walking art.

"I love to sing, dance, and make art," he told me.

Marc has several tattoos including those on the neck, shoulders, arms, fingers, back, legs—basically everywhere. I love the tattoos on his fingers, which spell "love art" on each knuckle, with the last knuckle having a heart.

Marc lives with his partner, their daughter, and cats.

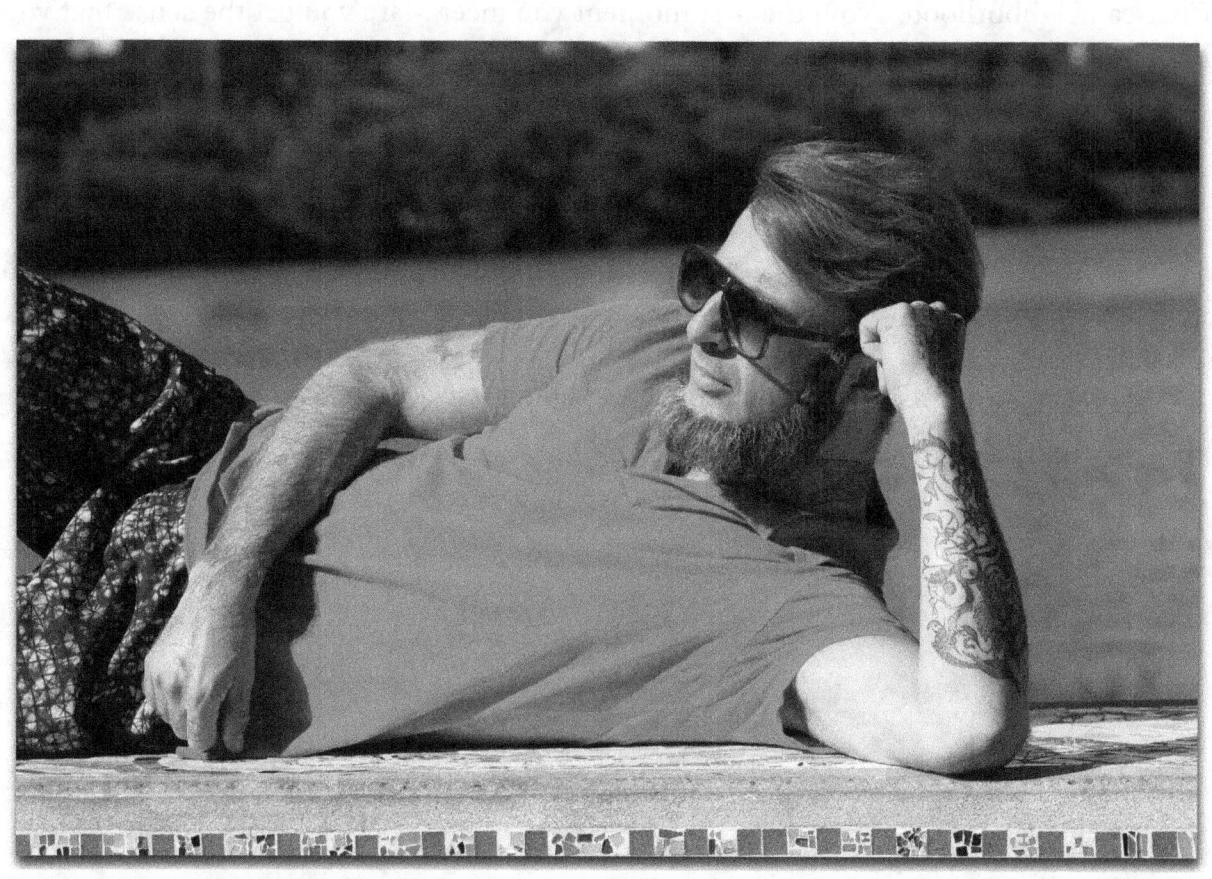

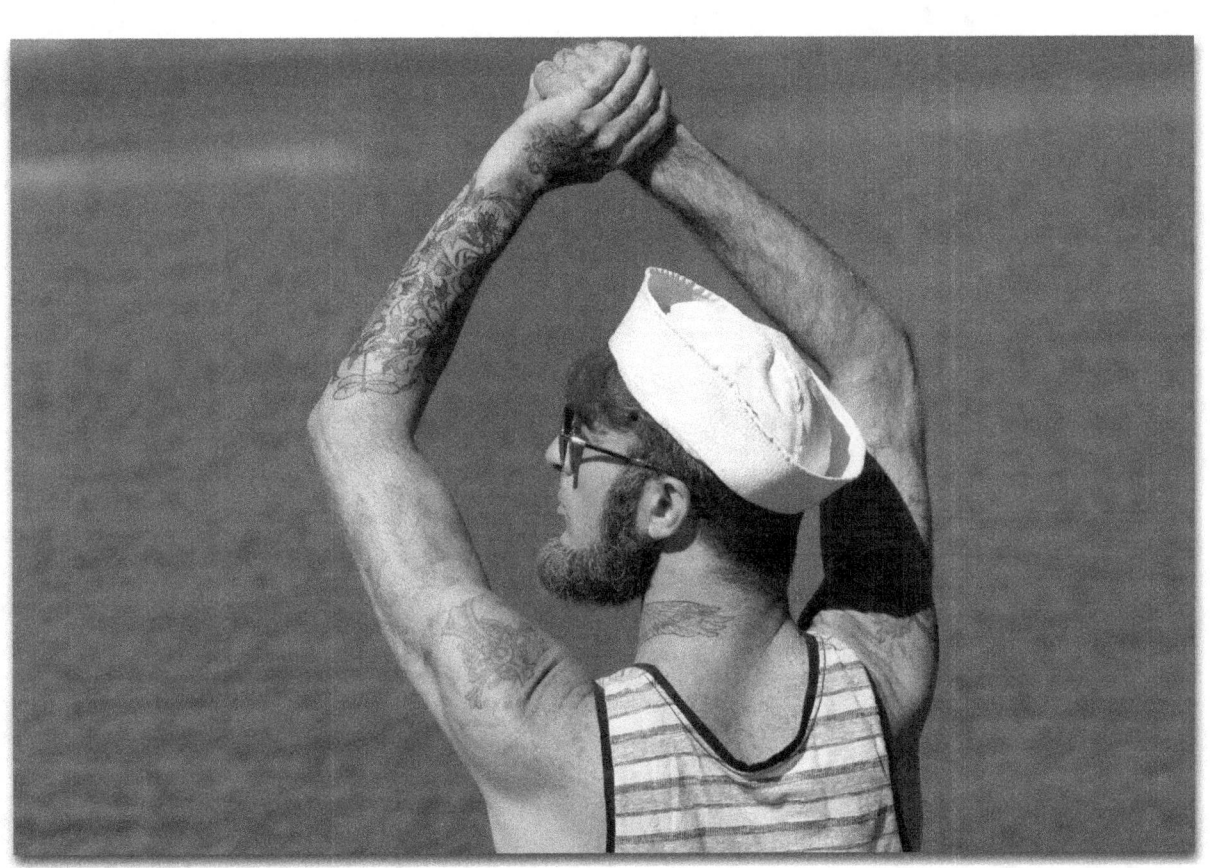

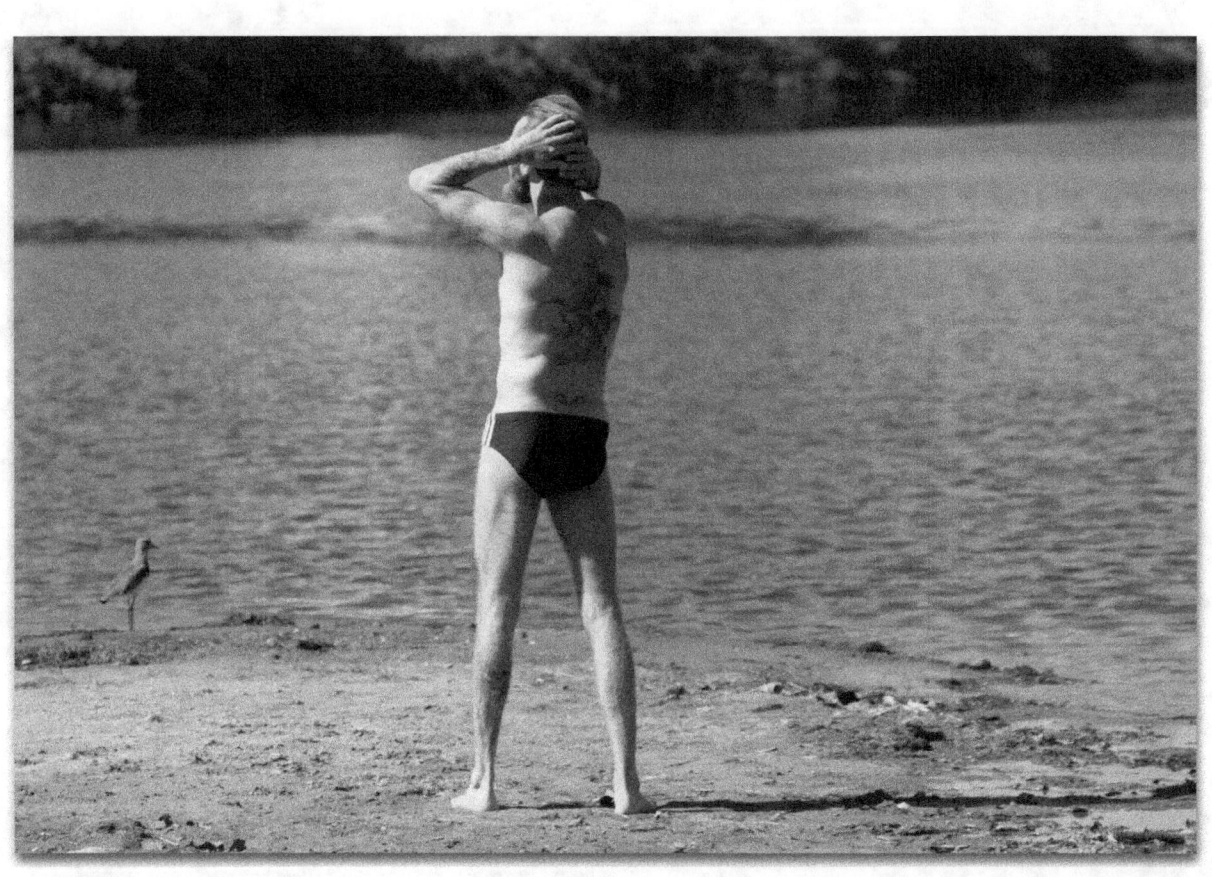

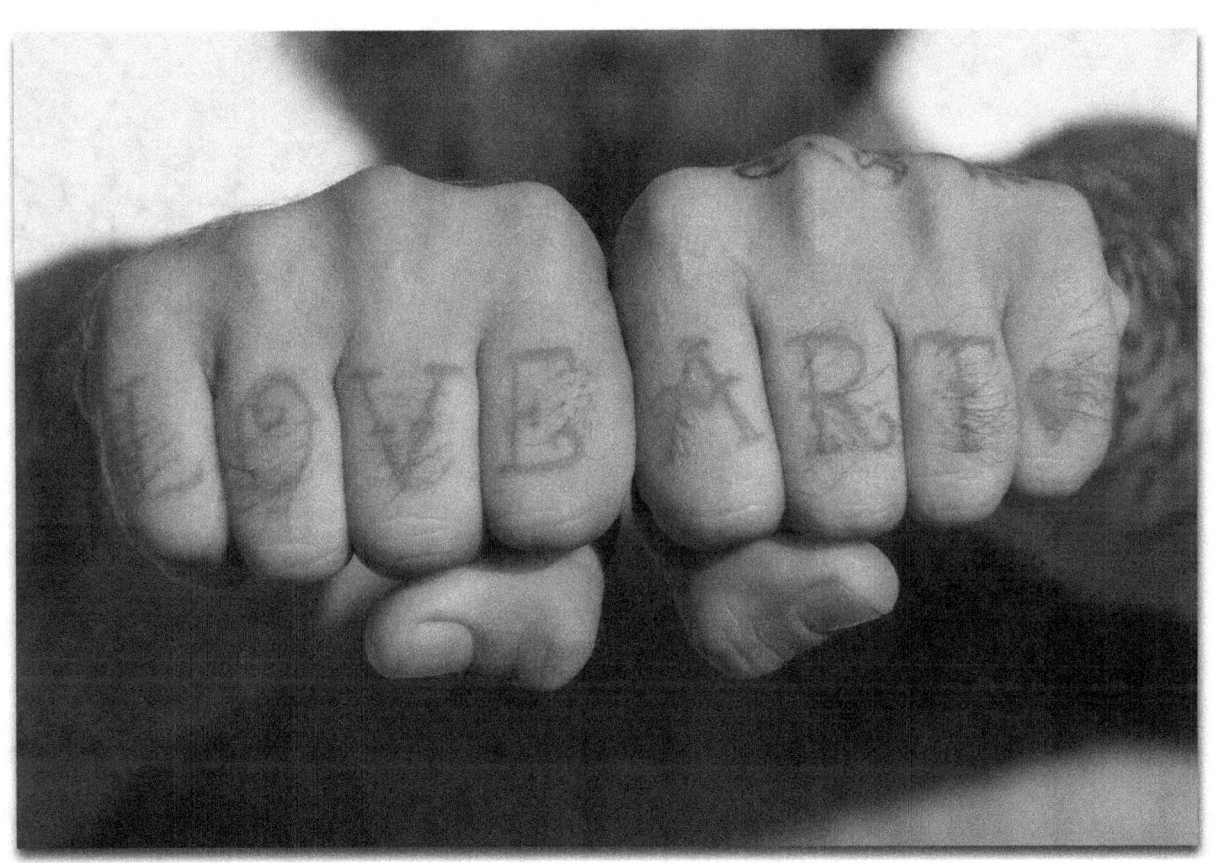

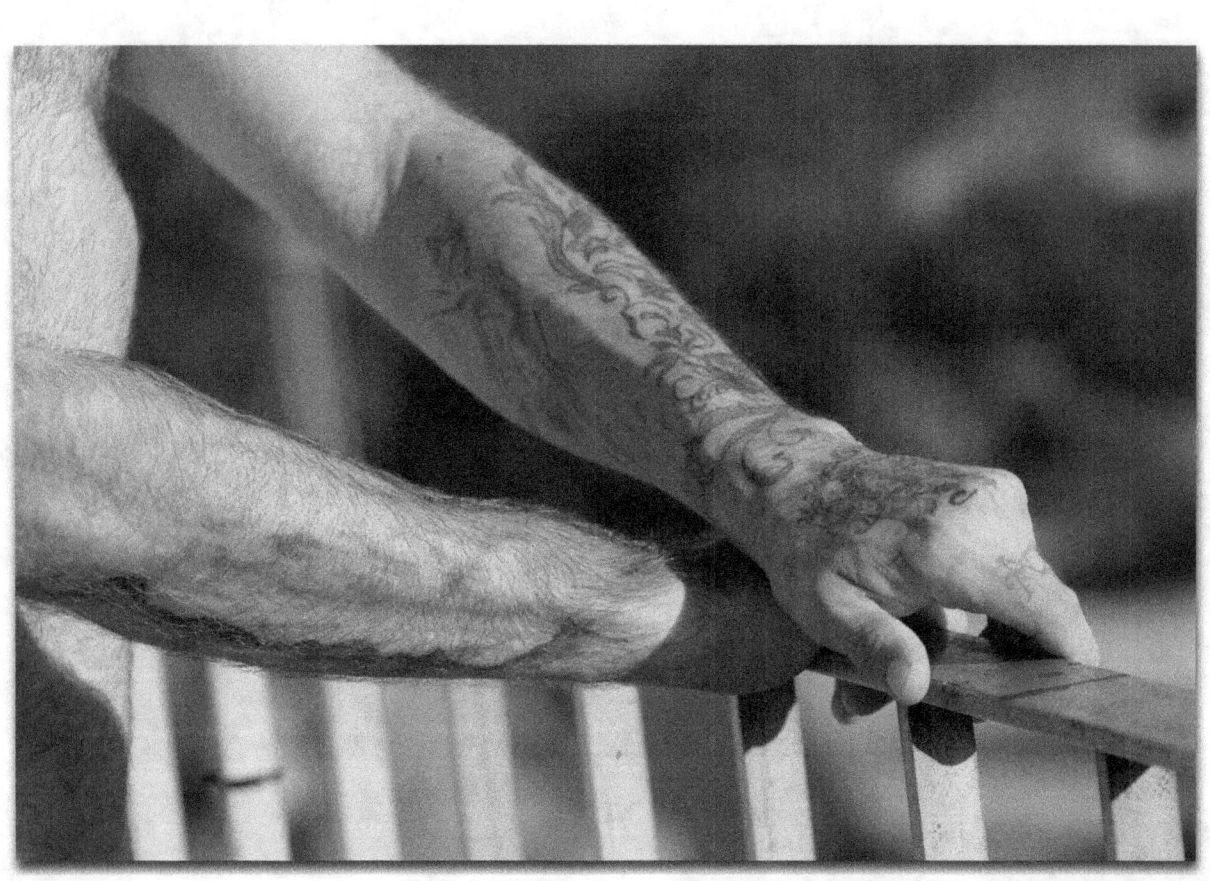

Gerson

Gerson was born in the state of São Paulo, and moved to Rio ten years ago.

"I moved to Rio because I wanted to make my dreams come to true," says Gerson. "I really needed to live in a city. I needed to be in a place where I could work in art, live with art, make art, and do everything with art," he adds, "I could live in São Paulo, but I prefer to live in Rio because of the sea, because of the nature."

Gerson is the author of three books, including the authorized biography of Gretchen, a pop superstar in Brazil.

He is also a dancer on a popular television show called *Amor e Sexo* or "Love and Sex" headlined by the gorgeous Fernanda Lima, one of the most famous personalities on television.

He's a big fan of music, but he also loves the Carnival.

Having been in Rio for so long Gerson says he is a carioca at heart. "I'm all the places where I lived," he says, and adds that every place he lived made him who he is today.

Gerson graduated in dance from the Universidade Federal or Federal University in Rio. For his final thesis, he chose a subject close to his heart: international music. He focused on Madonna's Reinvention Tour.

"I wanted to show that music can be more than superficial," says Gerson, who focused on each song of the tour and connected it to the arts in literature and cinema, for example. "I wanted to say that you could use music to reach people. The most important aspect of the tour for me the dialogue between what she was showing and the audience. She showed things that say 'this is what I believe, this is what I feel, and this is what I think.' It was as though she was telling them to choose freely. It was a real dialogue."

I photographed Gerson all over Rio.

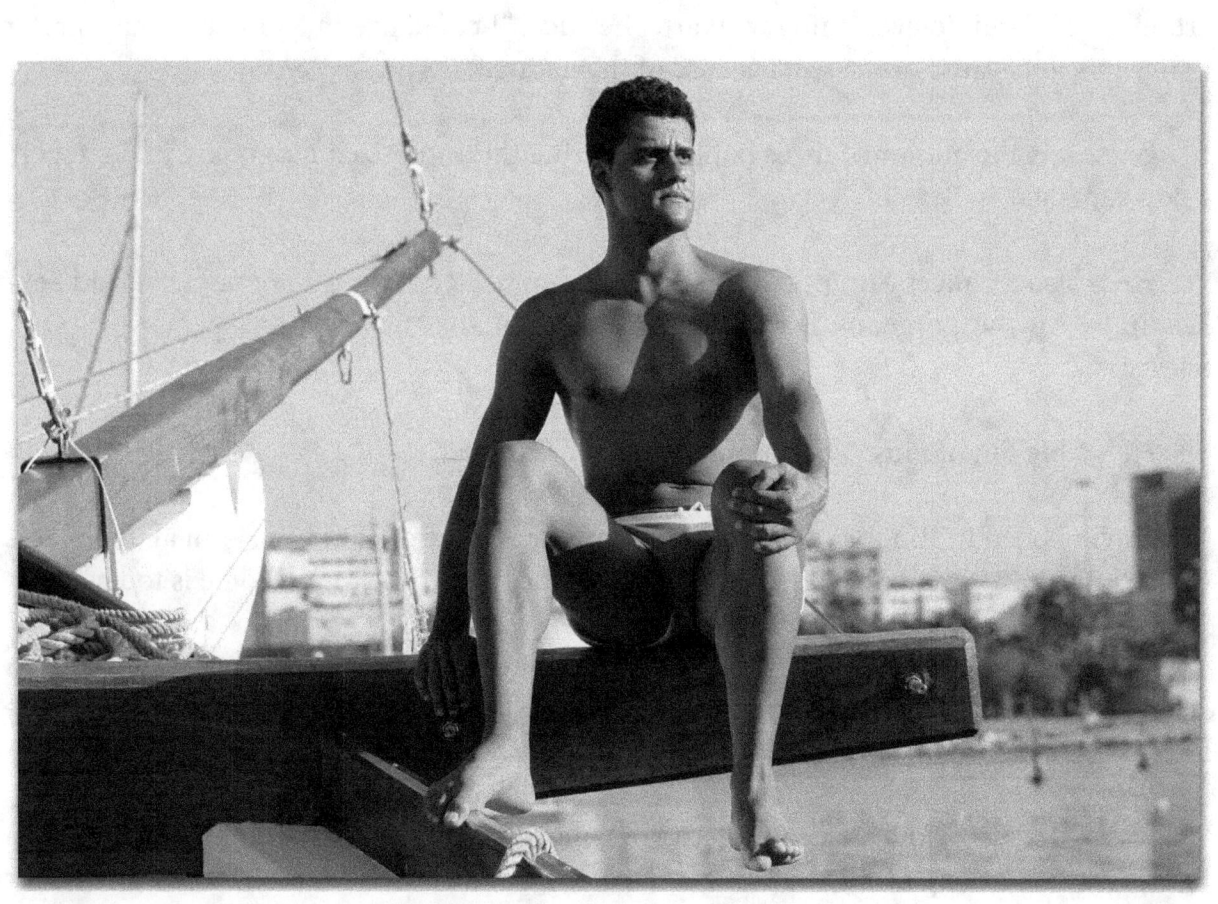

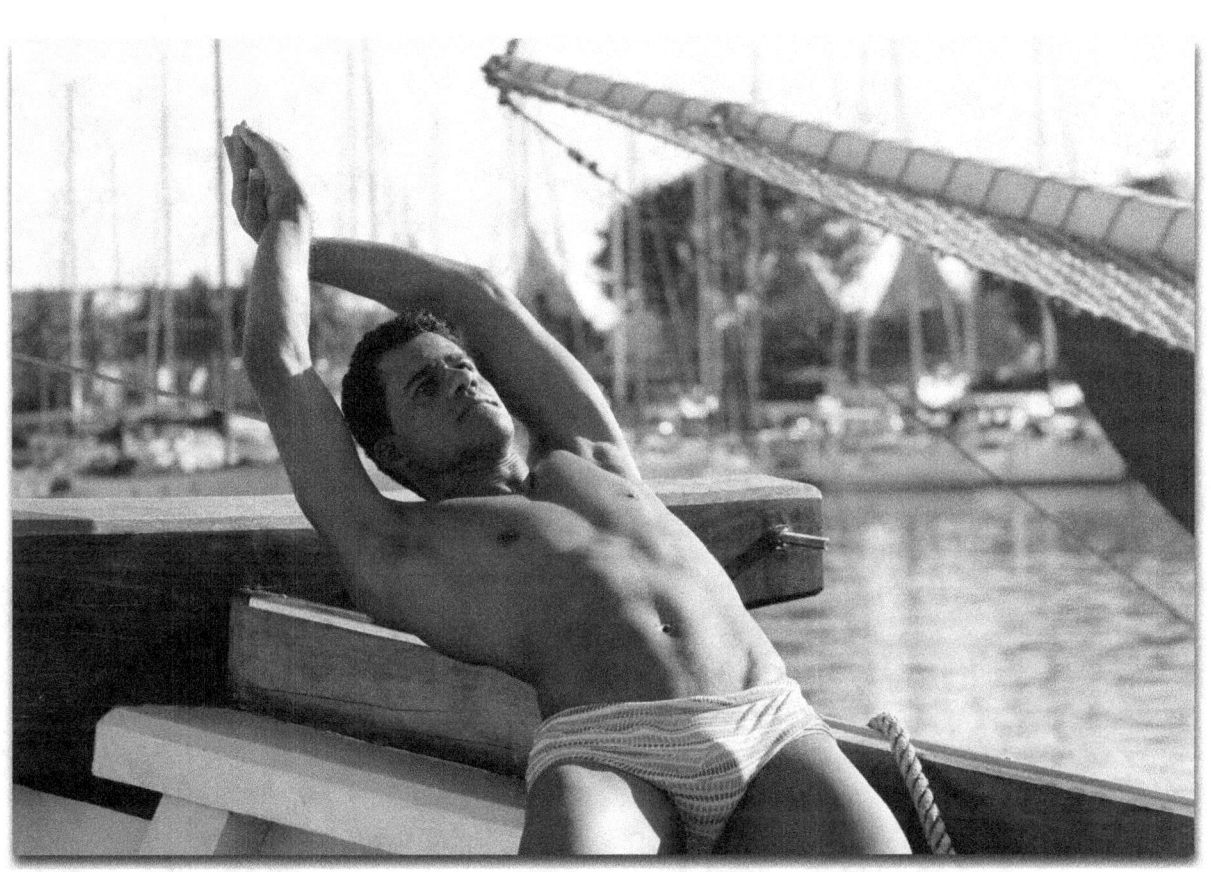

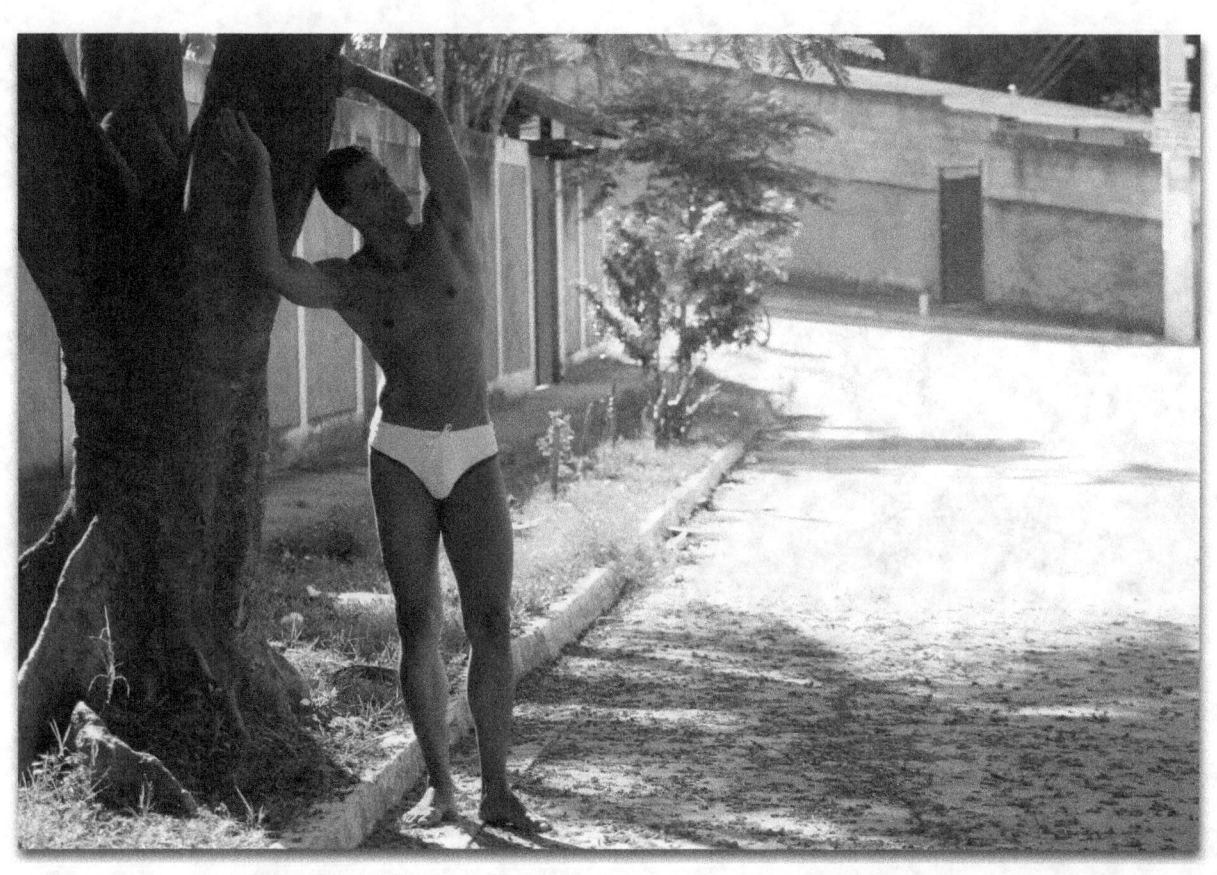

Kim

Kim is an ambitious young man.

He has big dreams.

But he is not just sitting there and dreaming, he is actively working to make his dreams come true. It was an agent friend of mine who turned me to him. She said he had what I was looking for, which at the time meant a young man who had dreams beyond being the cliché.

"His eyes say something," my friend told me over the phone, "I will send you his Facebook profile."

Kim and I started talking on Facebook that night because I saw what my friend saw. Although it was months later we would finally have the chance to shoot, it was nice to be able to stay in contact with him and hear about his ideas.

"I think everyone has dreams," he told me, which I agreed with, "I'm just following mine."

Kim, who was born and raised in Rio, was living in Centro when we started talking. Later when I arrived in Brazil, in São Paulo, he had already moved back to his mother's business, a hotel located couple of hours away from Rio. Yet, he made the time and he came for our shoot.

Very rarely do I meet young models that are on time, but Kim was on time.

"I'm always on time," he said.

He is a very professional kid.

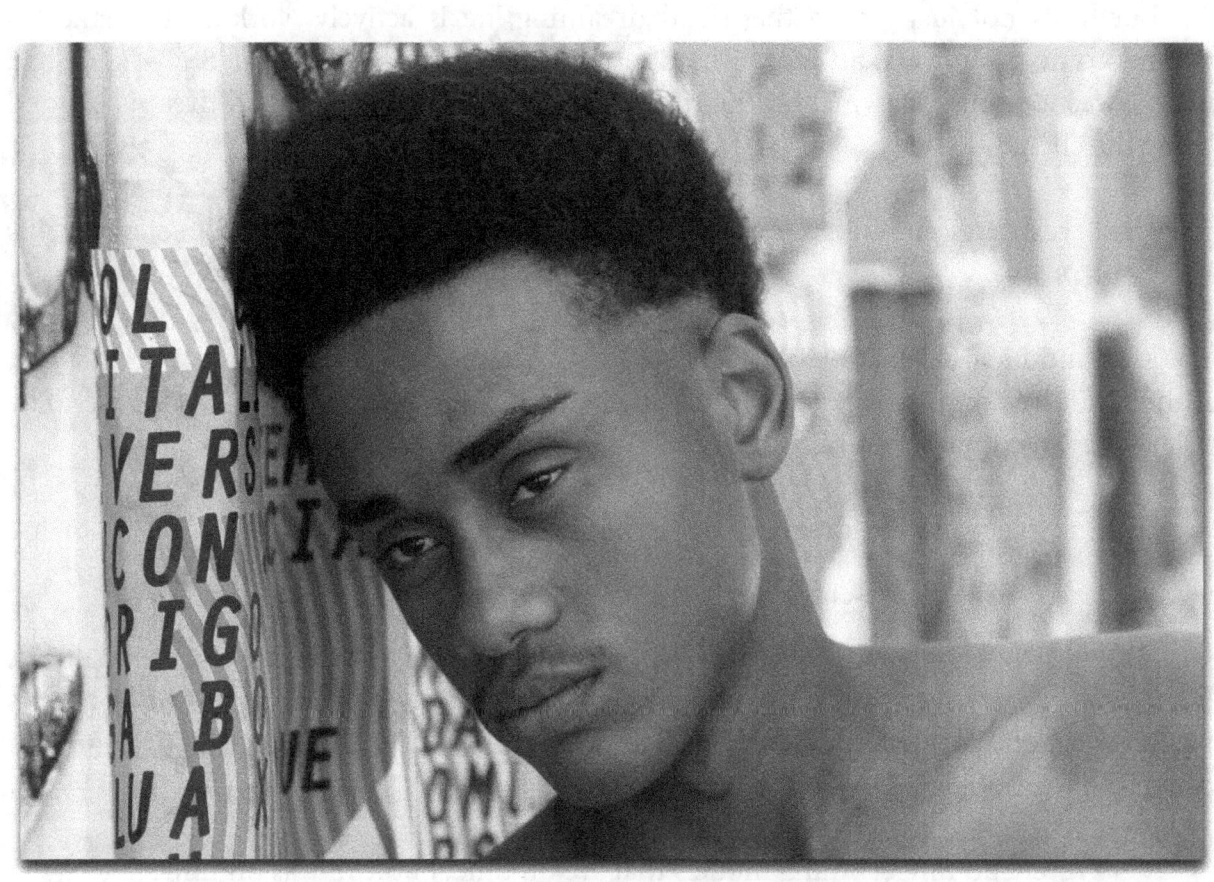

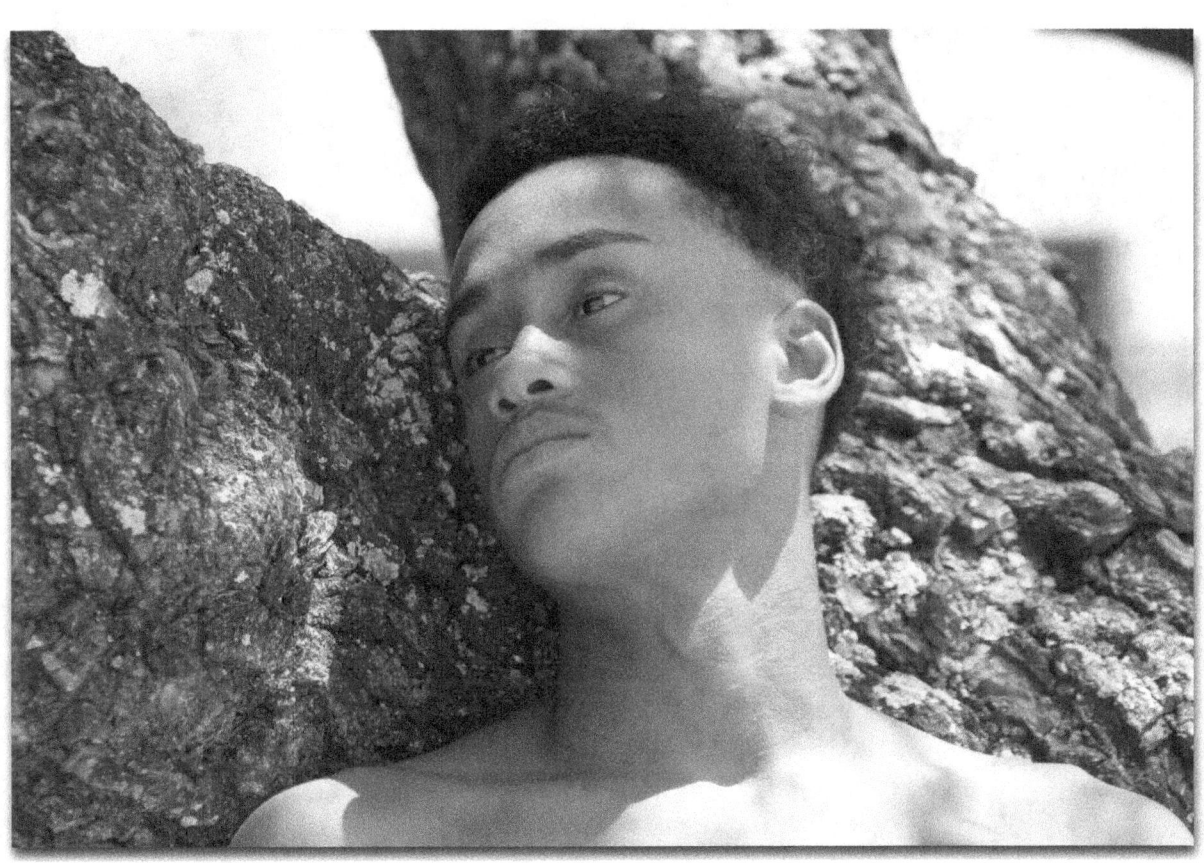

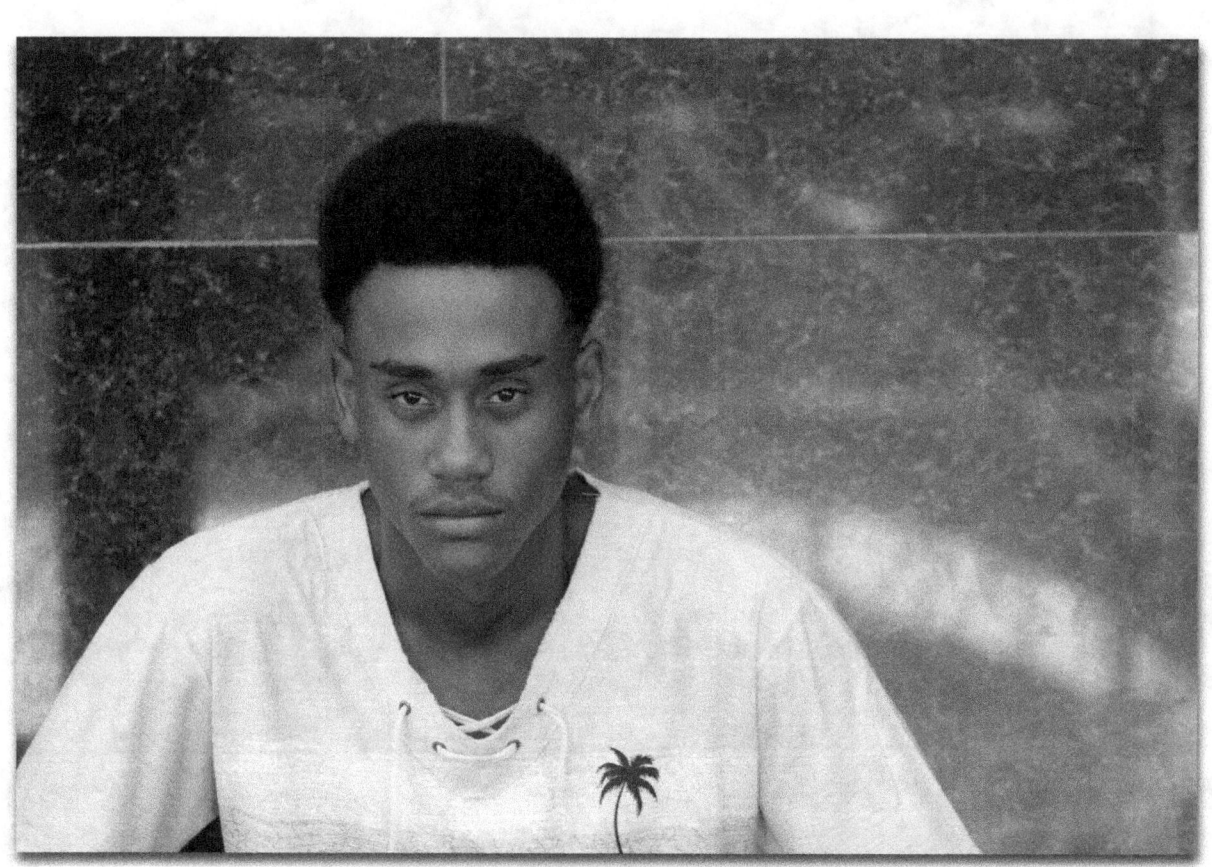

Lu

I met Lu on New Year's Eve in 2014.

We welcomed 2015 together, along with millions of others, in Copacabana.

I was so moved by his story of adventure. He is a Taiwanese young man who quit his job and decided to travel all over the world.

"I wanted to know what it is like to live in South America, Asia, or Europe," he told me, as we waited for the light show, "I wanted to have more experiences and to see what was going on in the world. I'm a mechanical engineer in Taiwan, and it's boring, really."

When I met him he had already been in most of South American countries and was in Rio to fly to Europe. The next day, on New Year's Day, we met and we went to Ipanema and had a shoot at the beach and around the neighborhood.

"I love Brazil," he confessed to me, laughing, "I think it's my favorite country in South America," he added, talking about how he loves the language, the people, the culture.

I met many tourists in Rio over the years, but not anyone like Lu. He seemed to really genuinely be interested in the people, in the culture, in the land.

May all the tourists in the world be like that.

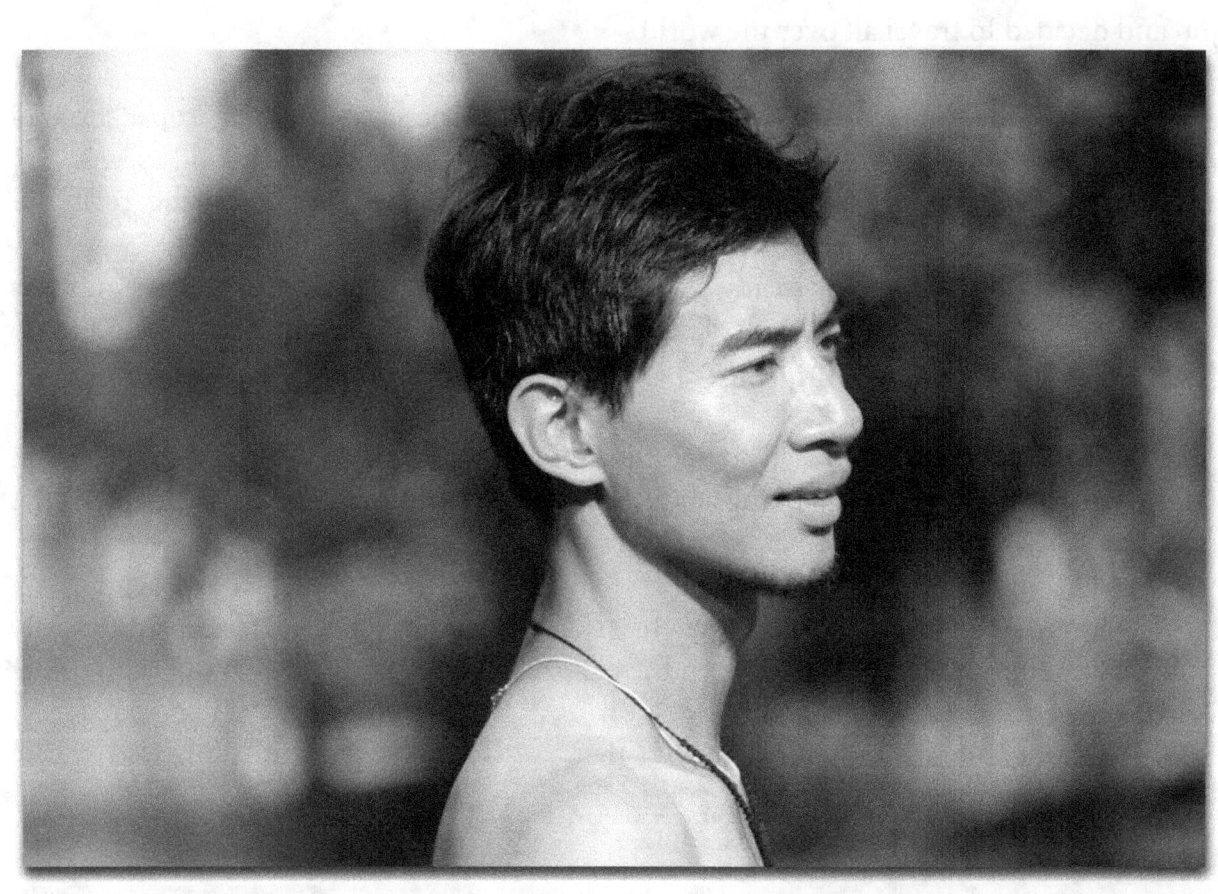

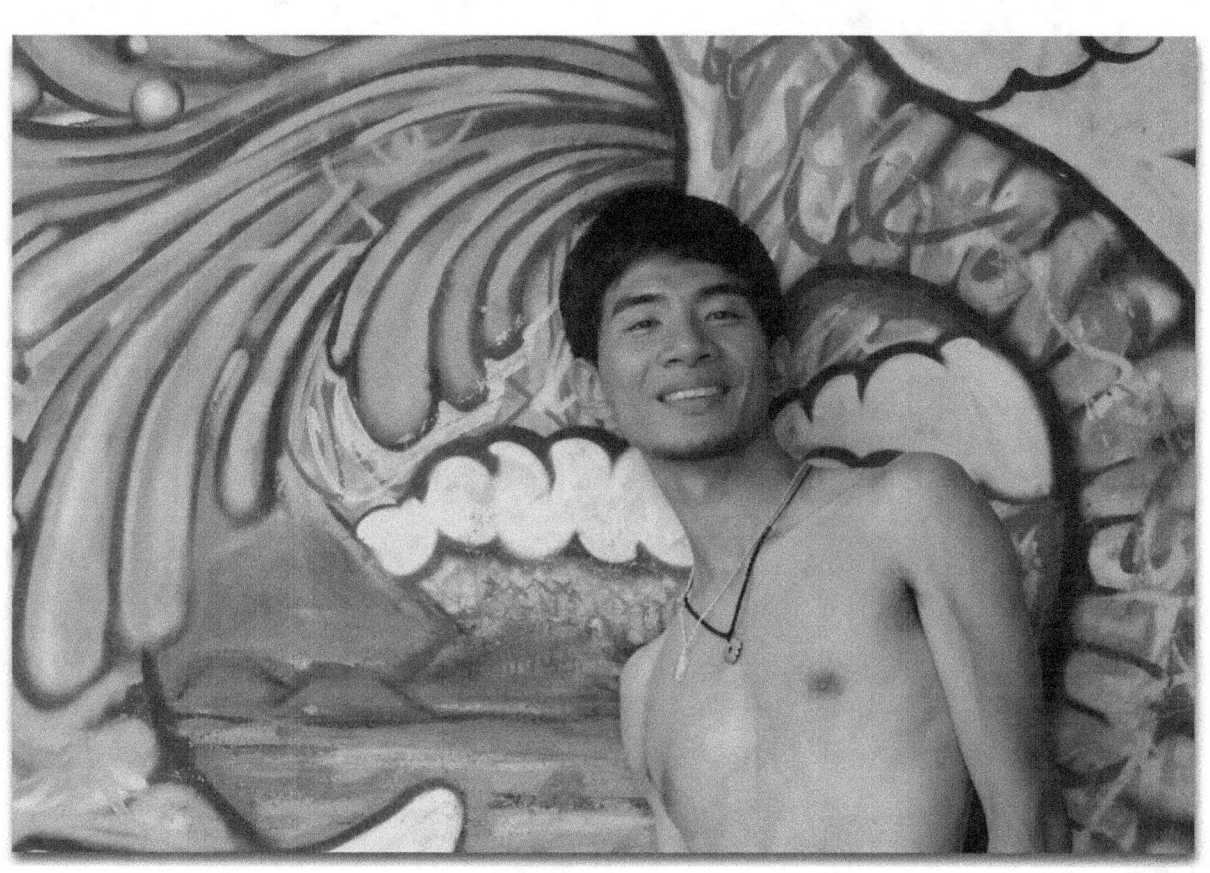

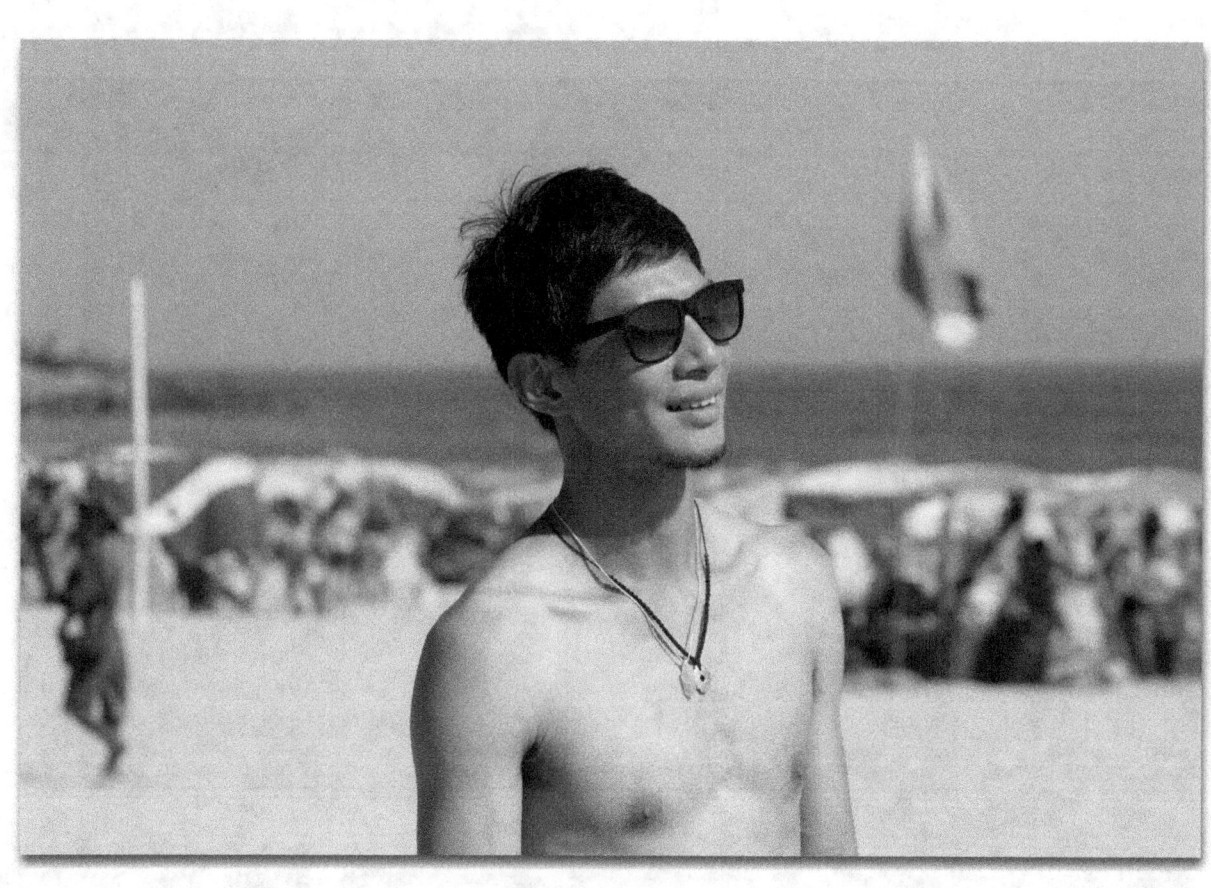

Culture

The culture of Rio, like that of Brazil, is a diverse culture.

It has its roots in Africa, Europe, and the Americas.

You can really see that in everything from architecture, to religion, to food, and everything in between.

You can see it in their films, and you can hear it in their music.

There is just a diversity that can't be denied in the culture.

"This city is full of culture," said João, after he and his girlfriend performed for me 'The Carioca,' a 1933-choreography from the film *Flying Down to Rio*.

Of course, it truly is impossible to discussed Rio's culture as much as it should in a book like this.

Nevertheless, in the following pages I will talk about beauty, festivals, religion, sports, food, and art.

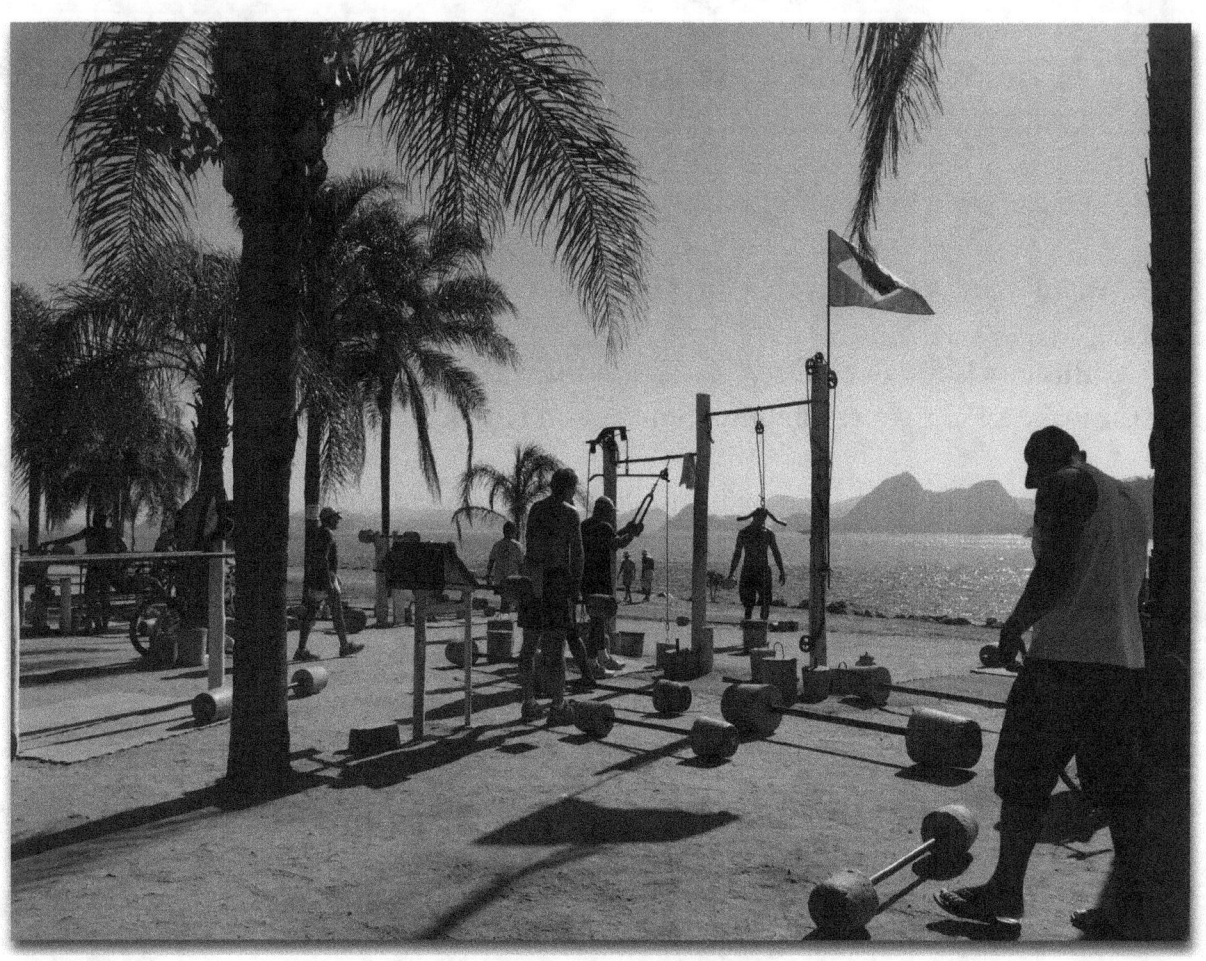
<u>Beauty</u>: The Cariocas are serious about their looks.

Beauty

Michelle Neri Rangel, a 27-year-old beauty dressed in a red evening gown with long curly hair, smiled brightly when her name was called as the winner of the Miss Talavera Bruce title.

Except, and totally out of place, right behind her was a grey-haired guard in a watchtower over a 20-foot wall.

Yes, the Miss Talavera Bruce Pageant takes place in a prison of the same name.

"This can only happen in Rio," said to me a young male editor at a fashion magazine who wanted to remain anonymous, "Beauty is everything to us. I think beauty is valued above all else for us. We go to church looking beautiful. So, even in prison beauty is important."

This editor had plastic surgery performed all over his body.

He has had 17 surgeries to date.

Everything from lips to breasts to the butt.

And, it really is normal here!

According to the Sociedade Brasileira de Cirurgia Plástica (Brazilian Society of Plastic Surgery) there were 276,000 plastic surgeries performed on men in 2014.

That means for every 2 minutes of every hour of the day a Brazilian man is going under the knife somewhere.

"I'm not surprised," said João, who said he would like to have eyelid surgery done when he has the money for it, "I know today in Brazil it's not a shocker for a man to have plastic surgery. Maybe ten years ago it was not like that at all."

João is right. In 2009 less than 100,000 Brazilian men had plastic surgery done, according to the SBCP.

Many of the Cariocas in the southern part of the city, I would say, are mostly doing beauty the traditional way.

People are working out at gyms, both private and public, and are just conscious of their physical bodies.

There are oceanfront boulevards that offer the space to be active.

As a result, I have to point out, that Zona Sul, or the South Zone, is full of physically fit people, attractive people, and even many who clearly enhanced their features.

However, I would argue, most people out of the southern portion of the city are average people like those anywhere else in the world.

It's just that the southern part of the city is populated with a lot of people in the entertainment industry, or industries dependent on that, and many of them are actually from elsewhere.

Beauty is a big business for Brazil, too, as a country.

With nearly 50 billion in beauty revenues Brazil is the third largest after the United States and Japan.

However, according to the global market research company Euromonitor, Brazil will overtake Japan in the coming years because in the past ten years Brazil's beauty industry grew nearly 150% while Japan's only grew by 40%.

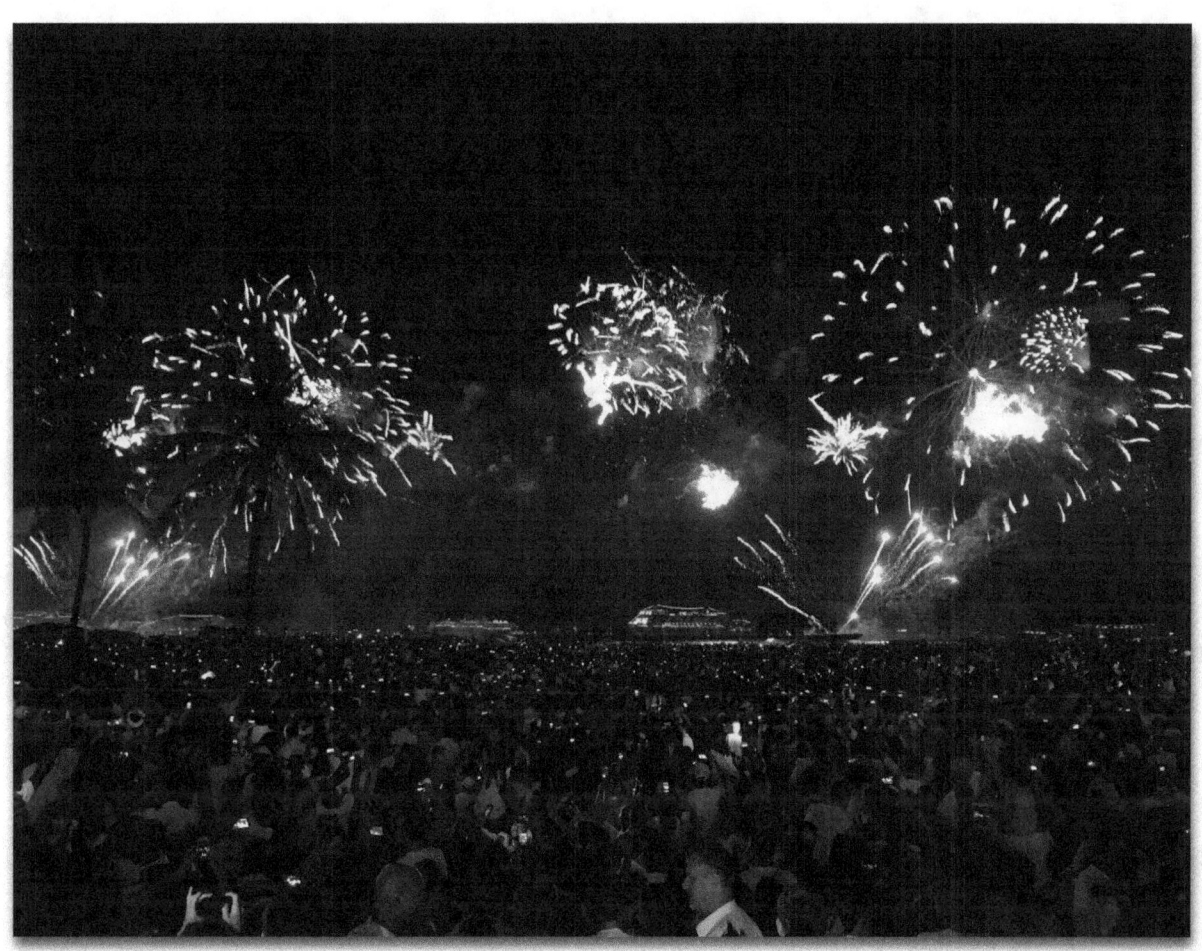

Festivals: New Year's Eve in Rio.

Festivals

Brazilians love to party.

Whether it is for religion, national interests, or for sports festivals make up a big part of the culture.

The Carioca year kicks of with **Réveillon**, the New Year Eve party in Copacabana. Millions of people descend upon the beach in white, which is for good luck, and celebrate the coming year with 20-minute long fireworks. Public transportation works all night, and the next day they relax at the beach to recover from the party.

Twenty days into the New Year and the Cariocas are in festive mood again with **Dia de São Sebastião**, or Saint Sebastian Day. There are parades from Tijuca to Centro. Religious people go to the church, while non-religious people will go to the beach. Sometimes there are parties at the beach because it is a public holiday. Saint Sebastian, who is the city's patron saint, is a revered figure here.

Then comes February with **Carnaval do Rio**, Rio Carnival, held all over the city. Carnival takes place between Ash Wednesday and the Friday before that. Those five days the world is on hold for the Cariocas. They party like it is no one's business. It is the only time of the year when you can get away with almost anything.

Carnival takes two shapes.

There is the one that is organized through the Escola de samba, or Samba schools, with colorful parades at the Sambódromo da Marquês de Sapucaí.

Then there are the Bloco carnavalesco, or carnival blocks, in the streets and in many neighborhoods, which now numbers in the hundreds.

May brings the football finals with **Campeonato Carioca** or Carioca cup. Whoever wins will head to the nationals, and with it brings much local pride and parties. Botafogo Club has a record of 33 wins, while Vasco da Gama, which happens to be the current titleholder, has 23 wins. Fans of the winning team will celebrate greatly throughout the city.

Festas Juninas, or June Festivals, come in the Brazilian winter. As such there are bonfires everywhere. The story behind this festival is that Elizabeth, the mother of Saint

John, made a fire to announce his birth. These days the festival actually celebrates three saints who were born in the month of June.

Dia da Independência, or Independence Day, falls on the seventh day of September. It is a national holiday, and the Cariocas are serious about their independence. Since 1822 they have been free from the Portuguese grip. The flag is everywhere. The beaches are full of happy people. It is just a day to party like you're free.

December brings **Natal**, or Christmas, and **Umbanda**, the day of the Goddess of the Sea Iemanjá.

The Cariocas are in festive mood during Christmas and one can enjoy the Árvore de Natal da Bradesco Seguros, which is a floating Christmas tree on the Lagoa. It's very similar to the Christmas in the United States.

Less than a week after Christmas the Cariocas take it to the beach in celebration of Iemanjá by lighting and decorating rafts full of gifts and setting them out to sea on the last day of the year.

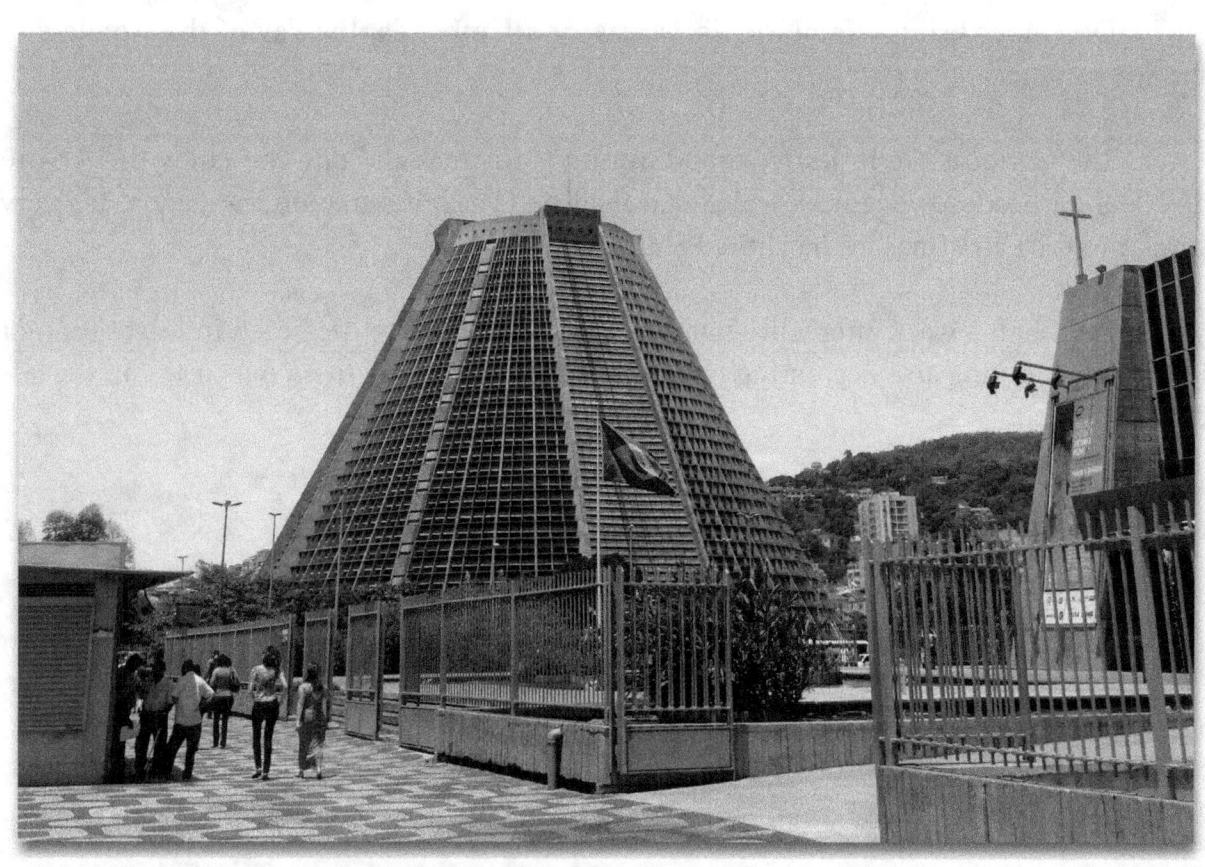

<u>Religion</u>: Saint Sebastian Cathedral in Centro.

Religion

Religion is a big part of Brazilian life.

Even when an individual may not be religious there are encounters of religion everywhere.

Religion is very powerful in this country. Brazil, regardless of the affiliation, is predominantly Christian country. According to an article by the *New York Times* Brazil was 90% **Catholic** in 1970 compared to only 65% in 2010.

In Rio those numbers shift to about half of the city being Catholic. Catholicism in Brazil goes back to Portuguese colonialism.

In the summer of 2013, while addressing Brazilian Bishops at the Archbishop's House in Rio, newly elected Pope Francis brought the issue of why Brazilians are leaving Catholicism in droves.

"At times we lose people because they don't understand what we are saying, because we have forgotten the language of simplicity and import an intellectualism foreign to our people," he told them, adding that without the simplicity that the Church "loses the very conditions which make it possible 'to fish' for God in the deep waters of his Mystery."

Where are all these Catholics going?

Protestant denominations have gained ground since the 1970s, accounting for about 25% of Rio's communities.

Pentecostals, Baptists, and the Adventists make up the largest Protestant faithful in Brazil in general.

Two Swedish missionaries founded the Pentecostals in Brazil, who account for the largest community of Protestants in the country and the largest community of Pentecostals worldwide.

The non-Christian communities of Rio include those who follow **Umbanda** and **Candomblé**, both Afro-Brazilian religions.

Afro-Brazilian religions are called as such because they mix aspects of West African religions like the Yoruba religion, Christianity and indigenous religions. Although these religions are more popular in the northeastern states like Bahia, where they were founded, there is growing number of followers in and around Rio. However, the more they grow the more they attract hostility.

"Afro-Brazilian religions face hostility from evangelical churches," wrote Dom Phillips for the *Washington Post* in February 2015 in an article about Afro-Brazilian religion in and around Rio. "Tactics range from propaganda blitzkriegs launched on blogs and YouTube videos to threats, violence and expulsions from drug gangs."

The good news for people practicing Afro-Brazilian religions is that Brazil is a secular country where freedom of religion is guaranteed to all citizens.

Islam and **Judaism** are also small but historical communities in Brazil. The Muslim community in Brazil dates back to the days of slavery when African Muslims were brought in as slaves.

"Muslim immigrants later came from the Middle East and South East Asia, mainly from Syria and Lebanon according to reports," wrote Fiona Hurrell for the English newspaper *The Rio Times* in June 2013, adding that according to "census conducted by the IBGE (Brazilian institute for geography and statistics), the number of Muslims living in Brazil has risen by 29.1 percent between the years 2000 and 2010."

Similarly the Jewish community of Brazil dates back to the early history of the country. The first synagogue in the Americas is actually located in Recife, dating back to the mid 1600s. As such Jewish life has always been part of Brazilian culture.

"The beautifully restored 1930s Grand Temple, once the center of Rio's Jewish life, sits in a quarter once known as Praca Onçe, which music aficionados might recognize as the putative birthplace of Samba," wrote Michael Kaminer for *Forward* magazine in April 2010, during a tour around the city's Jewish landmarks.

That said, around 14% of Cariocas are not religious, according to Instituto Brasileiro de Geografia e Estatística (Brazilian Institute of Geography and Statistics).

It should be noted this is almost twice the average for the national statistics.

Like anywhere else in the developed world Brazilians are becoming more and more detached from their religious backgrounds.

"The more we have people like Oscar Niemeyer the more many of us question religion," said Rafael, a young man who says he's an atheist, referring to the late famous architect. "We have more and more Brazilians who are not afraid to distance themselves from religion," added Rafael.

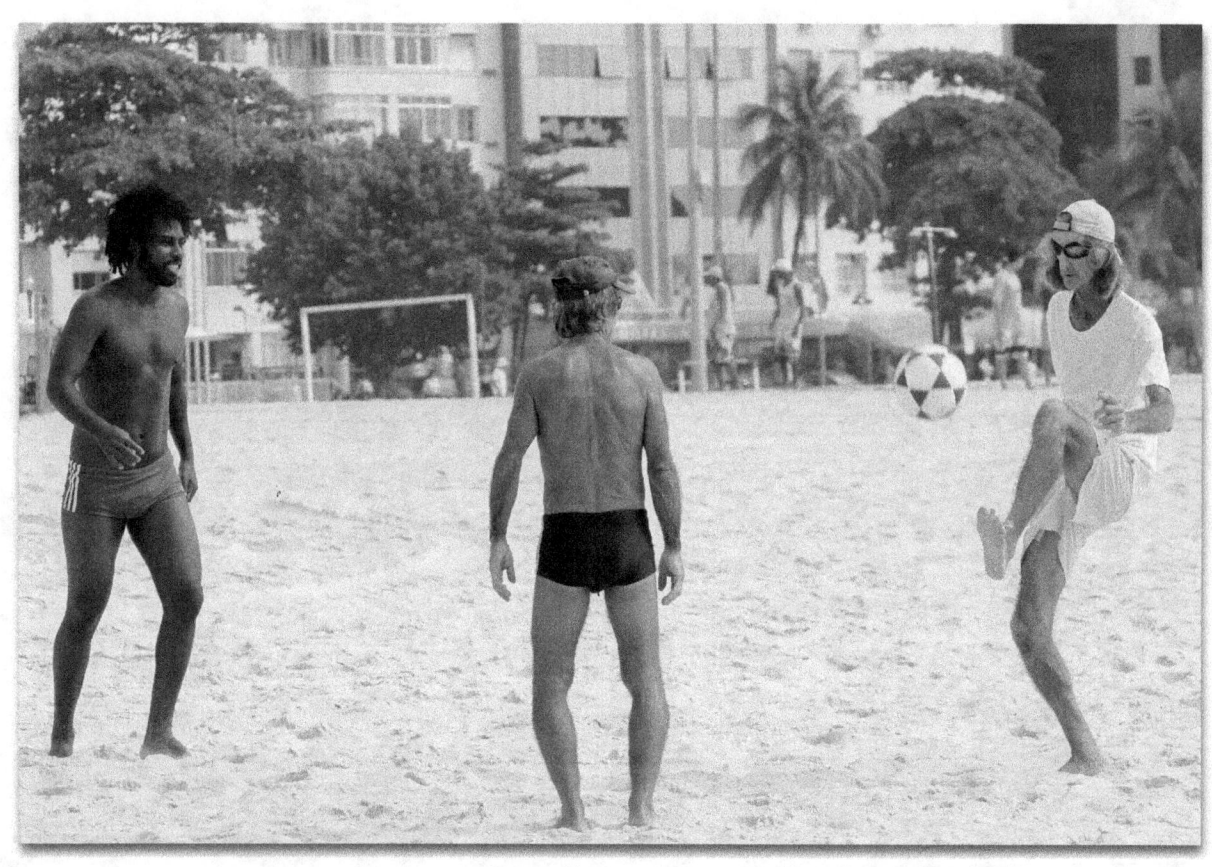

<u>Sports</u>: **Italo** playing football, or soccer, at Copacabana Beach.

Sports

Sports are truly one of the most important aspects of Brazilian culture.

I would say the most important sport is **futebol**, or football or soccer. Brazilians call their country "o País do Futebol" (the country of football), because almost every boy learns to play the sport growing up.

With over 10,000 professional players worldwide, for sure it is the country of football. I had just finished a shoot with Italo in Copacabana when I saw a couple of older men playing. I wondered if they would let him join for a last photo and they welcomed him.

In Rio there are many football clubs, almost every street has their own little club, but the four biggest and most important are Botafogo, Flamengo, Fluminense, and Vasco da Gama.

As mentioned under the Festivals section of this book the teams battle it out during football season and end their battles with the Campeonato Carioca, or Carioca cup, which takes place in May. The winner goes to the national competitions.

"Brazilian families place you in a football club by birth," said João, seriously. "If you belong to a Botafogo family, well, that is who you support throughout life."

There are three official stadiums in Rio.

Flamengo and Fluminense normally play at Maracanã, which is officially known as Estádio Jornalista Mário Filho so named for a famed journalist and writer who died in 1966.

While the other two teams will play at Maracanã on occasion, Vasco da Gama play most of their games at São Januário, which is officially called Estádio Vasco da Gama.

Finally, Botafogo play most of their games at Engenhão, officially known as Estádio Olímpico João Havelang named for both the 2016 Olympics (it also served for the 2014 FIFA World Cup) and the living legend and the 7th president of FIFA João Havelange.

Thanks to their beaches **Volleyball** is a big sport for Brazil. In fact, the country's men's team is the most successful in the world. Rio de Janeiro Vôlei Clube is the most successful women's team. Rio de Janeiro Vôlei Clube team play at Maracanãzinho, officially known as Ginásio Gilberto Cardoso, which honors a former president of the Clube de Regatas do Flamengo.

Throughout the city there are many young people who play volleyball.

Nearly all the beaches have nets set up to play volleyball and other related sports.

The Cariocas have created a new type of sport known as **Futevólei**, or footvolley, a mixture of soccer and beach volleyball.

Octavio de Moraes, a soccer legend who died in 2009, is credited as having invented the sport in the mid 1960s in Rio. By the 1970s most of the big cities in Brazil, including Salvador and Brasilia, have began participating and having their own teams.

Today footvolley is an international game with big clubs in South America, Europe, Asia, and North America, including the United States Footvolley Association. The Mundial de Futevôlei, or Footvolley World Cup, is now held.

Capoeira, which is another invention of this great country, is an Afro-Brazilian sport that combines martial arts with dance and music.

The name is composed of two Tupí words: *ka'a*, which means 'jungle'; and *pûer*, which mean 'it was.'

It is believed that runaway slaves in Brazil's interior began to practice this sport in the 1500s. Until 1930s it was illegal to practice Capoeira. It was couple of masters, whose Rio schools won several times around the country, who contributed to the proliferation of schools in the area.

Today Capoeira is a popular practice all over Brazil. In Rio there are literally schools all over the city that teach this sport. Federação Mundial de Capoeira, or World Capoeira Federation, celebrates the sport in the international spheres. UNESCO has granted a special protected status as "intangible cultural heritage" in 2014.

Beach of its many beaches **Swimming** is a big part of the sports culture here.

There are several competitions taking place throughout the year like Travessia dos Fortes, or Crossing of the Forts, in which many people swim between the two forts of

Copacabana, and the Rei e Rainha do Mar, or King and Queen of the Sea, which is a national competition of swimmers also taking place in Copacabana.

Swimming in Brazil consistently produces top athletes in the field such as César Cielo, who won three Olympic medals, six individual World Championship gold medals, and broke two world records.

Other major sports are international sports like **American Football**, **Basketball**, **Rugby**, **Skating**, et cetera.

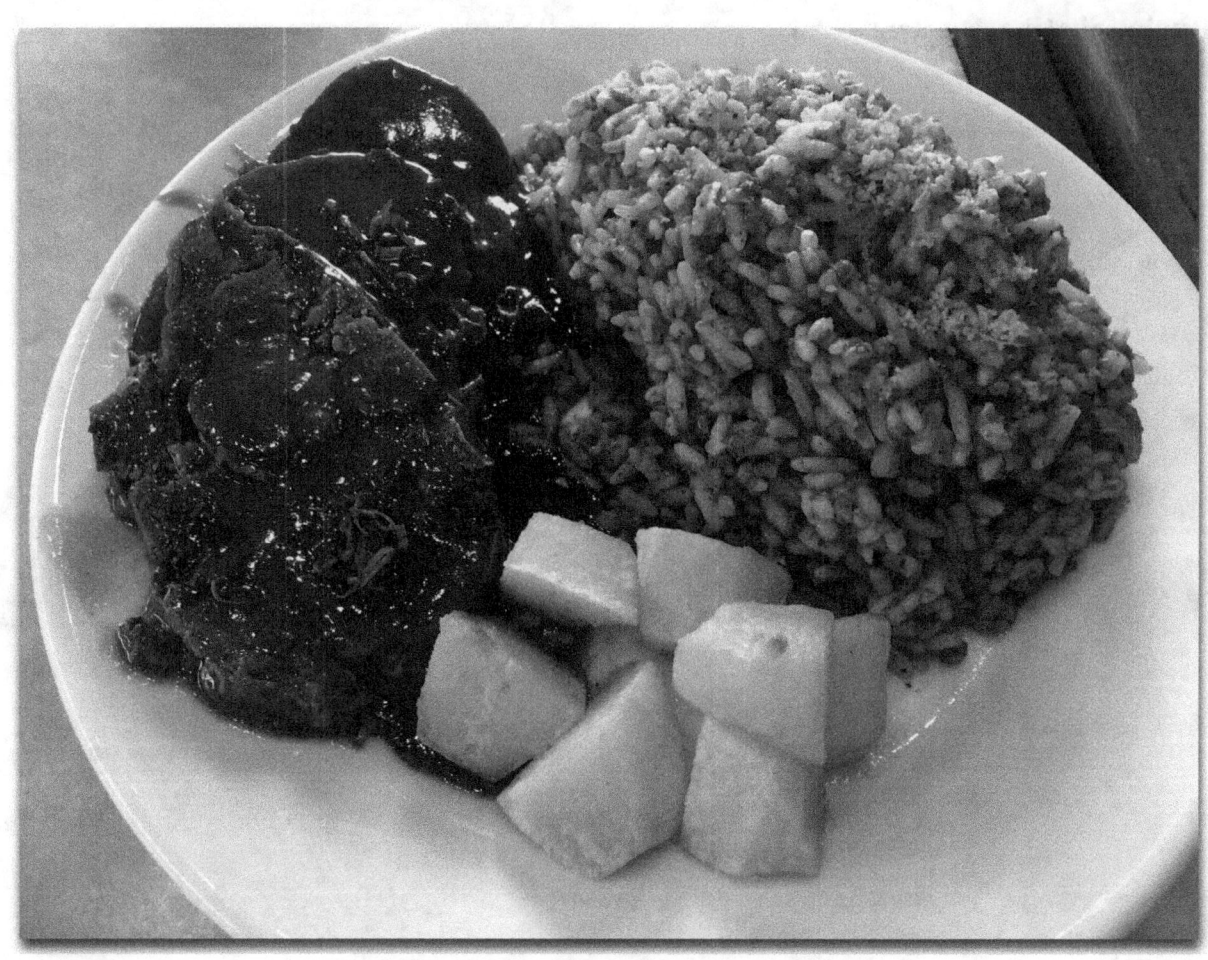

<u>Food</u>: **Feijoada Brasileira** in Copacabana.

Food

Brazilian cuisine is flavorful!

It is influenced by four distinct groups: the natives who lived in the land prior to European colonization; the Africans who were brought here as slaves; the Portuguese that colonized the country the longest; and the modern international world.

Brazil is home to the largest Lebanese and Japanese communities out of Lebanon and Japan. As such Arab and Japanese foods are not so foreign here, especially in these southern states.

As the cultural capital of the country Rio gets all of those influences. Therefore Brazilain local foods from other areas, such as the *coxinha* from São Paulo, *moqueca* from Espírito Santo, and *bobó de camarão* from Bahia, are popular in Rio.

Similarly Lebanese dishes like *tabouleh*, *kibbeh* and *hummus* are common in Rio thanks to the fast food chain Habib's, just as Japanese *sushi* and *teriyaki* dishes are equally as popular.

Do the Cariocas have their own local foods?

Yes and no.

Of course, Rio, like all areas of Brazil, has local foods. However, thanks to the nationalization of Rio culture, because of important cultural elements being based here such as popular television networks, the foods from Rio are rather known and enjoyed elsewhere, too.

My favorite Carioca dish is *sopa leão veloso*, which is a seafood soup whose name honors a famous politician of the past. This is basically a Brazilian version of the French *bouillabaisse* and rather a food of the elite. Unlike its French cousin this soup has local ingredients like annatto paste. This Carioca dish is now enjoyed in different parts of Brazil.

Like the soup above the *Filé à Osvaldo Aranha* is a dish that celebrates a famed politician. This is a large meal, to say the least. Because it requires high quality tender steak it is generally recommended to have it at high-end restaurants. Usually it is served with one side of friend potatoes and one side of rice, and mostly with farofa, and rarely with one side of vegetables. This is another dish of the Cariocas that made it to the other parts of Brazil.

Another local dish is *feijoada brasileira*, which is a dish made from meat and bean stew served with rice. Feijoada is actually a Portuguese dish, which is why it needs the "brasileira" (Brazilian) part added to differentiate this particular version because the dish is popular in most of former Portuguese colonies. However, in Brazil the dish is more or less local to Rio. Today, however, it is considered a national dish.

Street food, of course, is a big part of the cuisine here. In Rio it is composed of many easy to eat foods like the *salgados*, *empadas*, *pastéis*, *tapiocas* and many others. There are corner cafes, food trucks, and even people sitting on the street selling on tables. I find it that street markets tend to have good street food. However, many *sucos* or juice bars have menus too for quick foods.

There are restaurants of all levels in Rio. I prefer small, neighborhood restaurants that tend to have more local atmosphere. However, you can really choose any level you want. I have been with friends who took me to places that ranged from holes in the wall to Michelin starred restaurants in big hotels and resorts.

As the Cariocas say, "Bom apetite!"

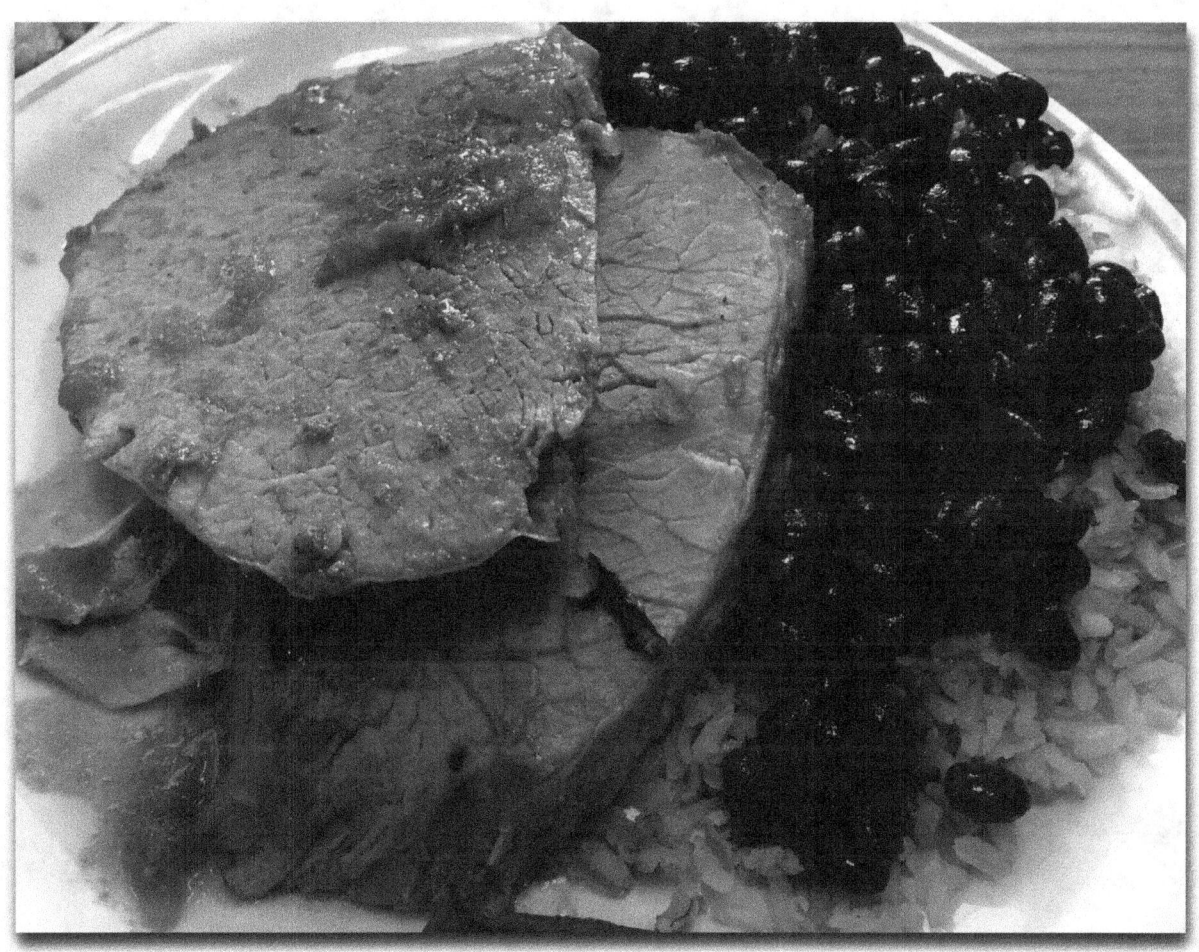

Carne Assada in Ipanema.

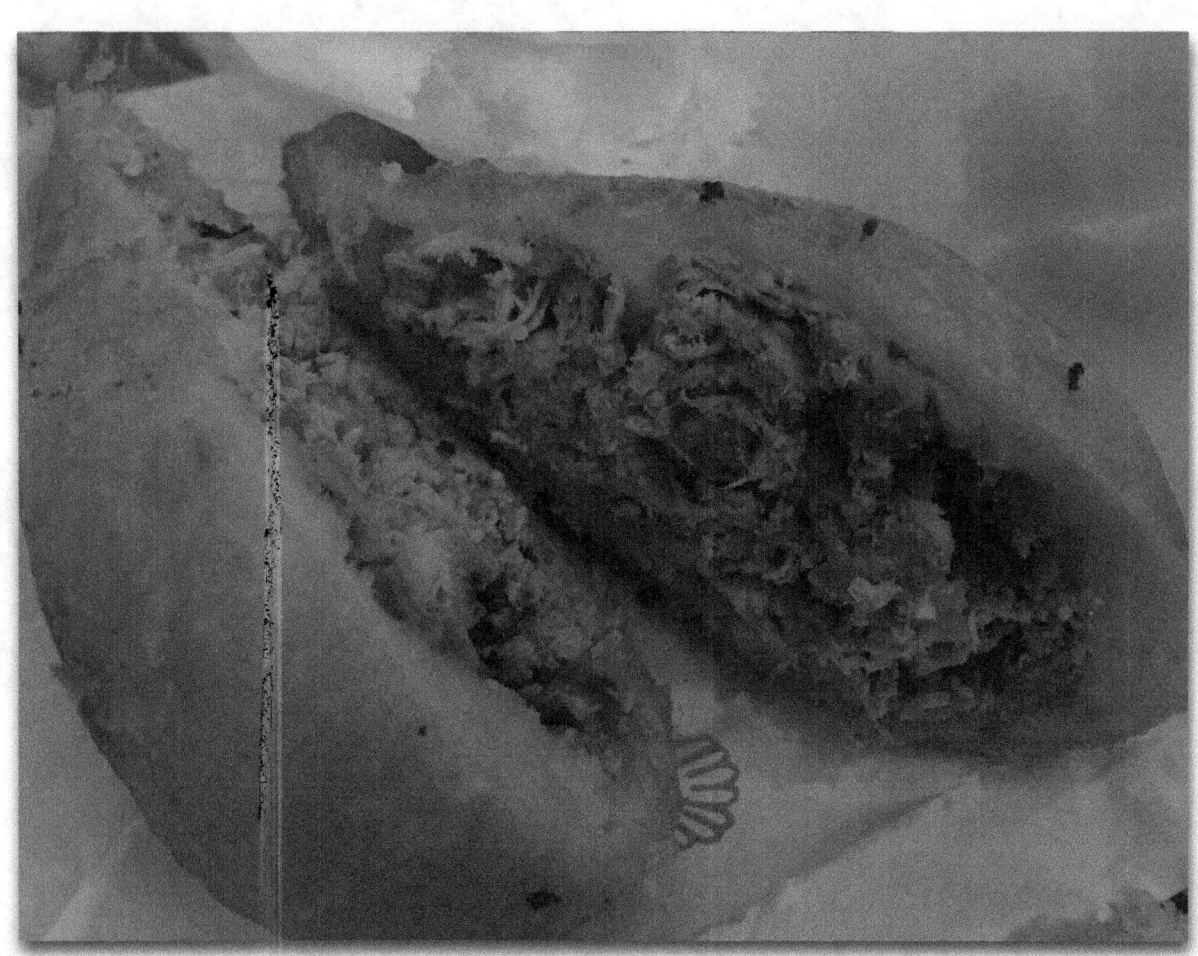

Coxinha in Centro.

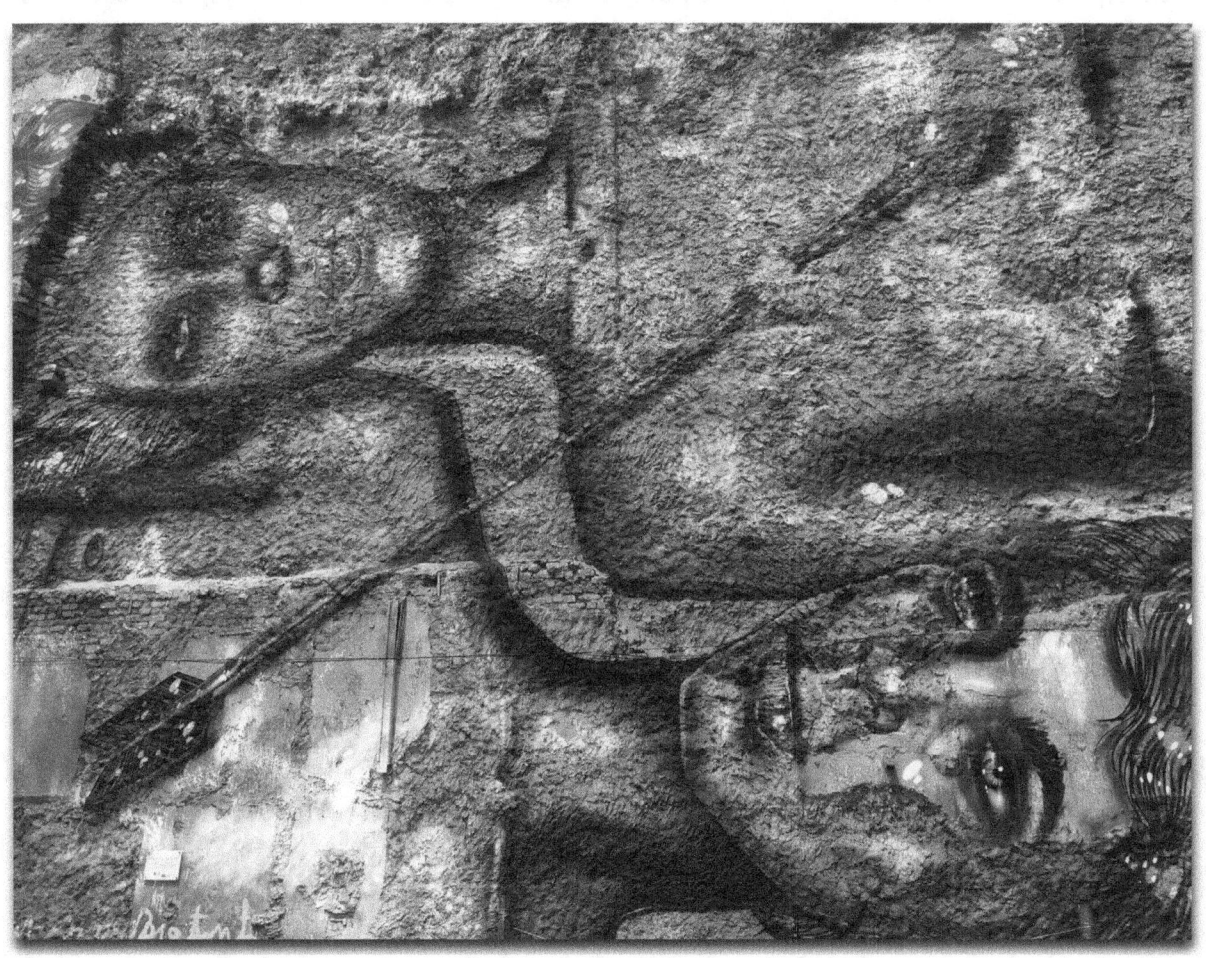

<u>Art</u>: Street art in Centro.

Art

The Cariocas love art.

When walking around certain neighborhoods you really do feel like you are walking in art. The architecture is beautiful. The streets are designed beautifully, sometimes by nature. The people dress artistically.

It is a very artistic city.

However, those of you who are seeking art you came to the right city. All you have to do is just grab a copy of *Mapa das Artes*, which is a map that gives you information about the art in the city. It lists museums, galleries, art spaces, and other art spaces like foundations. The best thing about this map is that it is free.

You can find it at tourist offices.

A lot of city's premier museums are located in the Centro or Zona Sul districts. The **Museu Histórico Nacional**, or the National Historical Museum, is a great place to start your visit. It was created in the early 1920s and contains hundreds of thousands of material dating back to the founding of the nation.

People travel all over the country to visit its 25 exhibitions, many of them permanent.

As part of the Brazilian Insitute of Museums, which is under the Ministry of Culture, this museum has been the ground zero for all other museums and therefore all other museums came out of it.

It is closed on Mondays, and it is open more or less until 5:30pm during the week and it opens at 10:30am. On the weekends, as well as public holidays, it stays open until 6pm although it only opens at 2pm. Entrance to the museum is free. It is located on *Praça Marechal Âncora* (and there is no number needed as it is a multi-complex location).

The **Centro Cultural Banco do Brasil**, also known as CCBB, is probably the most important venue for general art in Rio. There are other national locations in three other states. It is known for its artistic exhibitions of local, national, and international artists. It has shown the incredible work of Rembrandt, Kandinsky, and Picasso to many Brazilians who otherwise wouldn't have had the chance. It is free to enter. It is open 9am to 9pm daily, except Tuesdays when it is closed. The location for this museum is *Rua Primeiro de Março, 66.*

Very close to the CCB is the **Igreja da Candelária**, or Candelária Church, which is another good place to see art in Rio. This church dates back to the 1700s. The church brings together three types of art including Baroque, Neo-Renaissance and Neoclassical—all of which have been popular at some point in its history. The church's outside, which brings together Baroque and Neoclassical architecture, is attributed to artist Francisco João Roscio. In the late 1800s the artist João Zeferino da Costa was called to paint the church's story on the ceiling, and along with others brought more Neo-Renaissance to the church. It is an incredible piece of art that you must see. Sculptures by António Teixeira Lopes also decorate the church. Entrance to the church is free. The address is *Praça Pio X.*

The **Museu Nacional de Belas Artes**, or the National Museum of Fine Arts, is a museum that benefited greatly from a very interesting event. On November 29, 1807 the royal family of Portugal, along with nearly 15,000 people of its court, escaped to Brazil days before Napoleon invaded Lisbon. When the royal crown returned to Portugal the art collection was left behind. In the mid 1930s the museum inherited this collection through the National School of Fine Arts. These days the museum gets over hundred thousand visitors, many of them from around the country. The museum is closed on Mondays. During the rest of the working week it is open 10am to 6pm. On the weekends it is open from 12pm to 5pm. This museum charges about R$8 in entrance fees. The address is *Avenida Rio Branco, 199.*

After seeing the royal art collection you might decide to head over to see how the royals lived in the imperial times. **Paço Imperial**, or Imperial Palace, is where King John VI of Portugal lived. Between 1822 to 1889, while the country was under the Brazilian Kings Pedro I and Pedro II, the palace was used as a place of business rather than a residence. Nevertheless the palace gives a good idea of what royal life was like in that period. Entrance is free and it is open Tuesday to Sunday from 12pm to 6pm. The address is *Praça Quinze de Novembro, 48.*

There are several other places of interest for art lovers in other neighborhoods. The **Museu de Arte Moderna do Rio**, or MAM Rio as it is better known, in Flamengo Park in Flamengo. The **Museu do Índio**, Museum of the Indian, in Botafogo. The **Museu Casa de Rui** Barbosa in Botafogo. The **Museu de Arte do Rio**, better known as MAR, in Copacabana.

Of course, one of the best street art scene in the world is found in Rio. The Cariocas really enjoy their street art and the street artists here respect each other, rarely tagging on top of each other's art. The **Street Art Tour**, which was founded by two local young women, starts in Copacabana and ends in Leblon after going through Santa Teresa. In the meantime, if you don't feel like taking a tour you might want to check out the **Favela Painting Project**, a foundation started by two artists and which has been painting several neighborhoods.

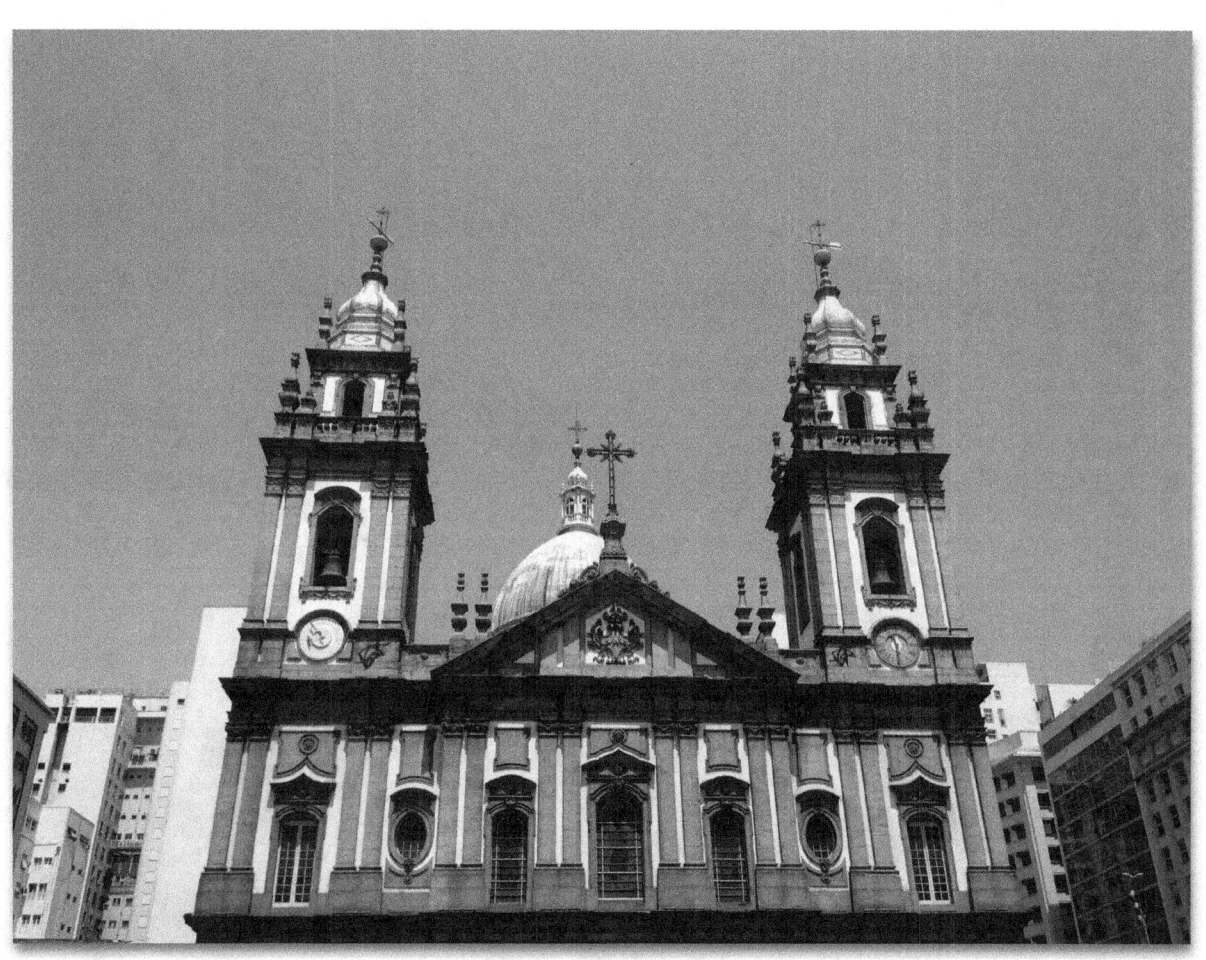

The **Candelária Church** in Centro.

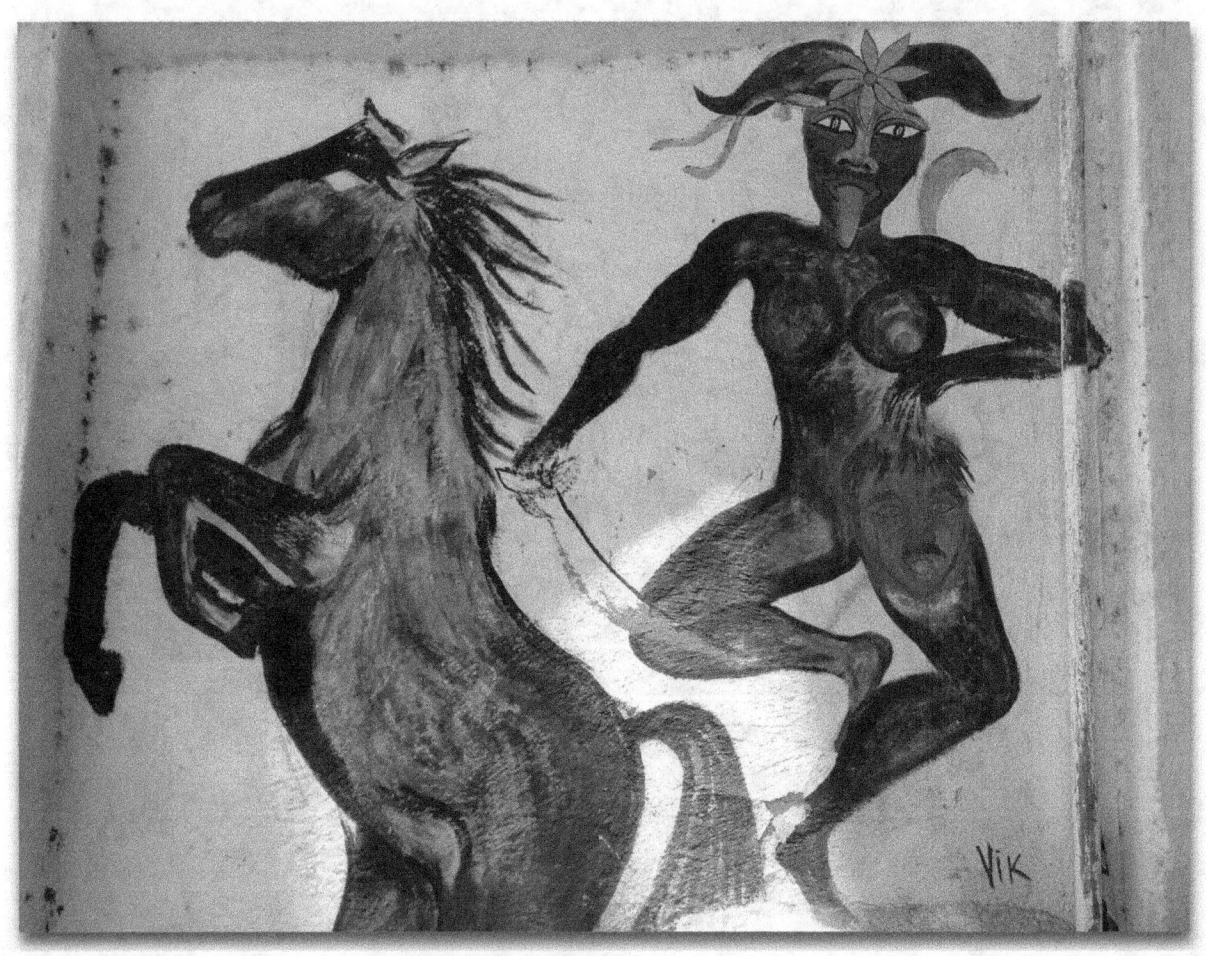

Street Art in Santa Teresa.

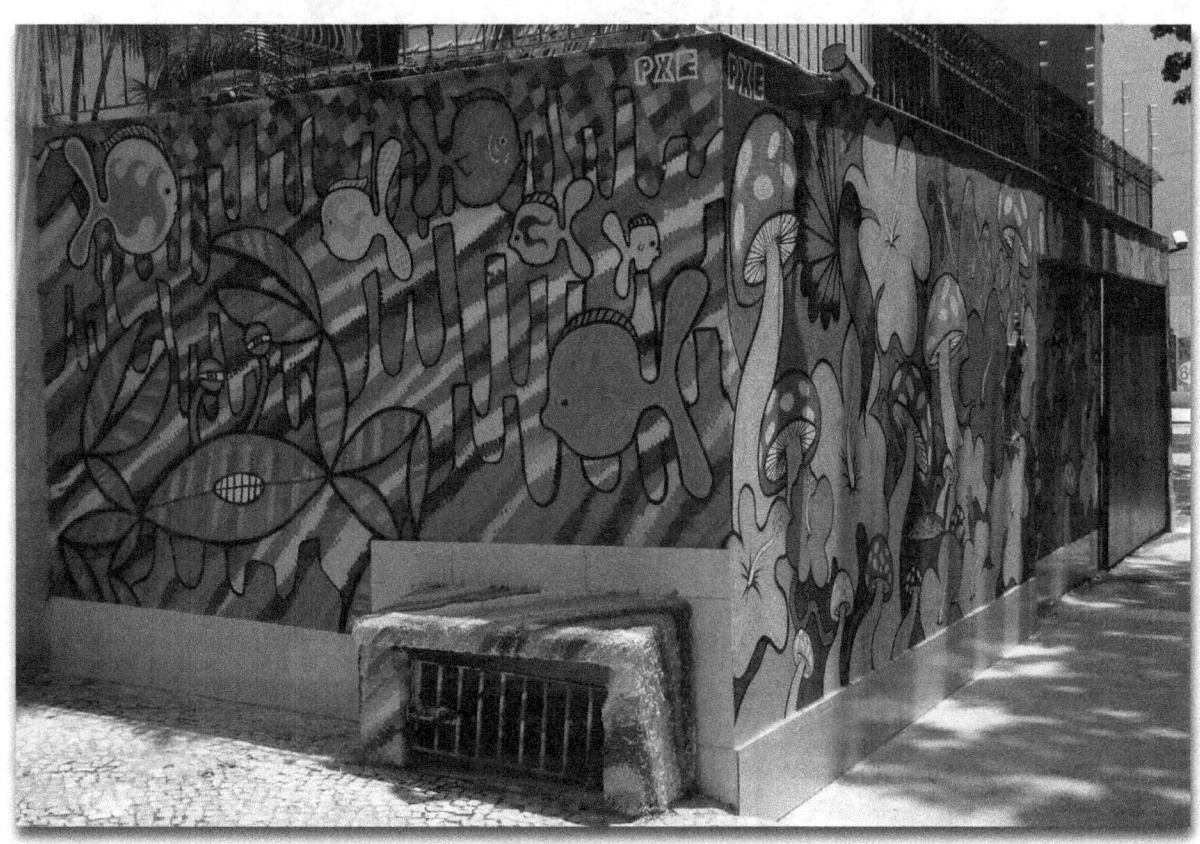

Street Art in Ipanema.

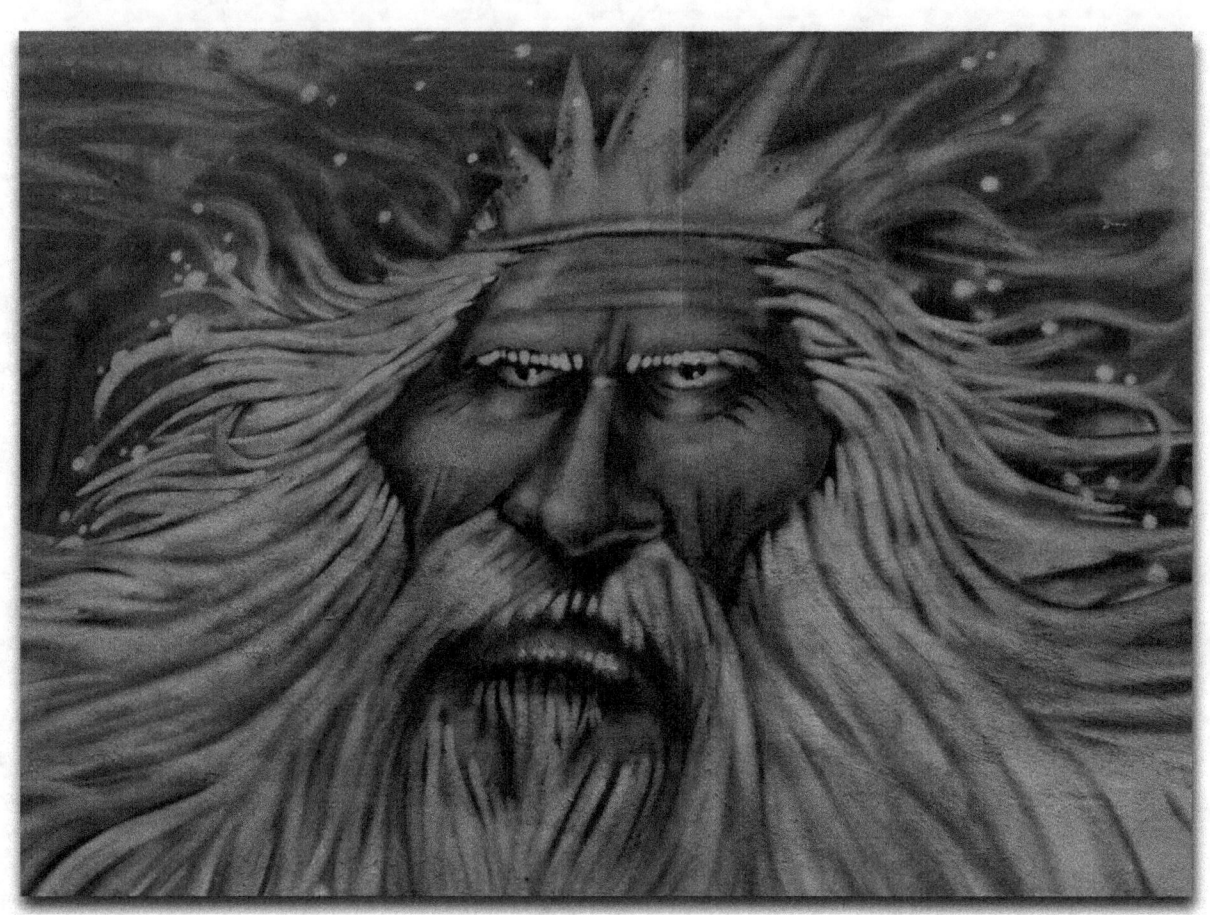

Street Art in Copacabana.

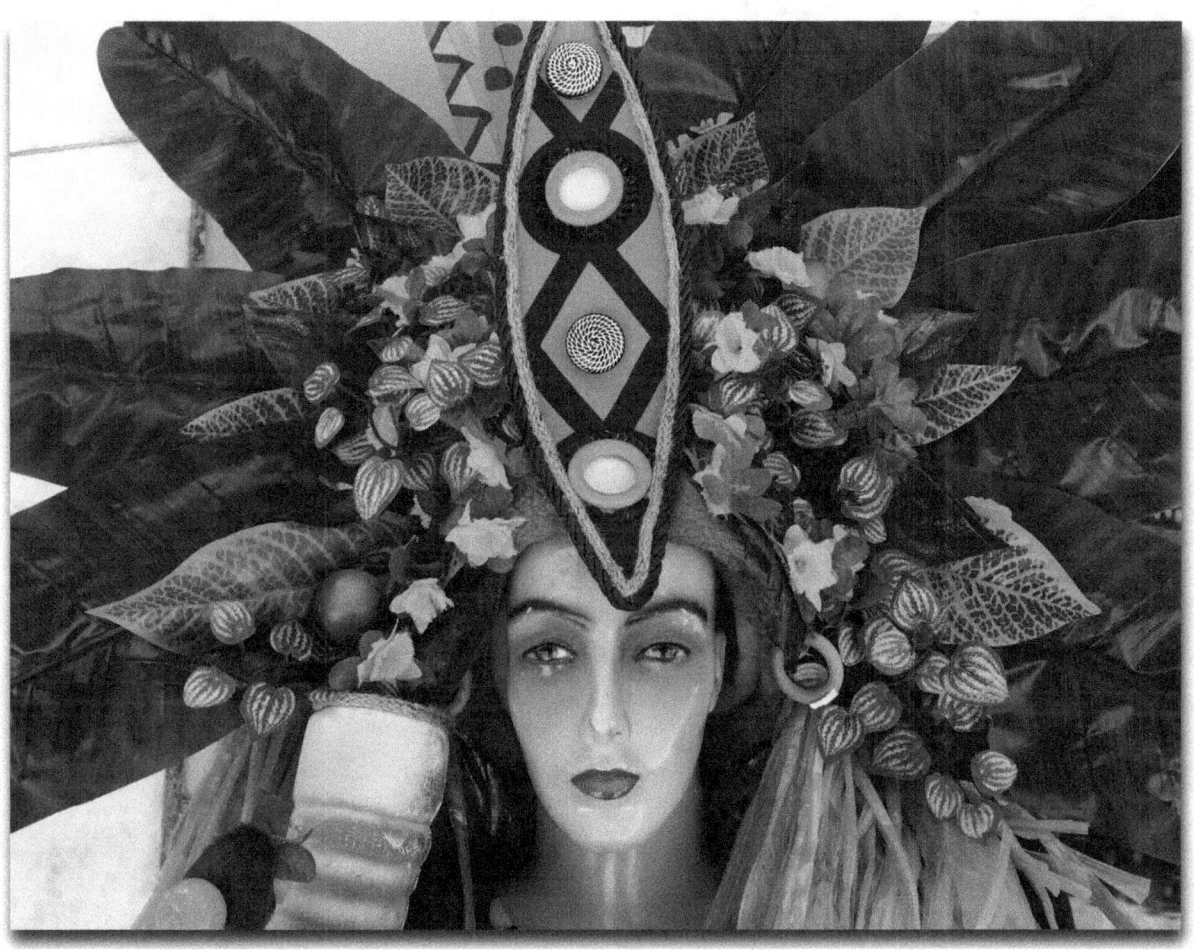

Mixed Art in front of a store in Leblon.

Thank You!

This book would not have been possible without the people who contributed deeply to its success. Thank you! Thank you to all the men! Thank you to all the people who let us work in their space! Thank you to all the residents of this gorgeous city!

About AJ Paris

AJ Paris is a New York-based photographer. His photo book "Men Around the World" shares the faces of the world's men, with men from all of the continents. He writes about his travels on his webiste www.ajparis.com and can be found on Social Media @ajparisphotos

www.ingramcontent.com/pod-product-compliance
Lightning Source LLC
Chambersburg PA
CBHW081559220526
45468CB00010B/2698